NATO at 40

NATO at 40

Confronting a Changing World

Edited by

Ted Galen Carpenter

INSTITUTE

Cato Institute, Washington, D.C.

Lexington Books
D.C. Heath and Company/Lexington, Massachusetts/Toronto

Library of Congress Cataloging-in-Publication Data

NATO at 40 : confronting a changing world / [edited by] Ted Galen
  Carpenter.
    p. cm.
  Includes bibliographical references.
  ISBN 0–669–21698–4 (alk. paper). — ISBN 0–669–21870–7 (pbk. :
alk. paper)
    1. North Atlantic Treaty Organization.   2. United States—Foreign
relations.—Europe.   3. Europe—Foreign relations—United States.
I. Carpenter, Ted Galen.   II. Title: NATO at forty.
JX1393.N67N34   1990
355'.031'091821—dc20   89–13417
                                CIP

Published simultaneously in Canada
Printed in the United States of America
Casebound International Standard Book Number: 0–669–21698–4
Library of Congress Catalog Card Number: 89–13417

The paper used in this publication meets the minimum requirements of
American National Standard for Information Sciences—Permanence of
Paper for Printed Library Materials, ANSI Z39.48–1948. ∞™

Year and number of this printing:

90 91 92 10 9 8 7 6 5 4 3 2 1

To Barbara, Lara, Amber, and Brian,
for their patience and encouragement

Contents

III Implications of a Changing Strategic Environment 111

IV Alternatives to the Status Quo 203

Foreword

Patricia S. Schroeder

I am delighted that the Cato Institute is taking a hard look at NATO
on its fortieth birthday. There are more sacred cows grazing in our
federal budget than in all of India, and one of the biggest is NATO.

NATO grazes on a wonderful green pasture, and I cannot blame our allies
for liking it. If I were in their place, I would like it too. If, for example, the
Canadians were to move 350,000 troops down here to protect us and spend
$160 billion a year for our defense, we would not object either. Likewise, we
would not be at all eager to share some of the expense with them. From the
perspective of U.S. national interests, however, it does not make sense for us
to continue to assume the majority of the cost of defending the European
allies.

I am very frustrated about this issue. For the past year, I have chaired the
defense burden-sharing panel of the House Armed Services Committee. The
panel has examined the military efforts of our allies, compared their contributions to ours, and discussed the future of the alliance. The reaction in Washington to our inquiries has been that we were asking the right questions but
our timing is off: "Now is not the time; this is not the day; this is not the year."
We have also been told that the United States cannot act unilaterally. Moreover, should the United States reduce troops in Europe, the Europeans will
no longer believe we are committed to their defense. A good example of that
thinking was recently displayed by Secretary of State James Baker. One of his
first actions was to tour the NATO countries and tell them not to worry, that
the United States was going to stay in Europe.

As an American, I am offended by that attitude. The reason this century
has been known as the "American century" is the creative leadership that we
have had. We have not allowed ourselves to be bound up in nostalgia. We
have always considered what we ought to do to position ourselves for the
future. We stopped thinking in that way about ten years ago, and we will be
in trouble if we do not get back to our traditions. The argument that the Europeans will feel totally undefended if the United States withdraws even a small
number of troops is an insult to American history. Twice in this century, the

United States came to the defense of Europe. At neither time did we have a single soldier stationed in Europe when the conflict began. Now that we are much more globally connected, it is absurd to argue that the United States would ignore a serious threat to Europe, that we would consider a threat to Europe as a threat to ourselves only if numerous American soldiers already stationed on the Continent were killed.

The second argument for retaining our current troop commitment is that without U.S. troops on the Continent, the Europeans will not "stand firm to stem the tide of communism." That assertion is equally unconvincing. Is there a German who does not understand what communism is all about? Germans live in a divided country, and they have seen their relatives try to escape from East Germany. If the Western Europeans were sold on communism, they would have capitulated long ago. The Europeans are raging capitalists. They are looking toward 1992 when they will create a unified economic market. It is not the case that should we bring home even one soldier, the Europeans will invite in the Soviet Union. The Europeans see major differences between the Soviet Union and the United States. Just as it demeans us to say we will not assist the Europeans unless our own soldiers are endangered, it demeans the Europeans for us to suggest that Europe will meekly surrender. Let us treat both sides with more respect.

To our great credit, we have never regarded NATO as an American empire. We have always treated it as an alliance, though we have borne the majority of the cost. Whenever we have made suggestions to them, the allies have felt perfectly free to say no. When we asked them to get involved in the war in Southeast Asia, they refused. When we asked them to get involved in the Persian Gulf, they refused. We asked them if they would help us out in the fight against terrorism, and they refused. If NATO had been an American empire, we would not have asked, nor would we have been refused. I challenge those who argue otherwise to cite even one instance in which our allies let us lead them where they did not want to go. They have always followed their own best interests.

Dwight D. Eisenhower was the last U.S. president who really understood the purpose of the alliance. Having been the commander of the allied forces in Europe during World War II, he should have known what NATO was created to do. Eisenhower clearly stated that the United States was not going to maintain a military presence in Europe in perpetuity. We were there to help the Europeans get back on their feet. He would be appalled to see how the nature of the U.S. commitment to NATO has changed.

There is nothing radical about asking a country to make whatever effort is necessary to protect its own borders. It is one thing for the United States to assist allies that are impoverished and cannot protect their borders, but it is hard to justify such assistance for prosperous allies capable of providing for their own defense.

When we look at the situation from the American perspective and from the perspective of the next century, it is important to realize that our military allies are also our trading competitors. While militarily it's "rumps together, horns out" against the enemy, on the trading plane we are going head to head with the Europeans. When engaged in head-to-head competition, it helps to have an even playing field. The playing field is not even if one of the competing nations is spending far more money for defense than the others. The allies know that and will not volunteer to pay more. If one competitor pays for the whole group, the others will be able to use their unspent resources to advantage against that competitor in the course of their competition.

We have tolerated this unjust situation in the name of "the Soviet threat." Our debt in the last eight years has increased by over $1 trillion, largely due to a massive military buildup to meet the Soviet threat. In terms of the percentage of gross national product, our allies were paying for more of their defense in 1980 than they are today. We have accumulated more debt in order to subsidize their defense. It is time to talk not just about the Soviet threat but about the threat of the debt. What effect will that debt have on our ability to compete in the international economic arena as the twenty-first century approaches?

There are other troublesome issues as well. One of them is the question of our overseas military bases. The Department of Defense (DOD) could close down any base abroad at any time because these bases have no congressional constituency. DOD, however, has not closed down a single overseas base in the past eight years except in places where the United States has been evicted.

In fact, the DOD will pay anything to keep overseas bases open. When allies such as Portugal, Greece, Turkey, and the Philippines demand more money, our response has been to ask them how much more. In fact, a significant part of our foreign aid is now disguised payments for base rights.

Another example of the bases problem occurred when Spain kicked out the 401st Tactical Fighter Wing. The 401st was in Spain to protect the southern flank of NATO, not to protect Florida. But where were our allies during the Spanish negotiations? Our European allies did not remind the Spaniards that they were part of the NATO partnership and should therefore bear some responsibility. Instead, the allies quietly watched us get kicked out.

It will cost a fortune to transfer the 401st to Italy. Having decided to move the planes to Italy, now we must decide what to do with the headquarters of the 16th Air Force in Spain if the planes are not there. The NATO allies have taken the position that moving the 16th Air Force headquarters is an American problem. Because the Spanish want to keep the headquarters, the allies refuse to pay any of the expense of moving it.

We are going to incur enormous costs when the 401st moves to Italy. Why should American taxpayers have to pay for all of that? This example can be replicated all over the world, and it demonstrates the magnitude of money we are spending overseas. If the NATO allies do not believe that their security is seriously threatened, why do they insist on our forces being in Europe? And if they do believe their security is threatened, they should be willing to bear a fair share of the costs.

Another situation illustrates the problem of the burden-sharing issue in Europe. Congressman Andy Ireland (Florida), the ranking Republican on the burden-sharing panel, and I have sponsored a bill that calls for a reduction of U.S. troops in Europe by the number of people who were sent there to maintain and operate the INF missiles. Although we have an INF treaty and the INF missiles were destroyed, the people we sent to take care of the missiles are still in place. It seems logical to us to bring them home.

The hostility of Washington officialdom to this bill has been overwhelming. We have been accused of acting unilaterally, though the INF treaty was negotiated multilaterally and everybody signed off. We have been told that doing this would be "a terrible signal to our allies." When we pushed the withdrawal proposal, proponents of the status quo came up with another excuse: the Italians do not want to provide base security when the 401st moves there. DOD then made the ridiculous proposal that the personnel assigned to the INFs should be transferred to Italy to provide security for the base.

How did we arrive at such an unsatisfactory situation in NATO? *American High: The Years of Confidence, 1945–1960* by William L. O'Neill, a book about the period when Americans were the kings of the planet, offers some insight. We enjoyed that undisputed dominance and are nostalgic about it. That kind of sentiment drives NATO partisans to preserve the status quo at any cost. There is also the influence of institutional perquisites. Officials find it much more enjoyable to travel to visit the troops in Europe than to see military bases in the United States. Those and other factors drive the "let's-keep-our-presence-over-there-no-matter-what" mentality.

The result of this complacency on the part of the U.S. policymakers is that we commit over 60 percent of our total defense budget, according to DOD, to defend Europe. That is a lot of money; it is even more than the amount of fiscal year 1988's federal budget deficit. It is important to reassess this situation.

As we look at the forty-year history of NATO at the end of the 1980s, these benchmarks should be an occasion for reflection. I speak on many college campuses and have been thinking about what I would pose to the students as an end-of-the-decade assignment. Then I came across a passage in a letter from Franklin D. Roosevelt to Winston Churchill in the mid-1940s. It said, "Mr. Churchill, I'm a sick man and I want to tell you one thing: how delightful it has been to share this decade with you." That letter has prompted me to ask our young people, "With whom are you glad to share this decade?" Frequently they say Mikhail Gorbachev. American young people admire Gorbachev so much because he is modernizing global strategy while all we seem to be doing is modernizing weapons. Gorbachev has realized how the Japanese have redefined global power; a country can be a global power without a large military. He had insight to understand that the Soviet Union could not be that kind of global power under the existing Soviet system and has started to change it. He may or may not survive. I do not know. It is interesting, though, that our young people have grasped Gorbachev's vision. Furthermore, they see that our only response to it is more of the same old policy clichés.

Initially a skeptical response may have made sense. When Gorbachev first announced that Soviet intentions had changed, our reaction was justifiably cautious. After all, intentions can change without warning. Indeed when considering security threats, intentions are irrelevant unless the country in question poses a threat in terms of its capability. The Soviet Union has always had that capability, especially in the military realm. But under Gorbachev, the Soviet Union has changed its actions, not merely its statements. Soviet troops have pulled out of Afghanistan. The Soviet Union signed the INF treaty. Gorbachev keeps formulating innovative proposals to ease the East-West conflict. U.S. officials must develop a more creative approach instead of reflexively clinging to the old institutions, such as NATO, with which we have felt so comfortable for forty years. It is time to reconsider our alliance strategy.

Although there is no present need for the United States to leave the alliance, the European members of NATO must become full partners instead of U.S. dependents. Their combined GNP is larger than ours, and they have nearly 100 million more people. We must stop telling our allies that they can just dial 1–800–USA, that we will go anywhere, and will take care of all their defense needs. In doing so, we have been bankrupting ourselves, while they have been outtrading us in the global market. If we intend to retain a prominent position in the next century, we must regain our economic competitiveness. A reassessment of our NATO commitments is an essential first step in that process.

Preface

s NATO celebrated its fortieth anniversary in 1989, there was an abundance of self-satisfied congratulations among alliance partisans on both sides of the Atlantic. According to the conventional wisdom, not only had the alliance preserved peace in Europe since 1949, but it had been responsible for keeping Western Europe out of the clutches of the Soviet empire. Moreover, transatlantic solidarity had never been stronger than it was at the end of the 1980s, if one believed the reassuring comments of many NATO supporters.

Although Western political leaders repeatedly reaffirm the importance of the alliance, there are mounting signs that such a complacent adherence to the *status quo* is unrealistic. Mikhail Gorbachev's diplomatic initiatives have shaken long-standing cold war assumptions to their foundations and, in the process, revealed serious fissures in NATO. The increasingly acrimonious debate over burden sharing is merely the most visible indication of the underlying problems afflicting the alliance. Although NATO has experienced episodes of disarray before, the perception of a looming Soviet threat always served to restore unity. This time, that vital solidifying element may no longer be present.

A growing chorus of NATO critics is making its views known. Such prominent statesmen as Henry Kissinger, Zbigniew Brzezinski, and Helmut Schmidt now advocate significant changes in the alliance's political and military arrangements. More radical critics assert that mere reforms are insufficient and that NATO is an expensive anachronism.

The contributors to this book address the most important questions facing the alliance on its fortieth anniversary. Is NATO still essential (if it ever was) to the security of the United States and the nations of Western Europe? Are the European allies contributing their fair share to the common defense effort, or are they free-riding on the U.S. security guarantee? Can the diverging interests of the United States and its allies be reconciled, or does the present discord foreshadow NATO's dissolution? Does the Soviet Union's more conciliatory and sophisticated foreign policy offer an opportunity to end

Europe's artificial division into hostile blocs, or is it a ploy designed to lull the West into a false sense of security? In discussing these and other vital issues, the authors greatly advance the debate about whether NATO can survive in a rapidly changing world.

This book is the outgrowth of a Cato Institute conference marking NATO's fortieth anniversary in April 1989. I wish to thank Edward H. Crane, William A. Niskanen, and the other officers of the Cato Institute for supporting the conference and this book. Their continued encouragement has been a crucial factor in making both projects a success.

I owe appreciation to Irving Kristol, Tom Bethell, and Karsten Voigt for their important contributions to the conference. I want to thank my collaborators in this book, who gave a tremendous amount of time and energy to their assignments and who exhibited an uncompromising insistence on quality. Paul O'Connell, the editor at Lexington Books, recognized the importance of this collection and diligently kept the project on schedule. Pat Felder and other members of the Cato Institute's word processing staff put in long hours without complaint to prepare the final manuscript. R. Channing Rouse diligently tracked down elusive citations, sparing various authors painstaking and time-consuming labor.

Most of all, I owe a great debt of gratitude to my assistant, Rosemary Fiscarelli. A talented young NATO scholar in her own right, she provided invaluable help in assessing and editing the chapters. The timely publication of this book and much of its quality are due to her dedication.

Introduction

NATO—the North Atlantic Treaty Organization—has been the keystone of America's security commitments since its inception four decades ago, and the alliance is still considered sacrosanct by many members of the foreign policy establishment. But criticism of NATO is mounting in both the United States and Western Europe. The Soviet Union's more conciliatory and astute foreign policy under Mikhail Gorbachev has intensified discontent with the alliance as concerned Americans and Europeans wonder whether NATO is relevant in the rapidly changing international environment.

American critics note that alliance commitments consume more than 40 percent (some estimates are as high as 60 percent) of the U.S. defense budget each year, and they question the wisdom of such a continuing financial hemorrhage when the federal government must grapple with chronic budget deficits. They also accuse the European allies of free-riding on the U.S. security guarantee instead of contributing their fair share to the common defense effort. Finally, they find the Western Europeans maddeningly insensitive to U.S. wishes on a host of out-of-area issues, from Middle East policy to the situation in Central America. These concerns lead a growing number of American journalists, academics, and policy experts to conclude that NATO—at least as presently constituted—no longer serves the best interests of the United States.

The Europeans also have an expanding list of grievances. In addition to long-standing complaints about U.S. domination of alliance affairs, they find Washington disturbingly unresponsive to Moscow's diplomatic initiatives. The Bush administration's insistence that NATO deploy a new generation of short-range nuclear missiles has perplexed and disturbed a sizable segment of West European, especially West German, public opinion. Concern seems to be growing on the Continent that U.S. leaders are wedded to the status quo, thereby missing an unprecedented opportunity to ease East-West tensions and perhaps even heal the wounds caused by the cold war—especially the artificial partition of Europe into hostile blocs.

The contributors to this book have examined the numerous issues that now trouble NATO. Some of the authors insist that the alliance has served the West well for forty years and will continue to do so in the coming decades with relatively minor adjustments. Others contend that fundamental reforms are imperative if NATO is to survive as a viable entity into the twenty-first century. Members of a third faction argue that vast changes in global political conditions have rendered NATO obsolete—an expensive and potentially dangerous anachronism.

In part I, three authors explore the causes of NATO's disunity. Despite their differing conclusions, they agree that the problems afflicting the alliance have been building for some time and are largely attributable to crucial changes in the international system.

Ronald Steel notes in chapter 1 that NATO has frequently been beset by economic, political, and military problems throughout its history. But the current disarray, he contends, is more serious, suggesting the existence of systemic disorder rather than a passing crisis. In particular, America's hegemonic status can no longer be sustained since the Western Europeans exhibit a growing reluctance to defer to Washington on important policy matters. Steel argues that NATO is an increasingly irrelevant association—a military arrangement designed to meet the dangers of another era.

Robert E. Hunter reaches a different conclusion in chapter 2, insisting that NATO remains indispensable for the protection of Western security interests. The alliance has preserved peace and freedom in Western Europe for four decades, Hunter asserts, and it should not be jettisoned casually. Moreover, NATO has previously displayed a surprising ability to overcome internal disputes, so its resilience should not be discounted. Even Hunter concedes, though, that preserving NATO does not mean a blind endorsement of the status quo. Reforms are needed, including taking steps to have the European members play a more vigorous and responsible role.

In the third chapter, I argue that the current tensions within NATO are the product of competing American and European security agendas that have existed since the creation of the alliance. The Europeans have sought to link the United States inextricably to Western Europe's fate in order to increase the credibility of deterrence. A large American troop presence on the Continent to act as a trip wire and a defense strategy that emphasizes a low nuclear threshold are viewed as tangible manifestations of that linkage, ensuring virtually automatic U.S. involvement in a European war. U.S. officials, conversely, have sought to maximize America's freedom of action and to contain any conflict if deterrence failed. The perception of a serious Soviet threat obscured the existence of these fundamentally divergent security interests, and the NATO members understandably avoided confronting their implications. But the apparent easing of the Soviet threat is now bringing divisive issues into the open, a development that bodes ill for the future of the alliance.

Part II examines the costs and benefits of NATO. Again, there is marked disagreement among the chapter authors whether the alliance is worthwhile financially to the United States. There is also a considerable divergence of views about whether NATO benefits the long-term interests of its European members.

Melvyn Krauss in chapter 4 asserts that incentives play a significant role in determining foreign policy behavior, just as they do in determining economic behavior. He contends that by taking responsibility for Western Europe's security, the United States has removed the needed incentive for the Europeans to make vigorous defense efforts of their own and to assess the Soviet threat in a prudent, realistic manner. U.S. policy has thereby turned prosperous and capable allies into resentful and irresponsible dependents who are increasingly inclined to adopt a policy of appeasement toward the Soviet Union. Change the incentives by reducing the level of the U.S. commitment, Krauss insists, and the Europeans will respond with a more responsible, self-reliant defense policy.

Josef Joffe emphatically disagrees in chapter 5 with Krauss's conclusion that U.S. disengagement would stimulate a more vigorous European military effort. Such action, he believes, would strengthen neutralist and pacifist elements throughout Western Europe, creating pressure for even more accommodationist policies toward the Soviet Union. A U.S. withdrawal could also lead to a revival of the national rivalries that have plagued Europe throughout its history and have frequently plunged the Continent into war. NATO has been a good bargain for the United States, Joffe insists, and although the European members can and should undertake more responsibility for the collective defense effort, it would be a grave mistake for Washington to curtail its commitments.

David Garnham next examines the European reaction to signs that the United States has already begun to scale back its NATO role. The response has generally been one of increased intra-European cooperation rather than a slide toward Finlandization. That is a gratifying development because Garnham sees mounting domestic pressure—primarily due to fiscal factors—to reduce the scope and expense of the U.S. military presence in Europe. In his view, the burden-sharing debate is merely one early manifestation of that process.

Alan Tonelson in the seventh chapter contends that current NATO arrangements are a poor economic and security bargain for the United States. His examination of spending patterns supports the thesis that the European allies have been free riding or at least "cheap riding" on the U.S. security guarantee. The Europeans have not lacked the economic resources to make a more vigorous effort, Tonelson contends; they have simply placed a higher priority on domestic welfare spending. The willingness of the United States to bear a disproportionate amount of the collective defense burden when

Western Europe was still devastated by the effects of World War II was at least arguably correct, but such a continuing subsidy to prosperous allies makes little sense from the standpoint of American interests. Indeed, U.S. trade and budget deficits are at least partly attributable to burdensome NATO military obligations, according to Tonelson.

Part III of this book deals with the implications of the evolving strategic environment. There is little doubt that the changes taking place in the Soviet Union and Eastern Europe are extremely important and confront NATO with a fundamentally new set of issues. It is less certain how the United States and Western Europe should respond to those changes, and the contributors to this part offer an array of views concerning that vital question.

Jeffrey Record examines in chapter 8 the U.S. troop presence in Europe and cites evidence of mounting domestic sentiment for a substantial reduction. He observes that America's security commitment to Western Europe has never entailed a specific troop level, and U.S. force levels have in fact varied widely since the early 1950s. Given that the Soviet threat has apparently receded, reducing the number of American soldiers stationed on the Continent may be both strategically and politically permissible, Record concludes.

Jed C. Snyder is cautiously optimistic about the prospects for a partial U.S. troop withdrawal within the context of NATO and Warsaw Pact conventional force reductions. Recent changes in Moscow's negotiating position significantly increase the possibility of that outcome. In chapter 9, Snyder emphasizes, however, that serious obstacles remain. Moreover, despite the apparent emergence of a less threatening Soviet foreign policy, NATO must stay vigilant and avoid steps that might prematurely diminish the deterrent capability of its conventional forces.

In chapter 10 Paul Bracken also sees improving prospects for the reduction of NATO and Warsaw Pact forces, as well as a less dominating U.S. role in the alliance. Moreover, the changing strategic environment in Europe alters the nature of deterrence, as well as its requirements. Bracken believes that a continuing U.S. military presence on the Continent is useful for crisis management and to facilitate the political changes taking place in Eastern Europe. He advocates a cautious approach to U.S. disengagement, periodically testing to see whether further steps are prudent. A gradual U.S. pullback, he insists, would lower "entrance barriers" for the Western Europeans, encouraging them to undertake greater defense responsibilities. It would also lower "exit barriers" for the Soviets, encouraging them to decrease their military presence in Eastern Europe and their political domination of that region.

William Lind argues in chapter 11 that focusing on such narrow issues as conventional force levels in Central Europe misses the significance of the changes occurring in the Soviet bloc, and indeed throughout the international system. He believes that those changes are sufficiently dramatic to warrant an entirely new grand strategy for the United States to replace the one that has guided U.S. policy since the 1940s. Future threats to U.S. and Western security, Lind maintains, are not likely to take place along an East-West axis, nor are they likely to be the kind of overt military threats that formal alliances and other aspects of America's existing grand strategy were designed to meet.

Stanley H. Kober shares Lind's conclusion that the changes taking place in the Soviet Union are likely to create an entirely new strategic environment. He detects increasing signs that Moscow's domestic political and economic reforms signify a systematic shift toward Western-style pluralism. If that trend continues, Kober concludes in chapter 11, it would eliminate any Soviet military threat to the democratic West and ultimately erase NATO's raison d'être. He urges U.S. and European leaders to encourage the Soviet reform process through a variety of innovative proposals to ease East-West tensions, including a mutual NATO–Warsaw Pact ban on conscription.

The authors in the final part of the book offer various alternatives to the status quo. All agree that significant changes are needed, but they diverge considerably about the nature and magnitude of those changes. Indeed, they disagree about the most fundamental question of all—whether NATO can or should be preserved.

David P. Calleo first argues that although the security of Western Europe remains important to the United States, some significant reforms in NATO's arrangements are imperative. Many of the economic competitiveness problems confronting the United States are at least partially the result of excessively burdensome alliance commitments, he insists. Calleo urges U.S. policymakers to begin devolving some of America's defense responsibilities to the European members of NATO. Devolution would include a larger Western European role in maintaining the alliance's conventional deterrent and the appointment of a European general as the commander of NATO forces. The United States should continue to play an important role in the defense of Western Europe, Calleo concludes, but it is essential that NATO become far more of a European-directed enterprise.

Earl C. Ravenal next contends that limited reform proposals will not prove sufficient. The changing international system renders alliance arrangements such as NATO and the Warsaw Pact increasingly ineffectual and irrelevant, in his judgment. Moreover, America's political and economic systems will no longer bear the enormous costs and risks of Washington's NATO commitments. The convergence of these international and domestic constraints, Ravenal insists, will ultimately leave U.S. officials with no alternative but to adopt a policy of strategic disengagement, severing the bonds that link the security policies of the United States and Western Europe.

Finally, Christopher Layne examines the implications of Europe's 1992 unified trade area plan for the United States and the Soviet Union. He believes that an economically integrated Western Europe would be an embryonic superpower that could pose problems for both Washington and Moscow. It is therefore essential for the United States and the Soviet Union to address some difficult issues while they still occupy dominant positions within their respective alliances. In particular, Layne urges the leaders of both super-powers to conclude an agreement for the mutual disengagement of their military forces now stationed in Central Europe. It is equally urgent, he contends, that steps be taken toward a political settlement that will heal the division of Europe, ameliorate the troublesome German question, and prevent the political ferment taking place in Eastern Europe from leading to turmoil that could result in a superpower confrontation.

Given the tremendous changes that have taken place—and continue to take place—in the international system, we should not be surprised that the viability and relevance of NATO are being called into question on the alliance's fortieth anniversary. Forty years is a long life span for any alliance, especially a peacetime one, and it is becoming evident that a reassessment is long overdue.

In determining whether the alliance serves the interests of either the United States or Western Europe, it is important to realize that throughout its existence, NATO has been a security arrangement between a senior partner (the United States) and an assortment of junior partners. The United States gradually assumed predominant responsibility for the security of Western Europe—at considerable cost and risk to itself—because of three important factors.

The first factor was that Western Europe seemed not merely relevant but vital to America's well-being. Extensive cultural and ideological ties played a role in that perception, as did the region's great economic importance. There was also the sobering fact that the United States had twice been drawn into European conflicts during a little more than a single generation. There was, in short, a significant incentive for the United States to ensure stability in Europe and to keep the Western European nations in friendly hands. Although critics as politically diverse as George Kennan and Senator Robert Taft questioned the need for U.S. membership in a comprehensive security arrangement—and offered trenchant arguments for less entangling alternatives—NATO enjoyed widespread American public support at its inception.

The second factor was the belief that a ruthless, expansionist power posed a serious threat to that vital region. Stalinist Russia seemed to validate the worst fears of Western statesmen on that score, and Stalin's successors did not materially ease those fears. Indeed, Kremlin policy frequently has been the glue holding NATO together. The invasions of Hungary in 1956, Czechoslovakia in 1968, and Afghanistan in 1979 restored at least a semblance of NATO unity following periods of marked disarray in the alliance.

The final factor was the realization that a Western Europe still reeling from the effects of World War II could make only modest efforts to defend itself. U.S. leaders were willing to compensate for that deficiency, at least temporarily, by undertaking extensive responsibility to shield Western Europe from aggression. At the same time, the Western Europeans were willing to accept a dominant U.S. role in the alliance, given the great disparity in both military and economic power between the United States and themselves.

Those were the crucial realities at NATO's birth and for a decade or so thereafter, but time has greatly altered the nature of all three factors. Western Europe is still important to the United States, but it has suffered a certain measure of relative decline. Strategically, the advent of intercontinental ballistic missiles reduced the region's significance as a forward staging area for the projection of U.S. military power. Economically, the nations of the Pacific Rim now exceed Western Europe in importance as America's principal trading partners.

Furthermore, Western Europe long ago ceased to be a war-ravaged community incapable of providing for its own defense. That realization has led to mounting irritation in the United States and an upsurge in debates about the question of burden sharing. A more subtle but equally important consequence is that the Western Europeans are increasingly reluctant to defer to U.S. policy preferences on a number of issues. As their economic power has grown, the Europeans have begun to assert themselves politically and to define their own set of vital interests.

Both changes have been apparent for some time, but as long as the perception of an unrelenting Soviet threat continued, the alliance could avoid confronting their implications. Such complacency is no longer possible, however; Moscow is pursuing a far more subtle and conciliatory policy toward the West. That shift in Soviet policy is an especially crucial development because the principal unifying force for any alliance is the existence of a dangerous adversary common to all the members. Remove that factor, and it becomes extraordinarily difficult to hold an alliance together. That is precisely the dilemma NATO faces at the end of the 1980s.

There is a diversity of views contained in this book concerning the current state of the alliance and prospects for its future. Despite the differing analyses and policy prescriptions, however, there is widespread agreement that the status quo is untenable. Profound changes in the alliance are almost certain—and not merely in the mists of the distant future but in the next few years. And the direction of those changes is reasonably predictable: toward a less extensive and dominating role by the United States. The principal areas of uncertainty are how far the processes of U.S. disengagement and devolution of security responsibilities to Western Europe will go and whether they will occur unilaterally or as part of an East-West grand settlement to end the division of Europe. The contributions in this book are presented in the hope that they will act as a catalyst for a badly needed reassessment of NATO on both sides of the Atlantic.

I
An Alliance under Stress

1

The Superpowers in the Twilight of NATO

Ronald Steel

I t has been argued that NATO is historically anachronistic, economically
absurd, militarily unviable, and politically obsolete. All this is, to some
degree, true. Nonetheless, in 1989 we commemorated—however improbable this would seem to NATO's founders—the fortieth anniversary of an alliance that has survived every proclamation of its inevitable and imminent
demise.

That it has endured so long is remarkable. That it will continue to flourish for even another decade is highly problematic. NATO is in a sense the
victim of its own success. It long ago achieved its original purpose—giving the
West Europeans a sense of security while they rebuilt their war-shattered
economies—and has become a bureaucratized institution worried about sur-
vivability.

It endured so long because the Soviets seemed rigidly hostile, the satellites
locked in their grip, the United States determined to carry the burden of
NATO at whatever cost. It hardly needs to be argued that all of these factors
have been profoundly changed. Today there are new elements in the equation—economic, military, and political—that have transformed the nature of
the alliance and of East-West relations.

First, there is the problem of economics. Ever since the Vietnam War, the
United States has refused to tax itself to pay for its extensive global commitments, let alone to provide the social benefits for its people that most Europeans take for granted. The problem became critical with the tax cuts and
massive deficits of the Reagan administration. Not long ago the world's
greatest creditor nation—a position of economic strength on which the alliance was built—it is today the world's major debtor. Deficits, declining overseas markets, and pressing domestic needs have made it far more difficult to
sustain the enormous cost of defending Europe, along with a policy of global
containment against various forms of radicalism and disorder.[1] What was an
easily manageable burden has now become a serious and even threatening
drain on American resources. The commitment to NATO, which consumes
an estimated 50 percent of the U.S. defense budget, or some $150 billion

annually, now has to be justified in terms of competing demands on American resources and the need to reduce budget deficits.[2]

In the search for expendable costs, NATO is a prime target. Shrill critics accuse the Europeans of being free riders and demand that these rich allies now pay for their own defense. Some of the more agitated demand that the United States pull its troops home forthwith and let the ungrateful Europeans fend for themselves.[3] Complaints echo across the political spectrum; all are inspired by annoyance with the Europeans, though the litany takes various forms.

Those on the right are annoyed at the Europeans for criticizing U.S. policy in places like Vietnam and the Middle East, trading imperviously with the Soviets, and running prosperous welfare states while the United States is mired in deficits. It is not so much the actual cost of NATO that seems to bother them. If it were, they would not have been such fervent defenders of Reagan's military budgets, including such multibillion dollar fantasies as the Strategic Defense Initiative. Rather, they find the Europeans too welfare statist, too independent, and too rich.

Those on the left are equally critical of NATO but approach the alliance from a somewhat different perspective. They see NATO Europe, with its anxieties about being abandoned by the United States in a nuclear crunch, as an impediment to a great power deal to slash nuclear weapons. To them the alliance seems more dangerous than it is worth. Also, being liberals, they believe that billions cut from the NATO budget could then be spent on items nearer to their hearts, such as schools, medical care, and pollution control. On both extremes—the resentful right and the romantic left—one can discern the old temptation of American unilateralism.

A more moderate position is taken by what could be called the burden sharers. Essentially loyal to NATO as it is, they nonetheless sense which way the wind is blowing and favor some reforms before the whole house comes down. Burden sharing is their answer: let the Europeans pay more for their defense. On the surface they have a point. On average the European allies pay about half as much for defense as does the United States.[4] But does this mean they pay too little—or that the United States pays too much?

The NATO allies spend about as much as they think they need to, and most of them draft their young men into compulsory service, which the United States does not do. One reason they spend less is that they have not seen the Soviets as threatening as Washington does. Another reason is that Third World radicals do not much bother them, and they see no reason to spend good money trying to get rid of them. Furthermore, the Europeans are not asking the United States to spend as much as it does on defense. The U.S. military budget is guided by factors other than Europe's welfare: the ability to intervene militarily anywhere in the world the United States chooses, to buy the fanciest military hardware, to pay for a volunteer army rather than draft conscripts, and to enjoy the privileges that go with being the protector of Europe and Japan.

Unilateralists, on both the right and the left, like the privileges but not the cost. They want the United States to enjoy full freedom of action—to disengage from Europe but still run its foreign policy, to defy the Soviets with impunity or sign separate deals with them—but without paying any political price for it. They want to shift the bill to the allies, assuming that the Europeans, though deprived of Washington's largesse, will still allow the United States to call the tune. They call this equity, but it may be nearer to wishful thinking.

Aside from the economic dilemma, which is relatively recent, NATO faces a recurring military one. From its inception, the alliance has rested on an American nuclear guarantee and an American threat to be the first to use nuclear weapons. Protection of the European allies, "extended deterrence" in the jargon, initially rested on the assumption of relative American nuclear invulnerability. But the growth of Soviet military power and the development of sophisticated delivery systems for nuclear weapons put both the United States, and the nuclear guarantee, at theoretical risk. During the Kennedy administration the threat of massive retaliation gave way to the more complicated strategy of flexible response, or a graduated application of force leading up to, but not necessarily invoking, nuclear weapons.

The strategy was designed to offer an escape from the spasmodic reliance on nuclear weapons inherent in massive retaliation, and also, to use a Kennedy-era phrase, a "wider range of options" in response to various perceived challenges. While it emphasized nuclear superiority over the Soviet Union and significantly boosted the U.S. missile force, it also premised a conventional buildup to prevent conflicts from escalating to the nuclear level. The ability to fight "limited wars," Kennedy told Congress on March 26, 1961, should be the "primary mission" of U.S. overseas forces.[5]

The emphasis on limited war was not enthusiastically received by the European allies. A strategy designed to spare the United States the ravages of nuclear war seemed, from the perspective of the NATO partners, to increase the chances of conventional war in Europe. "Flexible response was clearly an American strategy reflecting American preoccupations," one thoughtful critic has written.[6] The Europeans sought safety in persuading the Soviets that any assault on Europe would trigger a nuclear war that would engulf the Soviet Union itself. While they welcome a larger American army in Europe as a symbol of reassurance, they resisted any notion of a conventional war, let alone a nuclear one, actually fought in Europe. For them the more convincing was the prospect of escalation to nuclear war, the less likely it was that any conflict would occur. What they dreaded was the situation Ronald Reagan once mused about publicly early in his administration: a war between the Soviet Union and the United States confined to Europe.[7]

The military problem is in many respects a political problem, and this forms the third part of the equation. Extended deterrence is not just about weapons but about who decides and who takes the risks. Europeans want reassurance of American fidelity in the form of nuclear weapons, while the United States is rightly concerned about crises escalating to the nuclear level. As gestures of reassurance, the United States has, over the years, proposed various technical fixes, including the ill-fated NATO nuclear navy of the early 1960s, with its polyglot crews, and the Pershing IIs of the early 1980s. In every case the issue has been one of confidence and reassurance—in other words, psychological. But the attempted resolution has been in terms of hardware.

The political problem within the alliance has not been addressed directly in large part because it is so fundamental. For the Europeans, the Pershing issue was the expression of a political anxiety. They sought reassurance and some measure of control over U.S. strategy. The INF treaty signed in Washington in December 1987 resolved some of the military anxieties by securing the removal of the Soviet SS-20s, along with the U.S. Pershings, but did nothing to alleviate a European sense of being an instrument of American diplomacy.

The allies formally welcomed the INF accord, but it also reinforced the anomaly between political and military power within the alliance. The Europeans would like to secure greater control over American decision making insofar as the alliance is concerned while pursuing their own political and economic agenda in Eastern Europe, the Soviet Union, and elsewhere in the world. They do not want their military dependency to impede their diplomatic independence. They desire all the conveniences of protection by a powerful ally and none of the inconveniences associated with military dependency. Thus, they complain about American military hegemony but try not to let it get in their way. Apparently it is not so onerous that they want to do away with the need for it by providing for their own defense.

It is understandable that they want the benefits of both worlds. Why should they not? But this is not quite the bargain that they, or the United States, undertook in establishing NATO. That bargain was that the Europeans would relinquish diplomatic autonomy in return for American military protection. Nobody ever put this into writing, to be sure, but that was the bargain. De Gaulle understood this perfectly well, inveighed against it frequently, and pulled France out of NATO's integrated command because he wanted to pursue a diplomacy directed from Paris and not from the Potomac. For this he was pilloried by American officials, who considered him an egoist and an ingrate, and in a sense he was. But his great crime was in challenging Washington's monopoly on alliance diplomacy. He asked to be dealt in on the decision making, and when his bid was contemptuously refused, he set about to build a different creation, a Europe that extended not westward but eastward, one, in his phrase, "from the Atlantic to the Urals."

De Gaulle's weakness was that he spoke more as a Frenchman than a European, and France was in no position to substitute for the United States as Europe's protector. But that was a quarter-century ago, and today the balance within the alliance has changed. France is operating as a European, not a global, power; Western Europe is moving toward full economic integration in 1992; the Soviet Union is returning to the wider European state system of which it was once an integral part; and the United States no longer has the means to fulfill the measure of its global ambitions.

The Atlantic alliance, forged in another era, by its very nature resists adjustment to these changed conditions. Its tranquillity and even its relevance are hobbled by the disparity of power between the United States and its European allies, the inequality of risks among the members, the fact that the allies have no common diplomacy outside the NATO area, the determination of Washington to maintain political control over the alliance, the unwillingness of the Europeans to abide by what the Americans believe should be vows of diplomatic chastity, and the disintegration of the Soviet empire.

Mikhail Gorbachev has compounded, though hardly created, the problems, and his striking innovations at home and abroad have considerably loosened the glue of fear holding NATO together. His determined efforts to liberalize Soviet society, his willingness to withdraw in defeat from Afghanistan, his efforts at peacemaking in the Middle East and the Third World, his scrapping of the SS-20 missiles that gave Europeans such anxiety, his announcement of unilateral cuts of Soviet forces in Europe, his avowed willingness to reduce missile arsenals drastically and to negotiate political differences, and his acceptance of political pluralism in Eastern Europe—all this has had a profound effect on the European public and even on politicians and diplomats.

To many Europeans the cold war seems to be evolving into something far more familiar and manageable: a power rivalry between states based on such factors as balance of power and spheres of influence. The cataclysmic ideological conflict for the soul of the world now seems distant and improbable. Few take seriously the pretensions of communism, or of unregulated capitalism, for that matter. Everyone worships at the market. The problems facing industrial society are increasingly those of reconciling the demands of the free market system with social justice and welfare. The Europeans believe, with some reason, that they have dealt with this task better than the Soviets and even than the Americans. On both sides of what used to be called the iron curtain, the issue is how to make the market economy produce efficiently while maintaining an equitable system of distribution.

The Soviet threat has been redefined. For Europeans the task is to prevent the Soviets from sliding backward from the changes spurred by Gorbachev, to assist politically and economically the gradual political evolution of Eastern Europe, and to ensure European prosperity by protecting its economy from the dangers posed by the refusal of the United States to set its own economic house in order. Rather than trying to insulate themselves from a menacing Soviet Union, Europeans are increasingly engaged in the task of managing the transition of the Soviet Union from isolation and autarky into honorary membership in the European state system.

While the United States, like most other nations, faces threats to its security and well-being, those threats can no longer be defined exclusively, or even primarily, in terms of the Soviet Union. The United States must restore its economy to health and make it fully competitive within the world economic system, end the trade and budget deficits that cause turmoil at home and resentment among allies who believe they are obliged to pay much of its costs, and undertake the immense task of incorporating a demoralized, antisocial, drug-ridden underclass into the American social compact. In recent years there has been a sharp shift among Americans in the perception of threat. The greatest source of danger is no longer seen in Moscow but rather at home in the realms of education, crime, pollution, and drugs.[8]

Europe today seems a haven of safety and stability, but its future is clouded by unresolved issues. Among these is the future of Germany. The Atlantic alliance was created in large part to protect, and also to contain, the Germans. NATO, like the European Community of which the Federal Republic is the key continental member, was predicated on a Germany within a wider setting, one where it will neither threaten nor dominate its neighbors. De Gaulle tried to do this in the early 1960s by establishing a special relationship with Bonn, though with only limited success. When the chips were down, the Germans relied on Washington more than on Paris. But with Germany's new self-confidence and Europe's impressive prosperity, the balance is changing, and Germany's European identity is becoming more important to its younger leaders.

But if the Federal Republic now seeks its partners and its identity in the European Community, that entity, too, no less than NATO, is built on the existence of two Germanys. No European can affirm this formally, nor can any German who seeks a future in politics. Just as West German politicians must declare that reunification, however distant and even improbable, must never be ruled out, so must Germany's NATO partners continually pledge their allegiance to something they would prefer not to think about.

The unresolved contradiction within the equation is that the Soviets hold the keys to German unity. Would they be willing to see East and West Germans reunited? There is every reason to doubt it, despite the highly ambiguous offer Stalin made in 1952 in order to block German rearmament. But this does not prevent the Soviets from tantalizing displays of their German card. During his triumphant visit to the Federal Republic in June 1989, Gorbachev dropped a guarded hint that the wall between the two Berlins could perhaps come down "once the conditions that generated it disappear."[9] Whether the Soviets would accept the demise of their important East German ally, whether the government in East Berlin would allow itself to be dismantled, whether the West Germans would actually welcome the prospect of absorbing some 17 million ethnic cousins who for two generations have lived under a radically different social system, and whether Bonn would be willing to put at risk its place of honor within the European Community structure—all of these are matters of conjecture.[10] Yet the virtual defection of Hungary from the Soviet bloc, the Soviet acceptance of a noncommunist government in Poland, the flight of East Germans to the Federal Republic across the Austrian frontier, and the decision of Moscow to placate Bonn at the cost of antagonizing or even destabilizing the GDR has suddenly brought the issue of Germany's reunification to the forefront.

Whatever Germany's future, the fact that East Germany is militarily dependent on Moscow gives the Soviets a special position of influence in Bonn—one to which the Federal Republic's friends and allies must be sensitive. For these reasons Germany's situation within the alliance is unlike that of any other nation. Its strategic position on the front line between East and West puts it in a position of danger that is unique. Any war in Europe would immediately be fought on German soil, however improbable such a war may currently seem. This is why the Germans are particularly sensitive to NATO's nuclear strategy as defined by the United States and why there is such resistance even in the governing conservative party to Washington's insistence on modernizing short-range nuclear missiles along the border with East Germany. A current phrase, "the shorter the range, the deader the Germans," expresses not only anxieties about nuclear war but the growing insistence in Bonn that East Germans, on whose territory such weapons are targeted, are Germans too.[11]

Because of its history and geography, Germany is forced to look to the East as well as to the West. The political evolution of Eastern Europe is no abstract matter for Germany, as it is for Americans and even for the British and French. For years Bonn has quietly been pursuing a policy of engaging East Germany in a network of economic and political deals. Even if reunification in the foreseeable future remains unlikely, the two German states are deeply intertwined and will almost certainly become more so.[12] Increasingly the West Germans are faced with the difficulties of reconciling their Atlantic and European Community loyalties with their pan-German identity and their determination to forge closer economic and even political links with Eastern Europe. Once again, partly as a result of Moscow's loosened control over the "satellites", partly because of Bonn's great economic power as market and lender, the once-forgotten concept of Mitteleuropa—a Central European constellation focused on Germany—is now being openly discussed.

What has become known as Genscherism, named after the architect of Bonn's foreign policy during the Schmidt and Kohl governments, has elicited wide support across the political spectrum because it opens German policy toward the East while retaining loyalty to Germany's Atlantic and West European commitments. This policy preaches a restructured Europe with a reduced American (as well as Soviet) presence, a growing entente with Eastern Europe and with Moscow, and, through diplomacy and the evolution of NATO, the construction of the old dream of a Europe open to the Urals.

The dramatic changes in Soviet policy over the past few years both at home and abroad have virtually dissolved the cement of common danger that has held NATO together. While the alliance clearly retains utility as an insurance policy and while the Soviets themselves do not want an American withdrawal from Europe, with all the possibilities of instability that would entail,[13] the old structure of NATO cannot hold. If the alliance is not transformed, it will gradually disintegrate.

Essentially there are three possible courses of action. First, one can try to maintain the present system with a bit of tidying up around the edges in the form of more burden sharing by the Europeans. The basic problem with this approach is that it requires the continued infusion of a significant part of the U.S. budget into the defense of Europe. For all the reasons cited—the declining fear of war, the great prosperity of the Europeans, the economic troubles of the United States, and the increasing unwillingness of the American public to sustain the NATO burden—the old consensus has been undermined.

A second option is a considerably greater European role within the alliance, or "devolution." This means a European commander for NATO, a partial U.S. troop withdrawal, and perhaps some form of European nuclear deterrent. The virtue of such a plan is that it reflects the current economic balance within the alliance. The notion of two NATO pillars would move from rhetoric to reality. The major problem with this has been well expressed by one of NATO's most trenchant critics who has written that for the United States, devolution "combines aspects of commitment and decommitment. . . . We would have participation without authority, risk without control, involvement without the clear ability to defend, and the exposure without adequate deterrence."[14]

Creating a self-reliant Europe would eliminate the reason for American participation in the alliance. Devolution would be the end, not the reform, of NATO. This would be particularly true if the Europeans developed their own independent nuclear deterrent completely free from American direction. The United States would not relinquish the decision over war and peace to a European committee.

In any case, such a European deterrent requires an enormous degree of political will, along with an overwhelming sense of danger. Both are lacking in Europe today. So long as the Soviet Union continues along its path of political evolution, emphasis will be placed on engagement rather than confrontation with the East. An independent European nuclear deterrent may be an idea whose time has passed. The movement today is toward far fewer nuclear weapons in Europe, not more. It would take a dramatically aggressive change in Soviet policy to persuade the Europeans either to invest more in NATO or to believe that security lay in acquiring weapons that could never be used without destroying Europe itself. Increasingly in the world today, power and security are defined in terms of economics, not weapons.

One other possibility remains: the transformation of NATO into the cornerstone of a pan-European state system. NATO would find its apotheosis through its negotiated demise. Yet this can be done only in a way that protects the interests of the two superpowers, and indeed under their direction. Washington and Moscow have common interests to protect. The Americans want a Europe that will cease to be a drain on the U.S. Treasury yet is not endangered by Soviet pressure. The Soviets want a Europe that will help pull them out of their economic sinkhole, bail out the bankrupt satellites, while still allowing them a sphere of influence in an area they have always deemed vital to their security.

Both superpowers need a settlement in Europe. Their alliances are faltering, and their position, both politically and economically, is becoming weaker. Their extraordinary forty-year period of hegemony over Europe is now in its final days and cannot be resuscitated. They remain enormously powerful militarily, but their ability to use this power to shape the world has declined dramatically. National power today is measured more and more in terms of trade and productivity than in instruments of destruction. The key decisions in this realm are not being made in the Kremlin or the Pentagon but in such new centers of power as Tokyo, Frankfurt, and Brussels.

But why, it might be asked, should not the West Europeans simply carry on their own diplomacy with the Soviets over the future of their common house? The problem is that Europe does not yet exist. It is an ever more cohesive economic entity but still only a political dream. Who is to speak for Europe? Who is to carry on such negotiations with Moscow? The West Europeans do not have the political cohesion to back up their diplomacy. They do not, for that matter, yet have a diplomacy. NATO has been the instrument of their self-willed abdication from power. The Europeans have allowed the United States to speak for them because they have not decided who else should. Washington can represent European interests precisely because the United States is not a European power. It is a disinterested protector; it does not favor one European state over another. This is why, to borrow Canning's phrase, the new world was called into being to redress the balance of the old.

It is clear that a restored and self-reliant Europe cannot be attained by the Europeans themselves but only with the cooperation of the two great powers that still serve as their guarantors. In this regard NATO becomes important politically even as its military significance declines. The United States, rather than accept the continued diminution of its influence within the alliance, has the opportunity to use NATO as an instrument to negotiate a settlement with the Soviets to end the cold war in Europe.

In the twilight of their hegemony, the United States and the Soviet Union have the opportunity to draw to a close, on terms that protect both their common interests and European stability, the great confrontation that has divided the Continent. To dissipate that power is to lose control over the settlement and also perhaps to lose the stability that the rival alliances have, in their own way, produced.

Any such settlement must be based on the fact that the cold war alliances are of declining relevance. As the superpower condominium over Europe draws to a close, both Washington and Moscow must protect their interests over a continent that is more populous and richer than either of them. The partition of Europe is ending with a suddenness that few could have foreseen and with a momentum that the superpowers cannot control. Although the United States and the Soviet Union could not keep Europe divided even if they wanted to, their interests require them to negotiate a withdrawal that ensures European stability.

What form would such a settlement take? To sketch the outlines, it would provide for the gradual withdrawal of Soviet and American armies from the Continent, the removal of their nuclear weapons from Europe, and their agreement to respect the internal political evolution of the European states. The Europeans themselves would be forbidden from changing frontiers by force, acquiring aggressive military arsenals, threatening the security of their neighbors, and violating the basic rights of their citizens.

Such an arrangement would ease the transition from a bipolar to a multipolar world while reducing the dangers inherent in the release of old constraints. Such dangers are real. As Soviet power recedes in Eastern Europe, factionalism and anarchy are reappearing. In the West, the great postwar political and economic edifices are threatened by special interests and nationalistic goals. Thus, it is in everyone's interest that the cold war end in a settlement at the center rather than in a collapse along the frontiers.

The transition from détente to entente cannot be made by the Europeans themselves. It requires an accord by the great powers. Because the World War II settlements raised hopes that could not be fulfilled does not mean that great powers must never negotiate. Rather, it means that they must know how to define their interests, how to separate pious hopes from realistic equations of power, and to recognize that their common interests may now be greater than it was when the unique but now fading aura of their hegemony divided them.

Notes

1. On deficits, taxes, and benefits, see David P. Calleo: *Beyond American Hegemony: The Future of of the Western Alliance* (New York: Basic Books, 1987), pp. 109–13.

2. While it is extremely difficult to separate forces committed to NATO from the general military budget, a number of critics have made a serious effort to do so, most notably Earl Ravenal in, for example, "Europe without America: The Erosion of NATO," *Foreign Affairs* 63, no. 5 (Summer 1985), and *Defining Defense: The 1985 Military Budget* (Washington, D.C.: Cato Institute, 1984).

3. For the moderate "devolution" position see Calleo, *Beyond American Hegemony;* James Chace: "Ike Was Right," *Atlantic Monthly* (July–August 1987) and "A New Grand Strategy," *Foreign Policy* 70 (Spring 1988); Christopher Layne, "Atlanticism without NATO," *Foreign Policy* 67 (Summer 1987); and Ravenal, "Europe without America." For the more extreme ultimatum-withdrawal position, see Melvyn Krauss, *How NATO Weakens the West* (New York: Simon & Schuster, 1986), and "Let the Europeans Negotiate with Gorbachev," in Ted Galen Carpenter, ed., *Collective Defense or Strategic Independence? Alternative Strategies for the Future* (Lexington, Mass.: Lexington Books, 1989); and Irving Kristol, "What's Wrong with NATO?" *New York Times Magazine,* September 25, 1983, pp. 64–71.

4. In 1987 the following NATO nations spent on defense in billions of dollars: United States, 288; France, 34; West Germany, 34; Great Britain, 32; Italy, 16; in dollars per capita: United States, 1,185; France, 620; West Germany, 560; Great Britain, 567; Italy, 293; as a percentage of government spending: United States, 28; France, 20; West Germany, 23; Great Britain, 11; Italy, 5; as a percentage of gross domestic product/gross national product (1986): United States, 6.7; France, 3.9; West Germany, 3.1; Great Britain, 4.9; Italy, 2.2. Source: *The Military Balance 1988–1989* (London: International Institute for Strategic Studies). For a good discussion, see Stephen Walt, "Two Cheers for Containment: Probable Allied Responses to U.S. Isolationism," in *Collective Defense or Strategic Independence.*

5. For an extended discussion of flexible response, see Seyom Brown, *The Faces of Power* (New York: Columbia University Press, 1983), pp. 161–80; Kennedy quotation, p. 165.

6. Calleo, *Hegemony,* p. 46, and for the European reaction to flexible response, pp. 44–50.

7. General de Gaulle gave vivid expression to these anxieties in November 1962: "Who can say that if the occasion arises the two [superpowers], while each deciding not to launch its missiles at the main enemy so that it should itself be spared, will not crush the others? It is possible to imagine that on some awful day Western Europe should be wiped out from Moscow and Central Europe from Washington." Quoted in Brown, *Faces of Power,* p. 170.

8. According to a June 1989 poll conducted for the World Policy Institute by Greenberg-Lake/The Analysis Group, only 2 percent of adults polled listed Soviet aggression as "the most important problem facing America today," with education, inflation, environmental, and personal safety issues totaling 55 percent; among "potential threats from abroad" only 4 percent listed Soviet aggression, with 37 percent listing drug trafficking and 12 percent nuclear proliferation.

9. Michael Parks and William Touhy, "Gorbachev Ends Trip, Offering Hope That Berlin Wall Can Come Down," *Los Angeles Times,* June 16, 1989, p. I, p. 6.

10. For speculation that the Kremlin might be willing to accept a unified Germany, see Christopher Layne, "Toward German Reunification?" *Journal of Contemporary Studies* 7, no. 4 (Fall 1984): 22–25.

11. The fracas over short-range missiles that pitted Washington and London against Bonn and most of the European allies roiled NATO during the spring of 1989. The most serious dispute since that over the Soviet gas pipeline in 1982, it revealed an unprecedented degree of German resistance to the dictates of American nuclear strategy. It was calmed only when President Bush agreed to Gorbachev's call for discussions on deep cuts in troops and weapons in Europe and linked the missile issue to progress in reduction of conventional forces. Allied cohesion was restored, but at the price, in effect, of accepting Bonn's position with some window dressing. See Frederick Kempe, "West Germany's Ties with U.S. Become Increasingly Testy," *Wall Street Journal,* March 13, 1989, p. 1; Thomas Friedman, "U.S. Anger against Germans over NATO Stand," *New York Times,* April 30, 1989, p. 1; Joseph Biden, "Bush, Not Kohl, Is Undermining NATO," *New York Times,* May 7, 1989.

12. On Ostpolitik, See Calleo, *Hegemony,* p. 53; William E. Griffith, *The Ostpolitik of the Federal Republic of Germany* (Cambridge: MIT Press, 1978); Lawrence L. Whetten, *Germany's Ostpolitik: Relations between the Federal Republic and the Warsaw Pact Countries* (London: Oxford University Press, 1971); Angela Stent, *From Embargo to Ostpolitik: The Political Economy of West German-Soviet Relations, 1955–1980* (Cambridge: Cambridge University Press, 1981); Eric G. Frey, *Division and Détente: The Germanies and Their Alliances* (New York: Praeger, 1987). For a good overview of Europe's qualms regarding Washington's roller-coaster policies toward the Soviet Union, see Raymond L. Garthoff, *Détente and Confrontation: American-Soviet Relations from Nixon to Reagan* (Washington, D.C.: Brookings Institution, 1985), esp. pp. 1029–38.

13. During his June 1989 visit to Bonn, Gorbachev stated: "There is an understanding both in the East and the West of the role of the United States in Europe. I can't imagine a realistic policy of the Soviet leadership that would have the objective of pushing the United States out of Europe, of hampering the interests of the United States in Europe." *Los Angeles Times,* June 16, 1989.

14. Earl Ravenal: "Europe without America," p. 1030. Strong arguments for devolution, including an independent nuclear deterrent with German participation, can be found in Calleo, *Hegemony,* pp. 129–220, and Layne, "Atlanticism without NATO." For a more equivocal view, see Helmut Sonnenfeldt, "The European Pillar: The American View," *Adelphi Papers,* no. 235, "The Changing Strategic Landscape," part I. pp. 91–105 (London: International Institute for Strategic Studies, Spring 1989). Also see Michael Lucas: "The United States and Post-INF Europe, *World Policy Journal* (Spring 1988): 184–234.

2
NATO's Enduring Importance

Robert E. Hunter

There is nothing immutable about NATO. It was created to serve specific purposes. If and when those purposes—or new and valid ones—are fulfilled, it can and should cease to exist. Indeed, this fortieth anniversary of the NATO treaty is not just a moment symbolizing unprecedented success for a peacetime alliance; it is a time when major changes in the structure of European security have again become possible and when the core elements of security must be reexamined if what is important and enduring is to be preserved and adapted to changing times.

Creating an Alliance

The signing of the North Atlantic Treaty on April 4, 1949, was the culmination of a process of reinvolving the United States in the fate of the European Continent. There was as yet no military confrontation. Rather, America's new allies in Western Europe were mainly seeking a U.S. political commitment to underpin economic recovery in Europe that, if successful, would provide a greater capacity for West European states to resist threats to their domestic freedoms and political independence. The treaty was seen, at least by West European governments, not as a prelude to military confrontation but as added insurance to make the Marshall Plan work. The West European allies placed less emphasis than did the United States on the potential role of Soviet forces in shaping their future. Security was not essentially about military guarantees; at heart, it was about gaining a greater sense of certainty about the future of political developments.[1]

Indeed, the "O" in NATO was added only after the beginning of the Korean War, when it appeared that the Soviet Union, acting through North Korea, was prepared to apply military force to achieve expansionist political goals. Allied Command Europe was thus created, becoming active two days shy of two years after the North Atlantic Treaty was signed. Even then, it was some time before allied forces began to be prepared to respond to an attack from the East.

In this process, the emerging political division of Europe was militarized. To this day, it cannot be stated with confidence that, save for this act, there would have been aggression by the Soviet Union—just as the opposite proposition cannot be proved. But it was clear that emerging military confrontation created a much higher degree of certainty about security in Europe than there had been before. Deployed military forces were much more tangible than political disputes or economic challenge. And the addition of West Germany to NATO, plus East Germany to the Soviet alliance system, underscored the added certainty in calculations about European security that was represented by the division of Germany.

East-West relations in Europe became politically frozen in cold war. Yet for all the anxieties and fears that this entailed, the militarization of East-West conflict in Europe did provide a basis for predicting behavior on each side, for measuring it with some accuracy, and for understanding the limits of action and ambition. Militarization also imposed a logic of its own— analogous to that pertaining to deterrence of nuclear war—which exerts its demands to this day. This logic helped to ensure that American power would not be withdrawn after economic reconstruction was completed.

The goals of the alliance—then as now—have been quite simple: to prevent repetition of experience during the interwar period (although this time the potential aggressor proved to be the Soviet Union rather than Germany), to provide a secure political climate within which allied states could pursue their economic activities, to preserve the independence of each of the allies (and the freedoms of peoples in those that were democracies), to counter domestic political movements subservient to Moscow, and to contain the expansion of Soviet influence, regardless of the means that Moscow might employ. And at least in part, these goals were to be accomplished by involving U.S. power, in various aspects, for the benefit of Western Europe and the United States.

The Current Agenda

The logic of military confrontation has imposed severe requirements. Calculations of threat from the East have focused on capabilities rather than intentions; the context has been military, not political. Potential for Soviet–Warsaw Pact aggression has had to be measured in terms of the relative size of forces, character of equipment, dispositions, training and maneuvers, and what could be gleaned of Soviet doctrine. By the same token, the doctrine adopted by Western military forces has had to present a credible capacity to contain, by one means or another, any form of Warsaw Pact aggression.

Efforts required to meet the demands imposed by the logic of military confrontation have been clustered around two major considerations: gaining significant conventional force capabilities to retard (but not defeat) a Warsaw

Pact attack, especially in Central Europe, and to engage, and then make credible, the great equalizer represented by U.S. nuclear weapons. The alliance has always had more difficulty in dealing with the latter set of considerations, in major part because of two factors: none of the allies has been prepared to commit the material and human resources needed to guarantee that Warsaw Pact aggression could be defeated at the conventional level, and several of the allies, especially West Germany, have not been prepared to accept the possibility that a major war could be contained short of the initiation of nuclear hostilities.

Over the years, the reliance of NATO doctrine on the potential engagement of U.S. nuclear weapons has provoked a repetitive series of two basic difficulties. One has been recurrent opposition to nuclear weapons on the part of major sections of West European public opinion. The other has related to the difficulty of proving that the United States would use nuclear weapons on Europe's behalf, where that act could lead to America's destruction. In the latest full-blown political crisis over this issue during the early 1980s, the alliance underwent the torturous process of agreeing to deploy Pershing II ballistic missiles and ground-launched cruise missiles in Europe as a means of trying to "prove the unprovable" about U.S. steadfastness. And in 1989, some of the same basic issues were involved in the question whether Lance short-range nuclear missiles based in Europe should be modernized or bargained away.

In terms of the logic of military confrontation in Europe, therefore, the current agenda for European security is simple to describe. NATO needs to maintain robust conventional defenses, relative to the perceived Warsaw Pact military threat ("capabilities"), and it needs to retain in its doctrine a connection to the U.S. nuclear arsenal that is sufficiently credible both to deter the Soviet Union (long considered by most Western analysts to be relatively straightforward) and to reassure the West European allies (historically believed to be much more difficult). The former set of requirements can be achieved in one of two ways, or through some combination thereof:

1. By sustaining high levels of allied defense spending, adopting the use of high-technology weaponry, promoting rationalization, standardization, and interoperability, encouraging intra-alliance defense industry cooperation to improve the efficiency of resource use, and adopting doctrines and redeploying forces to maximize military effectiveness.

2. By gaining reductions in the Warsaw Pact threat, through either negotiated agreements or unilateral actions, such as a follow-on to those cuts now promised by the Soviet Union.

Issues relating to the role of the U.S. nuclear arsenal are more complex. In theory, if the Warsaw Pact conventional threat were reduced, the need for a U.S. nuclear guarantee would decline. But it is not easy to define the point at which this guarantee could be dispensed with. Furthermore, despite theoretical arguments about limited use of nuclear weapons, this engagement of the U.S. nuclear arsenal is in reality an either-or proposition: either NATO doctrine is based on the possibility that the United States would risk its own nuclear destruction, or it is not.[2]

So long as the potential use of nuclear weapons remains part of NATO doctrine, the logic of military confrontation argues either for making the U.S. guarantee as credible as possible or for finding a substitute. This logic lies behind the push to modernize Lance. There are two purposes involved in this effort, however. One is to increase the chances that the Warsaw Pact will be deterred from attacking Western Europe through NATO's retention of this particular rung in the ladder of escalation. Far more important is the role that short-range nuclear forces can play in reassuring the allies of U.S. stead-fastness, fundamentally a matter of the psychology of European allies.[3] Yet from the perspective of the United States, even without Lance or a successor, it would retain the capacity to destroy the same targets and demonstrate its nuclear commitment with weapons based elsewhere.

Extending these arguments, from a purely technical point of view, negotiating away land-based nuclear missiles based in Europe would not prevent fulfilling requirements of NATO doctrine. Politically, however, such an agreement—perhaps even the convening of East-West negotiations under the wrong circumstances—could be seen (erroneously) as removing nuclear weapons from NATO doctrine, with consequent uncertainties, risks, and apprehensions within the alliance.

Nor has there been anything inherently wrong in strategic logic with substituting a British or French nuclear deterrent in Europe for that of the United States. In terms of threatening escalation from conventional combat, either could suit perfectly well; indeed, either could help to ensure that the United States did not withdraw from engagement in European security, even if it formally rejected any linkage to its nuclear arsenal.[4] Yet the U.S. nuclear arsenal has always seemed to be a more credible deterrent than that of Great Britain and France, especially when related to the security of other states. Also, complications would attend the extension of a European nuclear umbrella over West Germany, with the risk of violating the almost universally accepted taboo against a German role in controlling nuclear weapons. The perceived greater reliability of the United States as a nuclear guarantor remains politically persuasive in Western Europe so long as the United States retains its essential political commitment to European security.

The Added Agenda

Security, however, entails more than defense and deterrence—the logic of military confrontation. That has been evident, for example, in the parallel development of West European integration through functional institutions, in the need for NATO to issue the Harmel report (1967), which held out hope for the success of *détente* in reducing tensions and ameliorating conflict, and in the increasing importance of prosecuting arms control—not just to promote military stability but to gain domestic political support for maintaining adequate military forces.[5] Indeed, adopting a two-track approach of arms control negotiations as a condition of deployments has become essential not just to make possible the modernization of nuclear weapons but also to sustain efforts in conventional arms.

With a new insistence, security in Europe has been moving beyond calculations of military balance and management of recurring defense problems to the exploration of political issues that have so far proved intractable. Several factors explain this change, including the policies of Soviet president Mikhail S. Gorbachev, fading memories of past conflict and instability, and competing demands for economic resources. But perhaps most significant, the effort to fulfill the logic of military confrontation has succeeded in the way that, politically, matters most. There has developed a deep sense of confidence in Western Europe that the process of containing Soviet power has worked to reduce the chances not just of war but of successful Soviet efforts to alter the internal character of Western states.[6] Virtually no qualified observer in Western Europe, civilian or military, believes there is more than a remote risk of war. This is not prelude to Soviet political encroachment, however. Notably, even with "Gorby-mania" in Western Europe, the term *self-Finlandization* has passed from discussion within the alliance.

Regarding the new agenda, the fulfillment of the logic of military confrontation has also been an essential backdrop to efforts to reduce conventional forces. For several reasons, talks in Vienna on Conventional Forces in Europe (CFE) hold out greater promise than did the old talks on Mutual and Balanced Force Reductions. Gorbachev has promised some unilateral force cuts and has accepted the principle of asymmetrical force reductions; the Warsaw Pact proposal first tabled in March 1989 was quite close to NATO's (including provisions for limiting the most threatening weapons); and there are economic pressures in both East and West to scale back military spending.[7] Most critical is confidence that East-West political stability in Europe has been achieved. Thus discussion can take place between the two sides about the terms in which the military element of stability is expressed, without the process itself seeming to hold out a serious risk of producing a new instability. Of course, it is possible, even probable, that European parliaments and perhaps even the U.S. government will make preemptive reductions in military spending and attendant force commitments to NATO defense. It is also possible that the Soviets, either in response or because of other developments, including turmoil in Eastern Europe, will revert to aggressive behavior. These possibilities pose significant challenges to Western leadership. Nevertheless, the risk of a recrudescence of intense militarized confrontation is today far smaller than at any other time during the past several decades.

This gradual working through the possibilities in the military aspects of European security is not the only key development. Equally important, it is also contributing to a gradual return to first principles: a renewed awareness of NATO's basic purposes (peace, independence, prosperity, freedom) and of many political issues regarding European security that were in play at a time when the overriding need to establish greater certainty in East-West relations in Europe froze them in place.

This renewed importance for the political dimensions of security also suggests that even greater emphasis needs to be put on the East-West negotiating track of security and political relations that parallels the force reduction aspects of the CFE talks. Indeed, in terms of creating a sound political basis for ending East-West confrontation and creating a new basis for security in Europe, the series of negotiations and conferences that are collectively referred to as the Helsinki process is a critical complement to efforts to reduce the role of military forces. All elements play an important role, including security- and confidence-building measures, commercial relations, flow of information, and a congeries of human rights issues. Because the evolution of political interests, concerns, and relations will largely determine the shape of any future security system in Europe, political aspects of the process of change must be accorded high priority from the outset.

What is happening is no less than a renewal of debate about whether Europe needs to be divided. This debate, of course, begs the question whether an undivided Europe is a natural state. Indeed, in the terms in which the concept has been expressed for the past four decades, it is without precedent in the modern world. Nevertheless, two factors are primarily responsible for making this issue more important than it has been for nearly forty years: the incipient reduction of political rigidities imposed by military confrontation and concern that the requirements of preserving the existing framework—significant levels of military spending, a large and modern nuclear arsenal, and a doctrine that implicitly embraces the possibility of mutual mass destruction—could themselves erode the West's confidence in lasting security. As a result, the time has come when some basic propositions regarding European security must be reexamined.

Criteria for Judgment

There must, however, be caution before leaping to the judgment that NATO can, in the relatively near future, be dispensed with or that the United States can divest itself of responsibilities for helping to preserve European security. The case for retaining the NATO framework and U.S. engagement, at least until there is a better means of providing for European security, mirrors the conditions for change. If a critical function of a militarized division of the

Continent has been to provide a high degree of certainty about European security, then any alternative must provide at least as much.

It is difficult now to detail the precise terms of an alternative structure of European security, but it is possible to discuss the problems that any radical change would entail. Some are already evident from negotiations on conventional forces; these include the lack of strategic depth in Western Europe, especially if any part of the Federal Republic of Germany were denied to NATO forces, immutable Soviet advantages over the United States regarding proximity to Central Europe, and consequently the West's greater dependence on nuclear weapons.

There are also several important longer-range considerations, beyond the technicalities of preserving and then transforming the arms balance. Three can illustrate the thought and effort required: evolution in Eastern Europe, the relationship between West European developments and ending the division of Europe, and the continuing relevance of U.S. power and presence.

Eastern Europe

Operating from the premise that no basic change in patterns of European security can or should take place without providing for a high degree of certainty, it is clear that the division of Europe cannot be ended so long as there is doubt about developments in Eastern Europe.

Politically, the cold war began as much over the future of these countries as over anything else. For the last several decades, implicit in the policies of NATO states has been the belief that the Soviet Union has and will insist on retaining primacy in Eastern Europe because of two propositions. First, the Soviet Union will not tolerate any interference with its capacity to protect itself from attack from the West, and to ensure this ability it will maintain a glacis in which its own troops will be stationed. Second, it will insist on preserving the leading role of communist parties in all satellite states, if need be through military force—that is, the so-called Brezhnev doctrine of 1968.

With efforts to export perestroika to some East European countries, there has been increasing speculation in the West that basic Soviet policy toward Eastern Europe is changing. At the United Nations in December 1988, Gorbachev did use a formulation that seemed to be a partial repudiation of the Brezhnev doctrine.[8] It is now at least conceivable that promised Soviet force cuts in Eastern Europe, plus other major reductions that could come as a result of a CFE agreement, could begin to erode the Soviet Union's capacity to impose its will on East European states, as much by signaling a lessening of intent as by causing a lessening of ability to act. Even before Gorbachev, the Soviets elected to deal with Solidarity through an "internal invasion" of Poland.

If there were a decisive change in Soviet policy toward Eastern Europe, it could even become possible to take a bolder approach than that set forth in the so-called Sonnenfeldt doctrine of 1976: the proposition that, in order to foster change in East-West confrontation, the West would have to accept an "organic relationship" between the Soviet Union and its Warsaw Pact allies.[9]

The risks associated with change in Eastern Europe must also be recognized. Whatever the Soviets now say to Westerners about their security preoccupations, a major transformation in one or more East European states could still provoke intervention. And such transformation—spontaneous, uncontrolled, creating major uncertainties—cannot be ruled out. During the next several years, Eastern Europe could prove to be, from the point of view of East-West concerns, the most dangerous part of the world. Thus even if the West does not admit to a Soviet–East European "organic relationship," it must develop its policies and approaches with an adequate appreciation of the legitimacy of Soviet security concerns, just as it demands that of the Soviets in the West.

In short, ending the division of the Continent, along with the stabilizing role of the two military blocs, cannot occur until there is a revolution in Eastern Europe. This must consist of several parts: internal changes in both economics and politics that reach a level of organic stability (that is, stability generated by the nature and operation of society rather than by military force), a willingness by the Soviet Union to tolerate, and to feel secure with, these changes, and a set of relations between states of Eastern and Western Europe that do not pose threats to regional stability or the Soviet Union's confidence in its security. These criteria may add up to a demand for democracy; certainly they represent the need for an unprecedented change in Soviet attitudes and behavior—far beyond, say, current Soviet encouragement for West German economic involvement in Eastern Europe; and they will need to apply fully to all East European states that are part of the so-called Northern Tier (Poland, Czechoslovakia, East Germany, and Hungary).

In addition, for change in Eastern Europe to permit a new security environment that is at least as stable as today's, there must be both political will and means to deal effectively with intraregional difficulties that are likely to become increasingly intense with the abatement of East-West military confrontation. There would be little promise for ending the division of the Continent if that would mean war between Hungary and Rumania over Transylvania or a restoration of the Balkans to its role as the precipitator of broader conflict. Here, too, there must be a working through of political and economic transformation before the evolution of Eastern Europe can meet the minimum requirements of altering security arrangements in Europe.

This will be one of NATO's major preoccupations during the next several years. Various allies are already significantly involved in Eastern Europe, the Federal Republic is demonstrating particularly intense interest, and there is a growing debate within the alliance about the proper course to follow: in brief, whether and on what terms to support East European economies, whether and if so how to discriminate among these countries, how to manage Western credit exposure and the export of high technology, and what opportunities to pursue (and limits to respect) concerning both internal and regional political developments.

For the foreseeable future, the process of change in Eastern Europe is less likely to be disruptive or to have a deleterious impact on a wider compass of East-West relations and security concerns in Europe if it takes place within the context of today's blocs. This does not mean that NATO should become the manager for all the allies' activities toward Eastern Europe. But because of the collective impact on the West if changing Eastern Europe leads to instability or to active threats to security, NATO must continue to be at least a place to compare notes, test propositions, and develop confidence in security, for both West and East.

Western Europe, Unified Europe

Progress toward ending the division of the Continent will also be critically dependent on developments within Western Europe. The year 1992, the target date for the creation of the single market, symbolizes the next major move toward European integration. It is an economic development but, like those that have come before, it also has profound political purposes. From the beginning, European integration had a major security objective: to make conflict among its members, especially between France and West Germany, impossible. By joining this process, Chancellor Konrad Adenauer made a fateful choice for his young nation: to choose ties with Western neighbors (a reality) over the possibility (most remote) of reunifying Germany.

Efforts to develop a defense personality as part of European integration came early and failed early with the collapse in 1954 of the proposal for a European Defense Community. It represented the ceding of too much national sovereignty too soon. In the 1970s, however, the community began its European Political Cooperation (EPC), an informal means of trying to coordinate foreign policy approaches in a few areas. With the Single European Act, EPC now has a formal basis and a mandate to consider issues in the area of security, notably, however, taking care not to conflict with the responsibilities of any community state that also belongs to NATO.[10]

This development highlights what could become a dilemma in moving beyond the current state of East-West confrontation in Europe. The European Community has acquired an integrity that includes progressive development of supranational political institutions, thereby implying movement toward a security identity in the broadest sense of the concept. If these institutions continue to expand in function and purpose, the community may be constituted as a bloc for political, if not also for military, purposes, and that expansion would be a significant factor in any change contemplated for East-West relations in Europe.

These developments must be set alongside another. Already, the European Community has been pursuing direct relations with the Council for Mutual Economic Assistance (CMEA), East German goods circulate freely within the community because of a special concession to West Germany in the Treaty of Rome, and the community is proving highly attractive to other East European countries. In the next decade, depending on Soviet attitudes, one or more East European states are likely to apply to join the European Community as full members or associates.

The possibility of ending the division of Europe thus entails an ambiguity regarding the European Community's future. Can Europe be "undivided"—even if NATO were abolished and U.S. power were removed—if the community develops a major security dimension? Beyond EPC's being upgraded in importance, other activities include the incipient composition of a European pillar within NATO. The Western European Union has been resuscitated and expanded to include Spain and Portugal. The Eurogroup countries have undertaken some cooperative ventures, there is an Independent European Program Group designed to promote efficiencies in defense production, and important bilateral arrangements exist, notably Franco-German defense cooperation. At the same time, there is pressure from the United States for its European allies to assume a larger share of common defense burdens, as well as proposals for the devolution of some security responsibilities to the allies.

These efforts, however, are very much part of what could be defined as the "old agenda"—a parceling out of traditional tasks according to a revised bargain between the United States and its European allies. In addition to the difficulties of gaining West European acquiescence, as prospects begin to develop for ending the division of the Continent, these new arrangements could become impediments to, rather than incentives for, change in the basic structure of European security.

The potential dilemma is most evident in the case of Germany. From the outset, a primary purpose of European integration was to anchor West Germany to the West, and the importance of that purpose has not diminished. Yet despite anxieties often expressed elsewhere, there is no reason to suspect West Germany of hankering for relations with the East that would have to be purchased at the expense of its ties to the West. It is fantasy to talk of a new "Rapallo"—in reference to the German-Soviet accommodation of 1922. Nevertheless, as West Germany increasingly develops its sense of self-identity and chafes at remaining formal impediments to its exercise of sovereignty, as opposed to self-imposed limits, its concern to redevelop ties with states in Eastern Europe and to secure a political position there calls for great sensitivity within the Western alliance. The Federal Republic's partners must continue to promote its integration in the West without foreclosing chances to foster economic, political, and human associations with East Germany and neighboring countries.

In general, while there could be merit in developing West European security relationships that are not subsumed under NATO and do not involve the direct engagement of the United States, beyond a point this step could be at variance with subsequent efforts to end the division of Europe and potentially that of Germany (German reunification is only conceivable in the context of broader, secure European reconciliation). Indeed, in West Germany in particular and in Western Europe in general, there needs to be careful thought about the wisdom of creating institutional arrangements in defense, separate from the wider NATO framework. That framework provides a basis for working with the East on new security arrangements embracing the entire Continent. By contrast, a subset of NATO that represents only West European states could retard progress toward change.

U.S. Power and Presence

Discussion of NATO's future always turns to the issue of U.S. involvement in European security. It is often argued that the United States will inevitably withdraw from direct involvement when its task—to help contain the spread of Soviet power, particularly that expressed in military terms—is completed. According to this reasoning, the task can be accomplished either if the threat from the Warsaw Pact is reduced to the point that there is little risk of conflict or if the U.S. role is replaced sufficiently by the military power, conventional and nuclear, of erstwhile allies in Europe.

But even if this definition of U.S. purpose in Europe is accepted, the time has clearly not come when the United States can safely disengage. It would be foolhardy to do so at a time when there is a possibility of working toward ending the division of Europe, a process that depends at every step on a climate of certainty about security arrangements. Nor is it apparent that any West European country or grouping of them could adequately substitute for U.S. commitment and involvement, for a variety of reasons, including the incapacity of the European Community or any subset of NATO nations—both now and for the foreseeable future—to reach the kinds of decisions that are required to conduct foreign policy and to employ military forces.

Even with steps in the direction of ending the division of Europe, there would remain value for the states of Europe to know that there is the potential for U.S. reengagement, as insurance against untoward developments. However much it restructures its foreign policy, the Soviet Union has not abandoned the practice of, reliance upon, or respect for power in its many forms. For the West in general, there is little to be gained and much to be lost by withdrawing the potential of a U.S. counterweight, even if this were expressed less in military terms than it is now.

In the midst of renewed expectations about change in East-West political and security relations, it is worth remembering that accounting for the problem of power is critical to transforming European security. It would require an extraordinary leap of faith to believe that any developments in Europe will invalidate the relevance of power, however expressed, even in the problematic event that there were constant progress toward the democratizing of all European countries.

As in the past, a central factor in considering change is the future of a reunited Germany. It is not necessary to resurrect memories of wars past to take care in developing a new security system in Europe that includes a united Germany in its midst. The future of Germany—as one or two states—need not be threatening to anyone and is most likely to entail a set of functional relationships rather than a merged sovereignty, but there would still be value in having the continued involvement of the United States as a committed European power. Indeed, the Soviet Union continues to show ambivalence about the U.S. role in Europe. Moscow works assiduously to reduce American influence, but it also is cognizant that the U.S. presence provides an added measure of stability. Implicitly, there has been a shared interest in the division of Germany; by the same token, if it is to be reunified, there must be shared support for new arrangements.

Unfortunately, debate in recent years about the U.S. role in Europe has tended to take on an either-or character: either it must be frozen as it is now or its credibility will be irretrievably diminished. It is important to change this practice for many reasons, especially because of growing economic pressures in the United States to reduce its military contribution to NATO. A significant part of committed U.S. forces is based in the United States, and some commentators argue that these forces might wisely be reduced first; other commentators, concerned about the need to protect U.S. interests elsewhere, believe that this would unduly weaken the U.S. strategic reserve.[11]

In this debate, it is important to understand the purposes of U.S. troops in Europe, the most visible aspect of the American commitment. Only one purpose is purely military: to help NATO maintain robust conventional defenses. Three others are essentially political: to give added credence to West Germany's domestic commitment to being able to defend as much of its territory as possible, to obscure the fact that the Bundeswehr is the largest Western military force on the Central Front, and to provide an earnest of U.S. intentions—to serve as hostages—in an act of coupling the U.S. strategic deterrent to West European security. Provided that there were a reduction of the Warsaw Pact military threat or an effective West European substitute for U.S. forces, there could safely be some reduction of deployed U.S. troops.

Indeed, their most important political function, coupling, could be accomplished at a much lower level of deployed personnel.

For simple prudence, however, the burden of argument is on the side of the United States' continuing to play a major role in European security. And the burden of argument is on the side of preserving a NATO framework through which that U.S. role can be effectively implemented. These conclusions will certainly hold true so long as conditions do not exist that will permit an end to the division of the Continent. After all, calculations of security are not just about trying to reduce costs; they are also about ensuring that major interests are not compromised. The U.S. role may evolve to become primarily a form of insurance. But measuring the stakes against the cost of the premiums, for the foreseeable future this is insurance worth keeping.

Notes

1. See Robert E. Hunter, *Security in Europe* (Bloomington: Indiana University Press, 1973); John Lewis Gaddis, *The United States and the Origins of the Cold War, 1941–1947* (New York: Columbia University Press, 1972); Robert B. Tucker, *Nation or Empire? The Debate over American Foreign Policy* (Baltimore: Johns Hopkins University Press, 1968); and Dean Acheson, *Present at the Creation: My Years in the State Department* (New York: Norton, 1969).

2. This is quite unlike the situation with conventional forces, where any reduction of capability can be done along a continuum. These points also indicate the flaw in propositions for a no-first-use pledge by NATO regarding nuclear weapons: once made, the deterrent value of a threat to retaliate with nuclear weapons is lost, but if Western Europe were being overrun, the U.S. president might still decide to use them. That calculation has always related to the intrinsic worth of Western Europe to the United States, not to any declaratory strategy. Thus a no-first-use pledge could increase the risks of war without reducing the possibility that nuclear weapons would then be employed. This is the worst of both worlds. However, with a profound reduction in Warsaw Pact threat, NATO may choose to make a no-first-use pledge for political purposes within the West—to counter any continuing domestic opposition to nuclear weapons. Such a pledge would theoretically be at odds with a consistent defense doctrine, but that might not seem to matter.

3. During the debate in the spring of 1989, the British government pressed for modernization, the French were ambivalent, and the West Germans, virtually across the political spectrum, favored postponement. See Robert E. Hunter, "Quit Pushing Bonn," *New York Times*, February 18, 1989.

4. Either European arsenal could have the ability to precipitate a general nuclear war, involving the United States, through a process that theoreticians once called catalytic war (a misnomer). See Robert E. Hunter, "After the INF Treaty: Keeping America in Europe," *SAIS Review* 8, no. 2 (Summer–Fall 1988): 164–65.

5. On the Harmel report, see *NATO Facts and Figures* (Brussels: NATO Information Service, 1984), pp. 289–91.

6. An analogous process in the field of U.S.-Soviet nuclear relations took place when both sides began deploying weapons that were nearly invulnerable—at sea and in silos. Even with the so-called window of vulnerability, there was no serious derogation from the proposition that both powers could dispense with a hair-trigger approach to nuclear retaliation. This development—dating from about 1960–1962—was a critical condition for *détente* in the political realm.

7. Of course, in discussing asymmetrical force reductions, the Soviets also propose that NATO make similar reductions in areas where it is ahead—such as strike aircraft; and some Soviet commentators have extended the concept worldwide in an effort to reduce U.S. advantages in surface seapower, including aircraft carriers.

8. "Everyone, and the strongest in the first instance, is required to restrict himself, and to exclude totally the use of external force. . . . The compelling necessity of the principle of freedom of choice is also clear to us. . . . Denying that right to the peoples, no matter what the pretext, no matter what words are used to conceal it, means infringing upon even the unstable balance that it has been possible to achieve. Freedom of choice is a universal principle to which there should be no exceptions." See *Foreign Broadcast Information Service/Soviet Union*, December 8, 1989, p. 13.

9. See text of hearing before the Subcommittee on International Security and Scientific Affairs on "U.S. National Security Policy vis-à-vis Eastern Europe (the "Sonnenfeldt Doctrine"), House Foreign Affairs Committee, 94th Cong., 1st sess., April 12, 1976.

10. See "Single European Act," Title III, Article 30, Section 6, in *Bulletin of the European Communities, Supplement 2/86,* Commission of the European Communities, April 1986, pp. 18–19.

11. See Leonard Sullivan, Jr., "Major Defense Options," pp. 97–114; Rhett Dawson and Paul Schott Stevens, "Defense Efficiency in the 1990s," pp. 115–28; and Anthony Cordesman, "Net Assessment and Defense Resources," pp. 129–49. *Washington Quarterly* (Spring 1989).

3

Competing Agendas: America, Europe, and a Troubled NATO Partnership

Ted Galen Carpenter

NATO's current disunity is not merely the result of Mikhail Gorbachev's effective diplomacy or disputes over specific issues such as burden sharing and the modernization of short-range nuclear missiles. Those problems are the symptoms of more serious cleavages in the alliance. The underlying problem is that the European and U.S. conceptions of NATO have always differed in fundamental ways. The paramount European objective has been to link the United States to the security of the Continent in the most secure manner possible, reducing or eliminating Washington's freedom of action. U.S. leaders, on the other hand, have sought, with somewhat less intensity and effectiveness, to retain that freedom of action and keep the nature of the security commitment limited.

Although the North Atlantic Treaty officially embraced U.S. preferences, for a variety of economic and strategic reasons, the European version of the alliance became dominant during the 1950s and 1960s. But the European members have paid a severe price for their victory—a humiliating and potentially dangerous dependence on the United States for their defense. That point became especially worrisome as the Soviet Union achieved strategic nuclear parity and eroded the credibility of the U.S. nuclear guarantee. Participation in NATO has also become increasingly unsatisfying from the U.S. perspective. Washington exercises alliance leadership to a degree never contemplated in the original treaty negotiations, but American taxpayers bear a burden of $125 billion to $160 billion each year to defend wealthy European allies and more than 300,000 U.S. troops remain on the Continent some four and a half decades after the end of World War II. Moreover, as the Soviet threat appears to be receding, the willingness of the allies to defer to U.S. policy positions is waning. The alliance has encountered crises before, but this time there is a far greater likelihood that the situation is terminal.

Negotiations in 1948–1949 leading to the North Atlantic Treaty underscored the competing European and American security agendas. European leaders, especially British foreign secretary Ernest Bevin, sought to entangle the United States as firmly as possible in arrangements for the defense of

Europe. As Martin Folly notes, "To rebuild European self-confidence, the British believed it was essential that there should be a written assurance that the United States would be militarily involved in a European war from the start, which would also involve them in prior planning of strategy and supply."[1] Conversely, the Truman administration remained undecided about even the need for formal U.S. membership in an alliance until the summer of 1948. Several officials, including George Kennan, argued against the need for any comprehensive security arrangements or at least insisted that an informal association with the Brussels Pact powers would be sufficient.

Although advocates of a more cautious U.S. security commitment to Europe lost out to the administration's Atlanticist faction, U.S. negotiators firmly resisted European demands for an automatic war clause and similar measures that would constrain the United States. Executive session testimony before the Senate Foreign Relations Committee revealed a pervasive assumption that America's NATO commitments would remain strictly limited. To reassure nervous Europeans and enable them to get on with their economic recovery programs under the Marshall Plan, the United States was prepared to pledge its support to Western Europe's security and to help rebuild the defense forces of the nations in that region. Beyond that assistance, the Western Europeans would be expected to assume responsibility for the bulk of their own defense, especially once their economic recovery was complete.

The treaty negotiations revealed that the European representatives had a very different conception of an alliance. They wanted a treaty requiring all participants to respond automatically with military force in the event of an attack on any member and sought a U.S. commitment for substantial arms aid to bolster their defenses. Some negotiators even suggested the desirability of increasing the U.S. military presence, with ground troops, on the Continent beyond the two divisions still stationed in Germany as part of the allied occupation force pending conclusion of a final peace treaty, although no one pressed that issue. Moreover, the Europeans wanted a long-term alliance commitment from the United States, seeking a treaty with an indefinite duration or one for at least fifty years. U.S. representatives insisted that the pact be binding for no more than twenty years and that it be subject to revisions after ten years.[2] One scholar of the period notes,

> Although the differences between the United States and its European allies kept being narrowed, they never disappeared entirely in the negotiations leading up to NATO. Washington continued to insist that the Europeans do as much as possible for themselves. The Europeans on the other hand wanted to make the American guarantee for assistance in case of attack as automatic as possible.[3]

In reality those differences only appeared to narrow; they have continued to be a serious problem throughout the history of the transatlantic partnership.

The gap between the European conception of an alliance and the attitudes of Truman administration officials and members of the Senate was obvious and significant. Several differences went to the heart of America's commitment.

One difference involved the automaticity of Washington's willingness to aid other NATO signatories in the event of war. In his executive session testimony before the Senate Foreign Relations Committee, Secretary of State Dean Acheson stressed the U.S. refusal to consider anything approximating an automatic war clause.[4] It became evident that even NATO's strongest supporters on the committee were opposed to anything resembling such a clause. Michigan Republican Arthur Vandenberg noted that the language regarding military action in an early treaty draft shown to committee chairman Senator Tom Connally (D–Texas) and him "stuck out like a sore thumb" and that both senators insisted on modifications. They did so despite "a storm of protest" from the Europeans that "we were trying to water this down to the point where there would not be anything involved."[5]

The insistence on maintaining America's freedom of action was apparent in other ways. During the executive session hearings, the question arose repeatedly whether the United States would respond to an attack on a European country in the same fashion that it would to an assault on the American homeland. Several senators emphasized that the responses would necessarily be different. At one point Vandenberg noted, "We accept the general obligation that the survival of France and the survival of Great Britain are essential to us, but we do not accept the basic thesis that an attack on Paris has got to be met precisely as if it were an attack on New York." Senator Theodore Green (D–Rhode Island) made the distinction even more explicit. In the case of New York, "[we] would use all military force immediately. In the case of Paris, you might stop to think things over."[6]

The committee's report recommending approval of the North Atlantic Treaty reflected that attitude. It emphasized that Article 5 of the treaty "clearly does not commit any of the parties to declare war." In that connection, "the committee calls particular attention to the phrase 'such action as it deems necessary.' These words were included in article 5 to make absolutely clear that each party remains free to exercise its honest judgment in deciding upon the measures it will take to restore and maintain the security of the North Atlantic area."[7]

To eliminate even the slightest doubt on that score, the committee specifically addressed the question of an attack on another member of NATO compared to an attack on the United States itself: "In view of the provision in article 5 that an attack against one would be considered an attack against all, would the United States be obligated to react to an attack on Paris or Copenhagen in the same way that it would react to an attack on New York City?" The committee report unhesitatingly responded that the answer was "no."[8]

Most advocates of NATO believed that there was a subtle but crucial difference between America's security interests and those of other nations, even valued allies. Although they considered noncommunist Europe important to the well-being of the United States, the survival of that region was not deemed equivalent to the survival of the United States itself. Therefore, an element of choice concerning the monumental issue of whether to go to war needed to be preserved. That preservation of choice was especially imperative in the new nuclear age when involvement in a European conflict might cause irreparable damage to American civilization. The American achitects of NATO showed no intention of forging a treaty that would give a future American president no alternative but to sacrifice Chicago to avenge a Soviet attack on Cologne. The contrast of those intentions with the subsequent evolution of NATO defense doctrine that quite intentionally eliminated any meaningful choice in such matters could scarcely be more graphic.[9]

Another factor distinguishing the U.S. and European conceptions of NATO was the issue of primary responsibility for defending the Continent. U.S. officials saw NATO as a predominantly European operation, with the United States offering support if needed. W. Averell Harriman, U.S. special representative to Europe under the Economic Cooperation Administration, typified that attitude when he expressed confidence that by assisting the Europeans to "help themselves in defending their own countries," there would be developed "a military establishment over a period of years which will help to establish a balance of power in Europe, *backed up*, of course, by the military establishment that the United States will have."[10] Others stressed the primacy of European responsibility to an even greater extent. One senator stated that U.S. officials must make it clear that American adherence to the North Atlantic pact "does not put upon us the responsibility of taking care of the whole of Europe in case of trouble."[11]

Still another difference between U.S. and Western European assumptions involved the duration of U.S. obligations. There were repeated suggestions by administration officials and the treaty's Senate supporters that even the relatively limited U.S. commitments should be temporary. Most treaty proponents seemed determined that the United States reap the eventual benefits of restoring a European balance of power. Secretary of Defense Louis Johnson expressed his hope that a strong European force would someday permit "a diminution of our own Military Establishment," although he cautioned that such an outcome was at least "3 or 4 years" away:

> My hope of reducing, and it must in some way be reduced, the great cost of the Defense Establishment lies in seeing these countries grow to the point that we can reduce. That is one of the most persuasive arguments with me in getting behind this program. It offers a chance to bring the cost down within the limit of our economy.[12]

When Johnson expressed the need to reduce the "great cost" of America's military, the defense budget consumed barely 5 percent of the nation's gross national product (GNP); the figure at the end of the 1980s is more than 6 percent.

The comments of NATO proponents underscored a fundamental difference in security interests between the United States and its European partners, despite the rhetoric regarding an Atlantic community. From the perspective of the European countries, the defense of their region was paramount since their very existence depended on its effectiveness. Western European security was important to American leaders, but they recognized that the United States could, even if the worst came to pass, survive Europe's fall.

Western European officials wanted a maximum, if not herculean, effort on the part of the United States to strengthen North Atlantic defenses, including ironclad commitments and military involvement on an operational level. Without that direct participation, the Europeans feared that America might fail to honor its pledge of assistance in the event of attack, however sincerely that promise may have been made originally. Even worse, Washington's restraint undermined the credibility of the U.S. nuclear guarantee, which the Europeans ultimately depended upon for their security. Any weakening of nuclear deterrence increased the likelihood of another major war, something that many Europeans considered an even greater nightmare than Soviet domination.

American leaders gave European security a high priority but balked at the allies' attempt to establish a suffocating embrace. They insisted upon maintaining a degree of flexibility and wanted to be certain that the alliance constituted an equal partnership, not a free ride for the Europeans. An unspoken assumption was that America would provide aid and protection only if the Western European nations made a vigorous effort to improve their military capabilities.

Most significant, Truman administration officials portrayed the North Atlantic pact to the Senate and the American public as though the U.S. conception of the alliance was accepted (at least grudgingly) by the other signatories. Not only did supporters offer repeated public assurances that nothing in the treaty obligated the United States to go to war on behalf of other signatories, they stated that no significant numbers of American troops would be stationed in Europe. One of the most graphic assurances came from Acheson in response to a question from Senator Bourke Hickenlooper. The Iowa Republican noted that Acheson had earlier confirmed that the Western Europeans would provide the vast majority of armaments for the collective defense effort. "I presume that refers also to the manpower," Hickenlooper observed. He then pressed Acheson on that point, asking if the United States would be "expected to send substantial numbers of troops over there as a more or less permanent contribution to the development of these countries' capacity to resist?" Acheson replied without hesitation: "The answer to that question, Senator, is a clear and absolute 'No.'"[13]

Acheson's assurance was only one of many given by Truman administration officials and other prominent treaty proponents. Senator Forrest Donnell, (R–Missouri) for example, asked Harriman if it would be necessary for American troops to be stationed in Europe in order to prevent the Soviet Union from overrunning the region, given its existing superiority in conventional forces. Not only did Harriman reject the idea of stationing U.S. forces on the Continent, he emphasized that he "never heard anyone in Europe suggest it." Moreover, he knew of no country there "that wants an armed occupation of United States troops."[14]

Critics of the treaty were skeptical of Harriman's statement that the European governments had never sought a troop commitment, especially since there had been several press reports suggesting the contrary. But General Omar Bradley echoed the comments of Harriman and Acheson. Not only did he deny any obligation to, or intention of, stationing additional U.S. forces on the Continent, he clearly regarded the occupation force in Germany as a temporary phenomenon. When Senator Arthur Watkins (R–Utah) asked him whether there was any intention of maintaining those forces during "the full 20 years of the pact," Bradley responded, "No, sir."[15]

Proponents of the North Atlantic pact therefore created a very specific image of the treaty and America's obligations under it. Senators who passed judgment on the document and citizens who followed the ratification debate were led to believe four important points about America's impending NATO membership. First, the treaty did not involve an automatic commitment to go to war if the allies were attacked; the United States would retain its ability to decide on an appropriate response. Second, there was no obligation or expectation that the United States would station troops in Europe. Third, following the initial phase in which the United States would help the European nations to rearm, Western Europe would become increasingly self-sufficient militarily. Finally, a strong Western Europe would ultimately enable the United States to reduce the scope of its own burdensome military efforts. The image of a pact outlining modest and, for the most part, short-term U.S. obligations was a potent one. It contributed significantly to the ease with which the North Atlantic Treaty passed through the ratification process.

Less than two years later, America's obligations mushroomed beyond any previous expectations, beginning the process of transforming NATO into an enterprise in which the United States would bear most of the responsibilities and burdens. Three factors in 1950–1951 acted as catalysts for that transformation: the slow pace of European rearmament efforts, a growing concern among administration officials that the Western Europeans could not forge an adequate conventional defense force without the addition of West German manpower, and the fear that the Korean conflict might explode into a global war at a time when the Europeans were not yet capable of defending themselves.

Under intense pressure from the European NATO members to make a more tangible demonstration of the U.S. commitment, the National Security Council (NSC) adopted NSC-82, which envisaged a significant expansion of the U.S. military role in the North Atlantic alliance. Concern about strengthening allied confidence in the reliability of Washington's commitment to Western Europe's security was evident:

> We are agreed that additional United States forces should be committed to the defense of Europe at the earliest feasible date in order that any doubts of American interest in the defense, rather than the liberation, of Europe will be removed, thus increasing the will of our allies to resist. We agree that the over-all strength of the United States forces in Europe should be about 4 infantry divisions and the equivalent of 1½ armored divisions, 8 tactical air groups, and appropriate naval forces; and that these forces should be in place and combat ready as expeditiously as possible.[16]

Such developments represented a significant departure from previous American policy, but NSC-82 tempered the change in several ways. Washington's willingness to assume a more visible and vigorous military posture was contingent upon the other NATO members' demonstrating a more serious devotion to the common defense effort:

> Plans to commit United States forces . . . are based upon the expectation that they will be met with similar efforts on the part of the other nations involved. The United States should make it clear that it is now squarely up to the European signatories of the North Atlantic Treaty to provide the balance of the forces required for the initial defense. Firm programs for the development of such forces should represent a prerequisite for the fulfillment of the above commitments on the part of the United States.[17]

The conditional nature of the new American obligations was equally evident with regard to the appointment of a supreme NATO commander. In an effort to encourage the creation of an effective multinational defense force, the United States would assume initial command responsibilities. But the Truman administration attached several important provisos, including the integration of West German manpower into NATO's defenses, and there was no inclination to maintain that role for an indefinite duration:

> It is our objective to assist the European nations to provide a defense capable of deterring or meeting an attack. When this objective is achieved it is hoped that the United States will be able to leave to the European nation-members the primary responsibility, with the collaboration of the United States, of maintaining and commanding such force.[18]

Truman's public announcement of his decision to dispatch additional American troops to Europe similarly underscored the contingent nature of the new U.S. commitments.[19]

Throughout the discussions about strengthening NATO in late 1950 and early 1951, the European allies seemed determined to link the United States to the conventional military defense of Europe in as thorough and rapid a manner as possible. Acheson and other U.S. officials resisted that pressure for the implementation of America's new NATO commitments before the Europeans agreed to German rearmament and a more vigorous military effort of their own. A continuing gulf between American policy and the desires of the allies existed on another important issue. Acheson stressed that closer European cooperative political action would be necessary to forge an effective integrated defense force and that the allies must be certain this problem was resolved "at the time when our troops . . . would no longer be necessary in Europe and went home."[20] The assumption that placing an American garrison in Europe and appointing a NATO commander was merely an interim measure until the Western European states achieved the requisite unity and military power to build an effective deterrent to Soviet aggression was not only Acheson's opinion, it pervaded American strategic thinking.

European officials viewed the matter differently, regarding a sizable contingent of American troops on the Continent as an essential, long-term method of linking America's strategic nuclear arsenal to Europe's defense. By ensuring immediate American involvement in any European conflict, a tangible U.S. conventional military presence would increase the credibility of NATO's deterrent function. Deterrence was the preeminent objective of the European allies because any war, nuclear or conventional, would be a calamity for their region.

The Truman administration's official hard-line stance proved to be more illusion than reality. Washington's determination to resist European pressure to proceed with additional troop deployments and the appointment of a supreme commander crumbled in late 1950 as an expanded Korean conflict created an atmosphere of global crisis. The Brussels conference in December 1950 ratified several crucial decisions that demonstrated how the North Atlantic alliance, and especially the nature of the U.S. commitment to the alliance, was being transformed. Council members established an integrated NATO force, assigned national military units to it, and ratified the choice of General Dwight D. Eisenhower as supreme commander.

The expansion of America's NATO obligations did not go unchallenged. A coalition consisting of noninterventionists who opposed the original NATO commitments, moderate critics who accepted the treaty's limited obligations but objected to the burgeoning U.S. role, and individuals who objected to Truman's attempt to implement such vast changes without congressional consent excoriated the new policy. Senator Robert Taft, former president Herbert

Hoover, former ambassador Joseph P. Kennedy, and others played prominent roles in the Great Debate of 1950–1951. Many of the arguments they employed foreshadowed the burden-sharing debates of the 1980s.

Despite a vigorous and often perceptive attack on the wisdom of the more extensive U.S. NATO obligations, the insurgents ultimately achieved only an anemic, nonbinding Senate resolution admonishing the administration not to send additional troops without congressional consent.[21] With the end of the Great Debate, the expansion of America's alliance commitments continued, not to be challenged in a serious manner until the Mansfield amendment controversy of the late 1960s and early 1970s.

In the years following, the initially temporary additional obligations the United States had assumed became indelible features of NATO. Although impressive conventional force goals were adopted at the Lisbon Conference in 1952, the Europeans conspicuously failed to attain those goals. NATO's deterrent became increasingly Americanized and nuclearized, and that suited the Europeans perfectly since it guaranteed extensive U.S. involvement in the Continent's security on an operational basis. The continuing presence of U.S. troops was a tangible symbol of that commitment and served the trip-wire function, ensuring American involvement at the outset of any fighting and providing an escalatory link to the U.S. nuclear arsenal, the most essential element of NATO's deterrent. By the end of the 1950s, the European conception of NATO had become dominant.

From the perspective of the late 1980s, the extensive alliance commitments undertaken by the United States in 1950–1951 have acquired such permanence that even to question their continuation is considered an exercise in radicalism. But it was not until the mid- to late 1950s that U.S. officials finally resigned themselves to an indefinite prolongation of the American troop presence in Europe and long-term command responsibilities for NATO's military forces. That development was less the product of deliberate policy decisions than it was a response to the constraints imposed by circumstances and manipulation by the European allies.

The 1950s was the decade when America's temporary NATO commitments were institutionalized, and the 1960s and 1970s were the decades when the issues that are now cleaving the alliance began to acquire high visibility. Western Europe's excessive reliance on an increasingly incredible U.S. nuclear guarantee, the continuing inadequacy of European conventional defense efforts, the diverging security interests and foreign policy objectives of the United States and such key NATO members as France and West Germany became evident. As in the case of earlier alliance controversies and contradictions, Western officials sought to evade or finesse such difficulties, and for a time they succeeded tolerably well. But they merely postponed the day when the centrifugal forces in the alliance could no longer be ignored. At the beginning of the 1990s, that day is fast approaching.

Ironically the Eisenhower administration's New Look defense policy, with its reliance on air power and nuclear weapons, although designed to ease the economic burdens of America's global military commitments, played into the hands of European leaders who wanted to make permanent the more extensive U.S. alliance leadership role. An explicit reliance on America's nuclear arsenal obviated the need to implement the Lisbon conventional force goals. That strategy also guaranteed that the United States would be immediately involved in any European war, thus giving the Europeans the automatic war clause (de facto, if not de jure) that they had sought unsuccessfully in 1948–1949. From the perspective of the Western Europeans, the continued presence of U.S. troops was important not as a serious addition to the strength of NATO conventional forces but as a trip wire guaranteeing the use of the U.S. strategic arsenal.

Not surprisingly, the other NATO countries endorsed a reliance on U.S. nuclear weapons, especially given the continuing failure to achieve the Lisbon force goals. As Thomas H. Etzold observes, "Of all the reasons for NATO's adoption of nuclear strategy, expected conventional force inadequacies weighed most heavily."[22] Alliance defense policy became formally aligned with that of the United States in the mid-1950s when NATO approved MC 14/2, a directive that called for the prompt use of nuclear weapons if the Soviet bloc attacked any alliance member. The new strategy viewed ground forces as little more than a means of slowing a communist offensive, thus giving Moscow time to reconsider before the West launched a devastating nuclear counterstroke.

Proponents of this massive retaliation doctrine emphasized its deterrent capability, not as a practical method of fighting a major war in Europe. The theory presupposed that the probability of subjecting the Soviet homeland to radioactive devastation, combined with ambiguity about the threshold that would trigger an American nuclear strike, would dissuade the Kremlin leadership from embarking on any aggressive enterprises. It also possessed the not inconsiderable benefit of making the continuing disparity of conventional forces between NATO and the Soviet bloc theoretically irrelevant. Nuclearizing NATO's strategy enabled the alliance members to avoid the kinds of difficult issues in the 1950s that have become so critical in the 1980s. According to Etzold, "It is clear that the turn to nuclear weapons averted serious allied quarrels over burden-sharing and over the reconstruction of conventional capability for the defense of Europe." He concludes that NATO "might well have failed to survive the decade of the 1950s" if compelled to confront those issues.[23]

French rejection of the proposed European Defense Community (EDC)—and the prospect that such rejection might scuttle West German rearmament—also served to deepen U.S. involvement in NATO. French negotiators insisted on crucial concessions from their British and American counterparts as the price for their consent to German rearmament outside the EDC. London was amenable, agreeing not to withdraw its forces stationed on the Continent without the consent of the other Western European Union (Brussels Pact) members. That move in turn placed enormous pressure on the United States to make its troop presence permanent. Washington, with some reluctance, offered assurances that the United States would keep its forces, including ground units, in Europe "while a threat to that area exists." The administration also agreed to view "any action from whatever quarter" that threatened "the integrity or unity" of the Western European Union as a threat to the peace and security of the North Atlantic region.[24] The latter item was an indirect promise to help prevent West Germany's withdrawal from, or domination of, the Brussels Pact.

Those guarantees represented a significant change in the foreign policy views of the Eisenhower administration. The president had long opposed any prolonged commitment to maintain American ground forces in Europe. Privately he still favored a substantial withdrawal of those units within a few years.[25] Yet policy constraints now compelled him to pledge to keep those forces on duty indefinitely.

The British and American assurances broke the protracted impasse regarding a military role for West Germany. In the process, however, the temporary troop deployment the United States had made in 1950, together with the assumption of command of NATO military forces, now became a commitment of indefinite duration.

The growing reliance on America's strategic nuclear power created a subtle but persistent problem. As the years passed, the European goal of linking America's nuclear deterrent as strongly as possible to the security interests of Western Europe became increasingly important, and by the 1970s and early 1980s it was fast becoming an obsession.

The principal reason for heightened European concern was the inexorable erosion of America's nuclear preponderance. As the Soviet nuclear capability grew, the credibility of U.S. pledges to use its strategic arsenal in the defense of third parties, even valued NATO allies, correspondingly declined. The Europeans were afflicted with two contradictory fears. On the one hand, they worried that the United States might renege on its promise to use nuclear weapons in the event of war. Indeed, even the perception that U.S. resolve might be wavering could erode NATO's deterrent and tempt Moscow. On the other hand, they worried that if deterrence failed, the United States might use its nuclear weapons, an action that, given Soviet nuclear capabilities, would turn Europe into a wasteland. This schizoid approach to the U.S. security guarantee characterizes European attitudes to this day.

At the root of such inconsistency is a pervasive European ambivalence about relying on the military power of the United States. The nations of Western Europe chafe at their dependence and the national impotence it implies.

At the same time, they also recognize that the American nuclear guarantee affords them inexpensive protection; without it, they would face dramatic increases in their own military budgets to create a conventional deterrent of the magnitude adopted at Lisbon plus a credible nuclear deterrent. Few European regimes relish that prospect, with its unpredictable economic and political consequences.

The depth of the European ambivalence has emerged on several occasions. For example, it surfaced when the Kennedy and Johnson administrations endeavored to shift NATO strategy away from its reliance on the doctrine of massive retaliation. Critics considered the policy too inflexible, especially in the post-Sputnik years when the expanding Soviet arsenal made it increasingly difficult to contemplate any American president's initiating a thermonuclear war, with devastating consequences for the American homeland, merely in response to an attack on Western Europe.

But when the Kennedy administration presented proposals designed to alter NATO defense doctrine, the European leaders clung tenaciously to the American nuclear shield, reaffirming existing alliance policy that a serious incursion against any member, even if purely conventional in nature, must be met by a retaliatory strike on the Soviet homeland. The continental governments considered the explicit threat of nuclear retaliation an indispensable element of deterrence; any dilution of that concept, they feared, would increase the probability of Soviet adventurism and the danger of a limited war between the two superpowers, with fighting being confined to the European theater. Washington acknowledged the primacy of nuclear weapons in any program of deterrence but emphasized that a conventional defense capability was essential to maintain a credible deterrent. Otherwise NATO's alternatives consisted of surrender or annihilation should a Soviet attack occur.

That fundamental difference about the nature of NATO's deterrent became steadily more intense during the 1970s and 1980s. Washington wanted a large, predominantly European conventional force to give NATO— and especially the United States—options other than the nightmare of a superpower nuclear exchange. But the Europeans never wanted the United States to have any other option because the very existence of options for their transatlantic protector would further undermine the credibility of the U.S. nuclear guarantee.[26] The desire to foreclose options is one reason that the European nations have always exhibited a distinct lack of enthusiasm for a serious buildup of conventional forces. It is not only in their economic self-interest to avoid such action; from their perspective, it is also in their security interest.

Persistent American pressure finally produced a change in NATO defense doctrine with the adoption of the concept of flexible response in 1967. Rather than threatening an inevitable nuclear counterstrike in the event of aggression, the NATO members undertook to establish an ability to respond in a variety of ways. This response might be confined to conventional means, it could escalate to tactical nuclear weapons, or it might be full strategic retaliation. This new policy represented a fragile compromise between European and American views on defense issues, and ultimately it was little more than an attempt to evade, or at least finesse, the erosion of America's strategic nuclear dominance and the problems that such erosion created for the credibility of Washington's nuclear guarantee.

European insecurity concerning the credibility of that guarantee emerged again in the late 1970s and early 1980s with the deployment of a new generation of American intermediate-range missiles. Ostensibly that deployment was designed to counter the Soviet SS-20s, which were targeted on Western Europe. In reality, it was to ensure immediate U.S. involvement in any European conflict on a strategic nuclear level. Because the INFs were American-controlled weapons that could strike targets in the Soviet Union, their use would automatically engulf both superpowers, thus preventing Moscow and Washington from waging a war confined to the European theater. By further eliminating any element of American choice concerning the level of involvement, the Western Europeans sought to reverse the crumbling credibility of the U.S. nuclear guarantee, thereby, according to their reasoning, enhancing NATO's deterrent and reducing the likelihood of war. Egon Bahr, one of the principal foreign policy spokesmen for Germany's Social Democratic party, candidly admitted the goal of constraining America's freedom of action. According to Bahr, "Europe does not want to allow America the freedom to decide when to put its own existence on the line, but rather wants to link the United States indissolubly, in an almost automatic manner with Europe's own destiny."[27]

At the same time, the NATO members pledged to increase their military budgets by 3 percent per year above the rate of inflation. This decision was a concession to U.S. views that NATO's continuing conventional inferiority in relation to the Warsaw Pact was a possible invitation to aggression. As they had done at Brussels in 1950, Lisbon in 1952, and several occasions thereafter, the Europeans attempted to placate the United States by acceding to U.S. demands for a more vigorous conventional defense effort. But the results again failed to match the promises. From 1979 to 1985, only one NATO member—the United States—met the target of 3 percent real growth in military spending each year. Some of the other members failed to achieve that target in any year, and as the 1980s progressed, inflation-adjusted military spending in several NATO countries actually declined.

The failure of yet another set of European conventional defense promises emphasized the problems afflicting the alliance in the 1980s. The bitter controversy throughout Western Europe concerning the deployment of American cruise and Pershing II missiles; ill-disguised grumbling in Congress about Europe's apparent unwillingness to fulfill existing military commitments or equitably share Western defense burdens; and serious differences regarding

Central American policy, arms control negotiations with the Soviet Union, and Middle East policy are other indicators.

NATO's growing dissension, epitomized most recently by the controversy over building a new generation of short-range nuclear missiles and disagreements about how to respond to Gorbachev's diplomacy, all suggest a terminal crisis in the alliance. Europeans increasingly wonder whether the dependence on the United States—despite the benefit of sparing the other NATO governments difficult choices about the adequacy of their own defense efforts, the creation of an independent nuclear deterrent, the status of Germany, and other troublesome issues—is a good bargain. American critics of NATO point to the annual cost of $125 billion to $160 billion of the NATO commitment and the risk created by the existence of a de facto automatic war obligation and ask the same question.

The need to make major changes in the U.S. security relationship with Western Europe is becoming increasingly evident and urgent. There is certainly little justification for perpetuating the expanded NATO commitments undertaken temporarily in the early 1950s. At the very least, U.S. officials should insist upon a return to the original concept of NATO: conditional U.S. support for a predominantly European defense effort, no permanent U.S. garrison on the Continent, and no automatic war commitment. If that level of American involvement was deemed sufficient in 1948–1949, during the most virulent phase of the cold war and at a time when the Western Europeans could afford to make only modest military efforts, it should certainly be sufficient in today's more benign international environment.

The opportunity also exists for the United States to adopt an even bolder policy change. NATO was created to bolster nervous Europeans whose nations still suffered from the devastation of World War II. But Western Europe achieved full economic recovery long ago and is now a prosperous and politically stable region capable of forging military forces adequate to meet any likely danger. NATO's principal purpose was to deter an attack by an aggressive, expansionist Soviet Union, a threat that at least seemed plausible under Stalin and his successors. But today the Soviet Union is preoccupied with its own severe internal problems. It poses, at most, a remote threat to Western Europe. Under such conditions, U.S. leaders should assess whether NATO is obsolete and should consider devolving full responsibility for the security of Europe to the Europeans.

Notes

1. Martin H. Folly, "Breaking the Vicious Circle: Britain, the United States, and the Genesis of the North Atlantic Treaty," *Diplomatic History* 12 (Winter 1988): 63.
2. U.S. Senate, Committee on Foreign Relations, *The Vandenberg Resolution and the North Atlantic Treaty: Hearings held in Executive Session on S. Res. 239*

and Executive L, 80th Cong., 2d session, 81st Cong., 1st session, 1973, pp. 123–24, 153.

3. Geir Lundestad, "Empire by Invitation: The United States and Western Europe," *Society for Historians of American Foreign Relations Newsletter* 15, no. 3 (September 1984): 8.

4. *Vandenberg Resolution and North Atlantic Treaty Hearings,* p. 88.

5. Ibid., p. 134. Analyses of the negotiations on the North Atlantic Treaty confirm the U.S. resistance to an automatic war commitment. See Timothy P. Ireland, *Creating the Entangling Alliance: The Origins of the North Atlantic Treaty Organization* (Westport, Conn.: Greenwood Press, 1981), and Escott M. Reid, *Time of Fear and Hope* (Toronto: McClelland and Stewart, 1977).

6. *Vandenberg Resolution and North Atlantic Treaty Hearings,* pp. 302, 303.

7. Senate Executive Report No. 8, 81st Cong., 1st session, 1949, pp. 13–14.

8. Ibid., p. 14.

9. For a discussion of how the element of choice for the United States has been virtually eliminated, see Christopher Layne, "Continental Divide—Time to Disengage in Europe," *National Interest* 13 (Fall 1988): 16–20.

10. *Vandenberg Resolution and North Atlantic Treaty Hearings,* p. 221 (emphasis added).

11. Ibid., p. 236.

12. Ibid., p. 228.

13. U.S. Senate, *North Atlantic Treaty Hearings* before the Committee on Foreign Relations on Executive L, 81st Cong., 1st session, 1949, p. 47.

14. Ibid., pp. 213, 217.

15. Ibid., p. 321.

16. *Foreign Relations of the United States, 1950,* vol. 3: *Western Europe* (Washington, D.C.: U.S. Government Printing Office, 1977), p. 273.

17. Ibid., p. 274.

18. Ibid., p. 277.

19. U.S. President, *Public Papers of the Presidents of the United States: Harry S. Truman, 1950* (Washington, D.C.: U.S. Government Printing Office, 1965), p. 626.

20. Memorandum of conversation with Sir Oliver Franks, October 25, 1950, Dean Acheson Papers, box 65, "Memoranda of Conversations, 1950—October" folder, Harry S. Truman Library, Independence, Mo.

21. For discussions of the Great Debate, see Ted Galen Carpenter, "United States' NATO Policy at the Crossroads: The 'Great Debate' of 1950–1951," *International History Review* 8 (August 1986): 389–415; and David R. Kepley, "The Senate and the Great Debate of 1951," *Prologue* (Winter 1982): 213–26.

22. Thomas H. Etzold, "The End of the Beginning . . . NATO's Adoption of Nuclear Strategy," in Olav Riste, ed., *Western Security: The Formative Years* (New York: Columbia University Press, 1985), p. 291.

23. Ibid., p. 311.

24. Dwight D. Eisenhower Papers, Ann Whitman File, Dulles-Herter Series, box 3, "Dulles, John Foster—February 1955" folder (2), Dwight D. Eisenhower Library, Abilene, Kans.

25. In May 1956, for example, he thought it important to make allied leaders realize that "our aid to the European countries must be drawing to a close." Memo

from Col. Andrew Goodpaster, May 6, 1956, Ann Whitman File, Dulles-Herter Series, box 5. After he left the presidency, Eisenhower continued to favor a substantial reduction in U.S. forces stationed on the Continent. Dwight D. Eisenhower, "Let's Be Honest with Ourselves," *Saturday Evening Post,* October 26, 1963, p. 26; *New York Times,* May 22, 1966, p. 17.

26. Christopher Layne, "After the INF Treaty: A New Direction for America's European Policy," Cato Institute Policy Analysis no. 103 (April 21, 1988), pp. 6–10. See also Layne, "Atlanticism without NATO," *Foreign Policy* 67 (Summer 1987): 22–45, and "Continental Divide," 13–27.

27. Egon Bahr, "Peace: A State of Emergency," in Rudolph Steinke and Michael Vale, eds., *Germany Debates Defense: The NATO Alliance at the Crossroads* (Armonk, N.Y.: M.E. Sharpe, 1983), p. 146. See also Karl Kaiser et al., "Nuclear Weapons and the Preservation of Peace," *Foreign Affairs* 60 (Summer 1982): 1157–70.

II
Costs and Benefits
of NATO

4
NATO: Take the Money and Run

Melvyn Krauss

More than most social scientists, economists recognize the role incentives play in determining human behavior. Given their income and tastes, consumers can be coaxed to buy more of a good only if its price falls relative to all other goods. Producers can be induced to produce more of a commodity only if the price system makes it profitable for them to do so. And changes in the economy's saving and investment behavior can be altered by policy-induced changes in the incentives to save and invest (by tax policy, for example).

But while the role incentives play in determining economic behavior is widely accepted, both inside and outside the economic profession, their role in determining what is generally considered to be noneconomic behavior is more controversial. For example, a growing number of economists believe that economic reasoning can be applied to the study of criminal behavior: criminals, like other economic actors, are rational beings who balance the expected costs and benefits of their prospective criminal behavior to determine whether to indulge in any given criminal act. If the society makes the expected costs of criminal behavior artificially low by passing laws particularly favorable to criminals, on the margin, more crimes will be committed than in the absence of such incentive. (This approach, it should be noted, contrasts sharply with that of sociologists, psychologists, and criminologists, who tend to treat criminals as irrational beings, incapable of either understanding or controlling their criminal impulses.)

Incentives Count

"Incentives count," then, is the message economists have for their colleagues in the other social sciences. In my book, *How NATO Weakens the West*, I attempted to use incentives reasoning to explain the behavior of America's allies within the context of the Atlantic alliance.[1] This behavior has proved disconcerting to many Americans of late for a variety of reasons. First, and

Table 4–1
Defense Spending Money for the Military Allies, 1987

	Defense Spending (billions)	As Percent of Gross Domestic Product	Defense Spending per Person	Gross Domestic Product per Person
United States	$281.10	6.8	$1,164	$17,174
France	28.46	3.9	514	13,007
West Germany	27.69	3.1	454	14,664
Britain	27.33	5.1	481	9,616
Japan	19.84	1.0	163	16,159
Italy	13.46	2.2	235	10,484
Canada	7.90	2.2	308	14,162
Spain	6.01	3.1	156	5,928
Netherlands	5.32	3.1	365	11,925
Belgium	3.40	3.0	345	11,436
Turkey	2.73	4.8	54	1,140
Greece	2.42	6.1	243	3,987
Norway	2.17	3.1	520	16,562
Denmark	1.65	2.0	322	16,118
Portugal	0.94	3.2	91	2,857
Luxembourg	0.05	1.1	145	13,439

Source: Department of Defense, *Report on Allied Contributions to the Common Defense* (April 1988): 88, 90, 124–5.

foremost, has been Western Europe's persistent underinvestment in defense. In 1987, the United States spent 6.8 percent of its gross domestic product on defense, while non-U.S. NATO spent approximately 3 percent (table 4–1). How can such underinvestment be explained? Do the European allies really view the Soviet threat differently than the United States does? (If they do, could NATO have lasted so long?) Are the Europeans less committed to Western values than the United States? (There is little convincing evidence of this.) Or is America inherently more warlike and Europe the "gentler and kinder" society? (Remember World Wars I and II?)

The answer, in my view, is none of the above. Instead, the explanation of inadequate European defense expenditure is to be found in incentives reasoning, particularly that part of it related to what economists call the theory of public goods.

Defense is a good that, once provided, benefits everyone within the defended area regardless of their contribution to defense costs. In an alliance, one country's defense expenditure benefits all; hence, there is an obvious economic incentive in an alliance to induce the other members to spend more on defense than you do. In the Western alliance, the Europeans have been able to get the Americans to bear the lion's share of Western defense expenditure by following a classic free-rider strategy.[2] By downplaying the Soviet military threat and generally taking a more neutralist line than they would if the United States did not pay the bills for them, the Europeans have created a mentality among U.S. officials that Europe has a different perception of the Soviet threat than does the United States. U.S. leaders then conclude that if the Americans did not make the defense expenditures, no one else would in the Western world.

Although they were not public goods theorists, at least two great statesmen of the post–World War II era—Dwight D. Eisenhower and Charles de Gaulle—recognized the inhibiting effect American defense support for Europe would have on Europe's own defense efforts. Eisenhower wrote in 1963 that "the maintaining of permanent troop establishments abroad will continue to overburden our balance-of-payments problem and, most important, discourage the development of the necessary military strength Western European countries should provide themselves."[3] In 1949, six months after the NATO treaty was signed, de Gaulle said: "France must first count upon itself, independent of foreign aid," and NATO "takes away the initiative to build our national defense."[4]

It should come as no surprise, then, that of all the West European allies, France, which is the least dependent on the United States for its defense, is the least accommodationist toward the Soviet Union, while West Germany, which is the most dependent on the United States for its defense, is the most accommodationist.

President de Gaulle's two critical foreign policy decisions of the 1960s—the withdrawal of France from NATO's military structure and its counterpart, the creation of an independent nuclear force—have insulated France from the neutralist disease. "No foreign weapons are allowed in France," writes Flora Lewis in the *New York Times*. "The pacifist movement in France, though it is growing, remains marginal because the French government retains full and exclusive control of its defense."[5]

Results of a 1983 opinion poll of national security elites in West Germany and France, conducted by the Science Center in Berlin, show German accommodationist attitudes considerably stronger than French attitudes:

- 66 percent of the West Germans and only 30 percent of the French agree that détente should be pursued independently of the military balance.

- 19 percent of the West Germans and 62 percent of the French agree on the question as to whether the West should agree on a list of economic sanctions to be used against the Soviet Union in case of such future actions as occurred in Afghanistan or Poland.

- 86 percent of the West Germans and 38 percent of the French believe the West should seek to increase trade with the East to establish a cooperative relationship and thus support the progress of détente in a mutual interest.[6]

Of course, the fact that antinuclear attitudes are strongest in West Germany and weakest in France is also consistent with the dependence thesis.

The public good interpretation of NATO defense expenditure implies that European and U.S. defense efforts should be inversely related: the greater the U.S. efforts, the less the European efforts, and vice-versa. There have been several econometric analyses of this issue, which confirm this seesaw relationship.[7] For example, L.R. Jones and Fred Thompson note that "during the 1970s when American defense spending dropped sharply in real terms and the U.S. nuclear umbrella over Europe and Japan became decreasingly credible, the West Europeans and Japanese markedly stepped up their own defense spending." The facts and figures of this period are as follows: the United States decreased its defense expenditure, measured in constant 1970 dollars, from $77 billion to $59 billion from 1970 to 1979, while during this same period non-U.S. NATO increased its real defense spending from $32 billion to $61 billion, and Japan increased its real defense expenditure from $2.5 billion to $6.5 billion. "On the whole," write Jones and Thompson, "our results are fairly robust. . . . What they show is that our allies are rational (that is, their defense efforts reflect both the Soviet threat and American contributions to the common defense) and that their demands for defense are apparently inelastic."[8]

The finding of inelastic European defense is crucial to the debate over whether U.S. troops should remain in Europe, for inelasticity implies that as defense costs rise to Europeans, they will continue to demand the same amount of defense as before the price increase. Thus, if the United States were to reduce its share of the common defense burden, Western Europe would pick up the slack even though its defense costs are increased.

This result undoubtedly surprises and dismays those who have vociferously argued against a U.S. troop withdrawal on the grounds that it would Finlandize Western Europe. For example, Richard R. Burt, former U.S. ambassador to West Germany, writes:

The Soviet Union remains the preponderant military power in Europe. The Soviet Union also continues to employ its military power to achieve political objectives, including the intimidation of Western Europe. In such circumstances, the withdrawal of American troops and of the American security guarantee would have the reverse effect from what Professor Krauss suggests. American withdrawal would leave Western European leaders with no realistic means to pro   for their national security except through accommodation with the dominant regional power, the USSR. American withdrawal would, as a result, depress, not stimulate, European defense efforts, while driving the U.S. into increasing international isolation.[9]

But Burt and those who agree with him are wrong, according to Jones and Thompson:

> Understanding the ability and willingness of our allies to take up burdens abandoned by the United States is the key to balancing risks and costs, because appropriate force thresholds depend not only upon the risks that policy-makers are willing to accept and the capabilities of the potential enemy, but upon available allied forces as well. For example, the United States continues to concentrate its ground and tactical air forces on the defense of Europe and Northeastern Asia. If, however, these contributions serve primarily to replace local defense efforts, their marginal value is practically nil. As Krauss explains, this implies a substantial misallocation of scarce resources. How, then, does one account for the magnitude of the American contribution to the defense of the areas? The best answer is probably simply inertia. But part of the explanation for the strength and stability of American commitments to Europe and Japan undoubtedly lies in the failure of American policy-makers to distinguish between marginal and absolute benefits (the defense of Europe and Japan *is* vital to American interests) and in the belief that the behavior of our allies cannot be predicted. Yet we know our allies are able to bear a larger share of the burden of defending Western Europe and East Asia than they do. . . . Krauss predicts that our allies would also be willing to bear a larger share of the burden of self-defense (the readers should note the distinction between willing and eager). The analysis presented here tends to confirm Krauss' prediction.[10]

The basic lever for European defense free riding has been the presence of U.S. troops in Europe. Not only do U.S. taxpayers bear most of the costs of these troops (an income transfer effect), but, even more important, the troops encouraged Western Europe to economize on its conventional forces at a time when the Soviets spared little effort in building up theirs (a behavioral effect). Thus, rather than redress the conventional imbalance in Europe, American defense support may actually have helped create the imbalance or, at the very least, prevented the conventional imbalance from being redressed by purely European defense efforts. A related point is that U.S. defense support, by substituting for local defense efforts, has reduced the nuclear threshold in Europe to a dangerously low level.

The nuclear threshold is that critical point in an armed conflict when one of the opponents is faced with the choice of either surrendering or using nuclear weapons. At present, the nuclear threshold is alarmingly low. If Moscow were to attack Western Europe by conventional means, according to the ex-NATO commanding general, Bernard Rogers, NATO could fight for "days, not weeks" before facing the doomsday decision. Why so short a time? Because Western Europe has economized on its conventional forces. And why has Western Europe economized on its conventional forces? Because of American defense guarantees.

What did the Europeans do with the funds saved by their defense free riding? They used them to build elaborate welfare states. In countries that are members of the Organization for Economic Cooperation and Development, welfare state expenditure increased by a healthy 12.7 percentage points of gross domestic product from 1955–1957 to 1974–1976, while defense expenditures actually fell by 0.8 percentage points during the same time period.[11] Thus, when Americans pay their defense bills, they are, in effect, paying for Europe's welfare state at the expense of their own.

This fact has not escaped the notice of liberal Democrats like Jesse Jackson, the only major party presidential candidate in the 1988 election to advocate a U.S. troop withdrawal from Europe. On the other hand, conventional conservatives have been less quick to grasp where their true interests lie in regard to the NATO issue. If the United States fails to pull its troops from Europe, the result could well be a substantial tax increase to redress the federal budget deficit. How many Americans, one wonders, would be willing to see their taxes increased so that Europeans can avoid a tax increase to pay for their own defense? Or how many Americans would be willing to endure a tax increase so that Europe could avoid a cut in its already bloated welfare state? To ask this question is to answer it. The only reason there has not been a revolt over NATO in the United States is that most American taxpayers are not fully aware of the issues.

Atlantic Unity and Europe's Defense Disincentives

The presumption—and it is little more than that—that the ultimate objective of the Soviet Union is to split the United States from Western Europe is a most important lever Europeans have over U.S. foreign policy.[12] To deny the Soviets their victory, Atlantic unity has been made the sine qua non of U.S. policy. An unintended, and unfortunate, consequence of U.S. attachment to Atlantic unity is to give the Europeans license to disregard U.S. interests. If the United States protests Europe's policies, the doctrine of Atlantic unity is waved in American faces by a coalition of European and U.S. Atlanticists who claim the United States needs Europe at least as much as Europe needs the United States.

Atlantic unity thus gives the Europeans an incentive to deny U.S. interests and policies, particularly those that conflict with the interests and policies of adversaries of the United States (such as Libya, Moscow, and the Palestine Liberation Organization). This result occurs because Atlantic unity prevents the United States from imposing costs on its NATO allies when they thwart it (as West Germany recently did by exporting poison gas technology to Libya), while U.S. adversaries suffer from no such symmetrical inhibition. This perverse incentive effect relates not only to defense policies but to other areas as well, such as high-tech exports and trade and credit subsidies to Moscow.

If Bonn, for example, were to refuse to extend subsidized financial credits to Moscow, the Soviets undoubtedly would make the West Germans pay in some way—if not militarily then by building a "bigger and better" Berlin wall or some such retaliation. On the other hand, if Bonn displeased Washington by extending overly generous financial subsidies to Moscow, Washington could be expected to complain but do little else.

As far as the issue of defense is concerned, on several occasions U.S. access to NATO bases in Western Europe has been denied because the European governments perceived the costs of crossing the United States to be less than the costs of crossing its opponents. The *Achille Lauro* affair is a case in point. When U.S. jet fighters forced the Egyptian airliner carrying the Palestinian terrorists to freedom to land at Sigonella Air Force Base, a NATO base in Sicily, U.S. troops surrounded the plane to transfer the terrorists to a waiting C-141 for transport to the United States. But the Italian troops at the base prevented the transfer by threatening the use of force against the American troops. President Reagan is reported to have personally intervened by ordering the ranking U.S. officer at Sigonella to hand the terrorists over to the Italians rather than risk a shoot-out with NATO allies.

The spectacle of U.S. and Italian troops squaring off at Sigonella should prove sobering for even the most enthusiastic NATO supporters. Why, bewildered Americans may wonder, did they spend $134 billion on NATO in 1985 alone if in carrying out a legitimate antiterrorist operation, U.S. troops are opposed by Italian troops—at a NATO base no less?

Of course, the decision to hand the Palestinian terrorists over to the Italian authorities proved to be a costly mistake. Within hours of the transfer, Rome released the mastermind of the hijacking, Muhammad Abbas, on grounds of insufficient evidence. At first, White House reaction to the release of Abbas was one of outrage, but when the White House issued a statement labeling Abbas's release "incomprehensible," it chose the wrong word to describe Italian behavior. Italian prime minister Bettino Craxi's reasons for releasing Abbas were no great mystery: Craxi feared the PLO more than he feared the United States. And how right Craxi was. A few days after Abbas's release, President Reagan sent his deputy secretary of state, John C. Whitehead, to Italy with an apologetic note.

Incentives for European Defense Cooperation

There can be no greater incentive for European defense cooperation than the withdrawal of American military support from Western Europe. This was made clear by the European response first to the Reagan-Gorbachev meeting in Iceland and then to the subsequent intermediate nuclear force (INF) treaty. According to a story in the *Wall Street Journal,* for example, "Common security fears following the Reagan-Gorbachev meeting in Iceland have prompted West Germany, Britain and France into an unprecendented agreement to coordinate their nuclear-arms-control policies. . . . Under the coordination efforts, Bonn, London and Paris aim to speak with one voice in arms control discussions with the superpowers."[13]

The *New York Times* reports that Prime Minister Margaret Thatcher has moved closer to her European partners as a result of Reykjavik:

> President Reagan's ability to manage foreign affairs and the durability of American commitments—especially conspicuous in the aftermath of the Iceland summit meeting—appears to have much to do with the urge to find an enhanced role for Britain in Europe. . . . A common fear that Washington might be tempted to negotiate away their deterrents leaves Britain and France, Western Europe's two nuclear-armed nations, with a sense of common interests on national security.[14]

A concrete step to increase military cooperation in Europe following upon the zero-option proposal (which became the basis for the INF treaty) was the formation of a joint brigade of French and German troops announced by the French and German defense ministers in July 1987. The 3,000-man brigade is to be headed by a French officer and kept outside NATO's integrated military command. Both Manfred Wörner, ex–West German defense minister, and his French counterpart, André Giraud, described the new joint brigade as an effective military force in the defense of Western Europe. "It will have an essential mission that we still have to define," Wörner said. "In the event of a crisis, it will fight alongside the other European and Atlantic forces, but it won't be part of NATO's integrated command." Although the French-German brigade had been in the works for some time, it is doubtful that it would have been approved by political leaders in the two countries had it not been for European fears of U.S. withdrawal from Europe's defense.

"There is more and more worry in France the closer we get to the total de-nuclearization of Europe," concludes former French foreign minister Jean François-Poncet. "Then maybe the U.S. troops will go, too." Indeed, the *Wall Street Journal* reports that "European fears have brought new urgency to the renewal of peaceful Franco-German ties that began in earnest a decade ago. Experts on both sides of the border say that relations between Paris and Bonn now are the best they have been since the war and that European cooperation on defense and other matters is no longer just a dream. This time, with the two nations united by their common security fears, rapprochement should last."[15]

But will it? Although there can be no doubt that the INF treaty has brought the European powers into closer military cooperation with one another, it is not at all clear that such cooperation can be sustained so long as U.S. troops remain in Europe. The American troops tend to comfort the Europeans when, in order to create an autonomous defense entity, the Europeans need to be provoked.

Zbigniew Brzezinski, President Carter's national security adviser, understands this point and argues that U.S. troops in Europe constitute a serious obstacle to the emergence of the autonomous European defense entity he favors. "Europe must be prodded if it is to move in the direction of increased military cooperation," writes Brzezinski:

> Left as it is Europe's cultural hedonism and political complacency will en-
> sure that not much is done. Even the modest 1978 NATO commitment to
> a three percent per annum increase in defense expenditures was not honored
> by most European states. America should, therefore, initiate a longer-term
> process to alter the nature of its military presence in Europe gradually, while
> making it clear to the Europeans that the change is not an act of anger or
> a threat . . . but rather the product of a deliberate strategy designed to pro-
> mote Europe's unity and its historic restoration.[16]

Brzezinski is undoubtedly correct that without the catalyst of a U.S. troop pullout, European military cooperation is likely to remain but another entry on the long list of European military cooperative efforts that have failed to materialize. The reality of Europe, after all, is division, not unity. The European peoples are divided by different cultures, different languages, different religions, and different economic interests. Moreover, historial antagonisms have separated one country from another. Only the ignorant would deny the dissonance and discord that have existed among the Europeans in the past and undoubtedly will continue to exist in the future as well.

Can it be said, then, that the nations of Europe are so hopelessly divided that they cannot make common cause with one another under any circumstances? Of course not. Those who preach the lessons of history should remember that mutual distrust between France and Great Britain did not prevent the two nations from joining forces to defeat the kaiser in World War I and Hitler in World War II. Nor did mutual national antagonism prevent the Germans and Russians from joining forces to defeat Napoleon, and so on. By themselves, national differences and traditional antagonism are bad predictors of how disparate and desperate nations will behave in any given situation. If history does have a message, it is that despite differences and antagonisms, the European nations can come together when there is a common interest to do so. The coalescing force in European politics most often has been the existence of a common enemy.

Since the Soviets are the common enemy today, the question arises as to why the European countries remain disunited. The answer is that Europe's gross defense dependence on the United States has voided the common danger that, in the absence of a U.S. defense commitment to Europe, could unite the European nations in common cause against the Soviets. Unwisely, the United States has pacified Europe to outside threats and thus removed the potentially congealing element from European politics. Should that pacification be discontinued, however, the political unification feared by the Kremlin could come about.

In 1992, the "year of Europe," remaining barriers to international trade and commerce between members of the European Common Market are scheduled to come down and disparate European laws and policies will be unified (or at least, harmonized) across countries. What better time could there be for Europe to announce a European defense force? The United States should target 1992 as the year of a substantial pullout of U.S. forces from Europe. This would certainly galvanize the Europeans into congealing action on defense as well as reinforce current European propensities for economic and political unification and harmonization. The contours of the post–post World War II period are shaping up. In this brave new world of European unification and independence, there is no place for permanent U.S forces in Europe. After forty years, it is time for the troops to come home.

The Gorbachev Factor

The evidence of quantitative public policy experts shows that European defense efforts are the result of a balance between European perceptions of the Soviet threat on the one hand and their perceptions of U.S. military strength and support for Europe on the other. Other things being equal, the greater the perceived Soviet threat and the lesser the perceived level of American strength and support, the greater is the European defense effort. The 1970s was a period in which both reduced real military spending by the United States and reduced credibility of the U.S. nuclear umbrella increased European real defense expenditures. The 1990s, on the other hand, promise to be a decade in which the Europeans sharply curtail their defense expenditures. The principal reason is the growing perception in Europe of a reduced Soviet threat due to the Gorbachev reforms.

Faced with the prospect of demilitarized allies intent on reducing their already undernourished share of the common defense burden, the United States would have no choice but to withdraw its troops from Europe—unless, of course, different perceptions of the Soviet threat on the two sides of the

Atlantic were so strong that the United States was willing to absorb an increasing share of the NATO defense burden. (Meager European defense efforts then could not be considered free riding but an implication of real differences in defense demand in Europe and America.) In that case, however, the absence of critical common ground—similar perceptions of the Soviet threat—would make it unlikely that NATO would be able to survive. The Europeans most likely would ask the U.S. troops to leave, and NATO would be finished. As German conservative politician Volker Ruehe recently remarked: "The softer Gorbachev sounds, the louder the noise of the [NATO] airplanes."[17] It is far better for the United States to leave on its own volition than to be kicked out.

Gorbachev's reforms threaten to destroy NATO. But with or without Gorbachev, the case for a U.S. troop withdrawal from Europe is clear. Without Gorbachev, the case rests upon European defense free riding. U.S. defense efforts merely substitute for local ones, and the marginal benefits of U.S. support are negligible, particularly when they are considered in relation to NATO's enormous costs (estimated at $160 billion per year). With Gorbachev, the marginal benefits also are low but not because of a defense substitution effect. Rather it is because the Soviet threat is perceived to be significantly reduced. In either case, the United States stands to save billions of tax dollars by withdrawing its troops from Western Europe. My advice to U.S. policymakers is to take the money and run.

Notes

1. Melvyn Krauss, *How NATO Weakens the West* (New York: Simon and Schuster, 1986).

2. This point was first made by Mancur Olson and Richard Zeckhauser in M. Olson and R. Zeckhauser, "An Economic Theory of Alliances," *Revue of Economics and Statistics* 48, no. 3 (August 1966): 266–79.

3. Dwight D. Eisenhower, "Let's Be Honest with Ourselves," *Saturday Evening Post,* October 26, 1963.

4. Quoted in C.L. Sulzberger, "Foreign Affairs: Poker as Played in Paris," *New York Times,* February 23, 1966.

5. Flora Lewis, "Missiles and Pacifists," *New York Times,* November 18, 1983, p. A-35.

6. Cited by Peter Schmidt, "Public Opinion and Security Policy in the Federal Republic of Germany: Elite and Mass Opinion in a Comparative Perspective," *Rand Paper* (Santa Monica, Calif.: Rand Corporation, 1984), p. 51.

7. See, for example, J.C. Murdoch and T. Sandler, "Complementarity, Free-Riding and the Military Expenditures of NATO Allies," *Journal of Public Economics* 25 (1984): 83–101 and "A Theoretical and Empirical Analysis of NATO," *Journal of*

Conflict Resolution 26 (1982): 237–63; T. Sandler and J.F. Forbes, "Burden Sharing, Strategy and the Design of NATO," *Economic Inquiry* 18, no. 3 (July 1980): 425–44.

8. L.R. Jones and Fred Thompson, "Is Krauss Correct: Does NATO Weaken the West" (paper delivered before the Association in Public Policy and Management Research Conference, October 29, 1987), p. 6, 7. Also see Fred Thompson, "Lumpy Goods and Cheap Riders: An Application of the Theory of Public Goods to International Alliances," *Journal of Public Policy* 7, no. 4 (1987): 431–49.

9. Richard R. Burt, "European Pullout Isn't Deserved or Desired," *Wall Street Journal,* March 28, 1983.

10. Jones and Thompson, "Is Krauss Correct?" pp. 13–14.

11. Organization for Economic Cooperation and Development, *Public Expenditure Trends* (Paris: OECD, 1978).

12. An alternative view is that the Soviet objective is to weaken Western Europe and to use a weakened Europe to weaken the United States. See Melvyn Krauss, "Let the Europeans Negotiate with Gorbachev," in *Collective Defense or Strategic Independence,* Ted Galen Carpenter, ed. (Lexington, Mass.: Lexington Books, 1989).

13. Peter Gumbel, Thomas F. O'Boyle, and Robert Keately, "Three European Nations to Coordinate Arms Control in an Unprecedented Move," *Wall Street Journal,* November 5, 1986.

14. Joseph Lelyveld, "Thatcher Is Quietly Moving Closer to European Partners," *New York Times,* December 6, 1986.

15. Thomas F. O'Boyle and Philip Revzin, "Nuclear-Missile Talks Lend a New Urgency to Paris-Bonn Amity," *Wall Street Journal,* November 5, 1986.

16. Zbigniew Brzezinski, "The Future of Yalta," *Foreign Affairs* 63, no. 2 (Winter 1984–1985).

17. Frederick Kempe, "West Germany's Ties with U.S. Become Increasingly Testy," *Wall Street Journal,* March 13, 1989, p. 1.

5

NATO and
the Limits of Devolution

Josef Joffe

NATO at 40 is an unmitigated success story. Alone among America's multilateral alliances, it has survived into healthy middle age. By contrast, the Southeast Asia Treaty Organization (SEATO), the Central Treaty Organization (CENTO), and the Australia-New Zealand-United States Alliance (ANZUS) have either disappeared or have turned into bilateral shells.[1] Far from waning away, NATO even picked up a new member, Spain, some thirty years into its existence. It has survived all of its crises—from the Suez war of 1956, when the United States humiliated its two oldest allies, France and Britain, to the "Euromissile battle" of the 1980s, when the alliance did manage to deploy Pershing II and cruise missiles in the face of fierce and protracted domestic revolt against new nuclear weapons. NATO did not founder when France pulled out of its integrated military structure in 1966, and it did not falter when two of its members, Greece and Turkey, unleashed their troops against each other in 1974.

So much for the good news. Yet there is no gainsaying the bad news, and it flows from three sources: the apparent decline of the Soviet threat, and the consequences drawn from that perception by the Europeans, on the one hand, and the United States, on the other. Surely the first and most important piece of bad news is a by-product of NATO's secular success: the apparent transformation of Soviet policy upon the accession of Mikhail Gorbachev in 1985. In a cynical, but quite à propos, aside, Georgiy Arbatov, director of the Soviet USA-Canada Institute, has put the matter thus: "We have deployed the ultimate secret weapon against you: we are removing the threat."

The point is well taken. The two most dangerous moments in the life of an alliance are their success and their failure. Obviously nothing is worse for the health of a coalition than defeat; there are no recorded instances of alliances that have survived beyond capitulation, which is the single most drastic proof of their failure. The Triple Alliance ended with World War I, and so did the Axis in 1945. An alliance is doomed when its founding purpose, victory in war, is frustrated by force of arms.

It is not so obvious why alliances should lose when they win. Why change a winning team? In fact, victorious coalitions historically have been hardly more cohesive than losing ones. The Triple Entente disappeared along with the Triple Alliance after 1918, and so did the Anti-Hitler Coalition in the wake of Germany's and Japan's capitulation. In the most general terms, alliances erode when they no longer serve the interest of their members and the burdens of alignment begin to exceed its benefits. As war ends in triumph, future costs tend to overwhelm present gains. The key cause of alignment disappears at the moment of the enemy's surrender, pushing diverging interests, previously suppressed, to the fore. If the partnership does not founder immediately, it will do so when the allies proceed to divide the spoils of victory ("his gains are my losses") or begin to contemplate a future in which yesterday's comrade-in-arms might turn into tomorrow's foe.

NATO did not "win" in the way the Triple Entente did in 1918. Not a single shot has been fired in anger since 1949, and today the Soviet Union is in no sense vanquished. If anything, it is a more powerful opponent today than forty years ago when it was neither a true nuclear power nor fully recuperated from the ravages of World War II. What is gnawing at the sinews of NATO is victory in terms of deterrence maintained and aggression forestalled. Furthermore, Soviet behavior and rhetoric have changed in ways thought inconceivable in 1949, an early peak in the ups and downs of the cold war.

This point—as opposed to the long-term objectives of Soviet policy in Europe, which may not have changed at all—need not be belabored. Europe at the threshold of the 1990s is a different place from the Europe of 1949. At that stage, the Soviet Union had firmly subjugated Eastern Europe and appeared ready and willing to move beyond the Elbe river. From the Berlin Blockade to the Berlin Ultimatum, Western positions in Germany were endlessly assaulted by means short of violence, a process that did not abate until the Berlin Wall was built in 1961. Thereafter, until the mid-1980s, the contest was dominated by a relentless Soviet arms buildup, the "moral equivalent of war" in an age where the real resort to the ultima ratio has been suppressed by the paralyzing fear of all-out nuclear escalation.

How has Soviet behavior changed? Where SS-20 missiles used to be fielded at the rhythm of one per week, there is now an agreement in place providing for the complete elimination of all intermediate-range nuclear forces. On the conventional level, frozen by sterile Mutual and Balanced Force Reductions negotiations for fifteen years, a new set of arms talks began in March 1989, shaped by two unexpected Soviet concessions: the admission of the Warsaw Pact's superiority in certain areas and the declared readiness for asymmetrical reductions, something the West had been demanding in vain since 1973. The setting appeared no less benign. At home, Mikhail Gorbachev had begun to loosen the strictures of totalitarian rule in ways far bolder than contemplated by any of his predecessors. Abroad, the Soviet assault against Afghanistan, which had made explicit cold war II (circa 1979–1986), came to an end in early 1989. Also at that time, Mikhail Gorbachev announced the unilateral reduction of Soviet armed forces by 500,000 men, followed by the announcement of a small nuclear cut (500 warheads) in the spring. In short, from Angola to the Middle East, from Afghanistan to Europe, the Soviet Union began to act as if it were prepared to return to the community of responsible great powers, which revolutionary Russia had left in 1917.

If this is the case and if the transformation of Soviet behavior at home and abroad proves to be lasting, then it might be said that the West has won in the sense originally defined by George F. Kennan. In his classic statement of 1947, Kennan had postulated that "the United States has it in its power to increase enormously the strains under which Soviet policy must operate, to force upon the Kremlin a far greater moderation and circumspection . . . and in this way to promote tendencies which must eventually find their outlet in either the break-up or the mellowing of Soviet power."[2] This was the founding idea of NATO and containment, whence it would follow that the "mellowing" of Soviet power defines the point of both "victory" and transcendence. If containment has achieved its purpose, are the means—such as alliances—still necessary?

This question precedes the accession of Mikhail Gorbachev, but it has gained urgency in the aftermath of his rise to power. To be sure, there is no respectable voice on either side of the Atlantic that would demand complete retraction from the alliance. But whether on the left (usually in Western Europe) or on the right (usually in the United States), the critics would, at a minimum, want to reduce the burdens of alliance. The logic is simple: if the demand for security has fallen, why not reduce the price paid for this collective good too?

In the United States, the call takes the form of devolution: let the Europeans take care of themselves. This version of neoisolationism (isolationism was always directed against Europe, not against the entire world as such) might be conveniently split into two: the fiscal and the nuclear variant. "Fiscal neoisolationism,"[3] taking note of America's endemic external deficits, would seek to "reconcile geopolitical pretensions with fiscal discipline" by "renouncing primary responsibility for directly maintaining the Eurasian territorial balance."[4] "Nuclear neoisolationism" proceeds on the premise that the U.S. nuclear guarantee for Western Europe in an age of "peril parity" might entrap the country in a suicidal war for the sake of other nations; it takes the following form:

> There are few Americans, however much they cherish Western Europe, who are actually willing to engage in mutual nuclear annihilation with the Soviet Union in retaliation for non-nuclear Soviet aggression against Western Europe. This means that NATO, as currently structured is an archaic institution, that the defense of Western Europe will become primarily a West Euro-

pean responsibility, that Western Europe will have to gird itself to fight and (hopefully) win a conventional war against the Soviet Union—with American help if needed, but not with a recourse to nuclear weapons.[5]

In Western Europe, dreams of devolution—or, more precisely, emancipation—are similarly informed by the escape from either dependence or entrapment in unwanted conflicts, and they range from the practical to the highly visionary. On a practical level, partial emancipation has already become a multifarious reality, and its shape is "alliance à la carte." The first and most dramatic instance was France's departure from the integrated military structures of NATO, and it is perhaps no accident that this step was taken in the mid-1960s, the first détente that unfolded in the wake of the Cuban missile crisis.

On the periphery, Greece and Spain have since followed in de Gaulle's footsteps, yet they stopped short of eliminating all U.S. forces from their soil. Denmark refuses to host any U.S. nuclear weapons, and in Norway the proscription applies to their deployment in peacetime. More recently, the West Germans defied American and British pressures to consent to the modernization of short-range nuclear forces (the Lance missiles), postponing a decision until 1992. Overall the trend is toward the reduction of the military burden of alliance, extending from low-level training flights to large-scale maneuvers.

On the visionary level—emancipation pure and simple—we have a voice of the German "national left" to make the point in all its baldness:

> If we succeed in turning *Mitteleuropa* step by step into a zone, where nuclear, biological and chemical weapons are no longer stationed, while simultaneously diminishing the conventional superiority of the Warsaw Pact . . . through appropriate troop reductions and the restructuring of forces for strictly defensive purposes, then the member states of the Westeuropean Union (WEU) will be capable of assuring sufficient deterrence on their own.[6]

In this scenario, the ancient problem of the European military balance— how to hold in check the Soviet Union without American help—would no longer matter. If achieved, the new system would merely render explicit "the Soviet Union's . . . paramount interest in a partnership-like cooperation with Western Europe. It is obvious that the strongest-possible security guarantee for Western Europe derives in the long term precisely from this interest."[7] This would be so because under Gorbachev, "the Soviet Union is in the midst of a fundamental reorientation of its foreign policy. It will have to decide whether its status as a world power is not better served by its opening toward, and cooperation with, Western Europe than by the obsolete condominium over Germany and Europe as shared with the Americans."[8] In short, Western Europe's security problem will disappear because the Soviet Union will balance its own power, as it were, through a consistent policy of self-denial.

Though different in substance, the underlying aspiration of Europe's "neoisolationists" is not far removed from that of their American counterparts. On both sides, the critics have begun to react against the strictures of bipolarity that spell options forgone and dependence assumed. The quest is for freedom—from the expenditures of "imperial overstretch," from the existential nuclear risks of extended deterrence, from subjection to a system that has bought security at the cost of Germany's and Europe's partition.

The dream of devolution and emancipation is surely as old as the alliance itself, and again, we have George F. Kennan to make the point. "Some day," he mused in his *Memoirs*, "this divided Europe, dominated by the military presence of ourselves and the Russians, would have to yield to something more natural—something that did more justice to the true strength and interests of the intermediate European peoples themselves."[9] Today that dream has gained more urgency as well as reality, for two reasons. On the side of urgency, few people on either shore of the Atlantic believe that the U.S. conventional and nuclear presence will persist at current levels, and so Western Europe may soon have to do with less of both and to rewrite the Continent's postwar security equation. On the side of apparent or emerging reality, there is the "new thinking" of Gorbachev's Soviet Union, which might yet flower into something more than marginal reform at home and marginal disarmament abroad. Might the Soviet Union then be content with the role of posttotalitarian *primus inter pares,* ready to exchange military intimidation for economic interpenetration with Western Europe and willing to let the countries of Eastern Europe take different roads from socialism (to use a term coined by Seweryn Bialer) as long as they respect their role as security buffer for the Soviet Union?

But even a democratizing Soviet Union will—indeed, cannot help but—pose an enduring security problem in and for Europe. It will remain a nuclear superpower with vast conventional assets, dwarfing all other comers. Merely by virtue of its weight and propinquity, it will dominate the rest of the continent in the absence of sufficient countervailing power. And its enduring geostrategic interests bid the Soviet Union to seek some form of domination, though that need involve neither conquest nor satrapy. At a minimum, Western Europe must not pose a strategic threat to the Western flank of the Russian empire; at a maximum, Western Europe would gestate into a "good conduct zone," refusing to challenge Moscow politically and yielding to it a steady flow of technological and financial benefits. These interests are surely givens of Soviet policy; they transcend Gorbachev, and they are not compatible with an enduring Western interest: the autonomy of Western Europe. This is the underlying security problem of the Continent; it will be muted, but it cannot be eliminated by a reformed Soviet Union.

Neither the European nor the American critics of the alliance deny the problem of power. The difference between them derives from their different conceptions of Europe's future order. The "neoisolationists," whether fiscal or nuclear, contemplate essentially the same order but without the United States as an integral part of the system. In their scheme, the Soviet Union still would have to be counterbalanced, albeit by a combination of West Europeans only (scenario A). The visionaries of the West European, primarily West German, left contemplate an order where military power no longer matters because other forms of power (economic—of which the West Europeans have plenty) will devalue the currency of arms or because the Soviet Union will contain itself (scenario B).

In scenario A (devolutionist Europe), Western Europe will raise the supply of military security; in scenario B (accommodationist Europe), Western Europe will lower its demand for security. In either case, whether supply side or demand side, equilibrium is thought to rule even in the face of America's withdrawal from the Continent's security equation. American supply siders presumably do not want the demand-side scenario to be realized because that would inevitably deliver to the Soviet Union a position of paramountcy, if not hegemony, in Europe—something the United States has labored hard to prevent since 1945. It is my contention, however, that the pursuit of scenario A will necessarily lead to, or accelerate, the implementation of scenario B, at great risk to America's well-considered interests in European and global stability.

Why should this be so?

The supply siders assume that Western Europe, once robbed of the free gift of American-provided European security, will swiftly move to make up for the deficit. In their view, it is only America's munificence that has kept the West Europeans from doing what necessity demands and their resources permit. And so, the assumption goes, only an American policy of retraction and devolution will force Western Europe to ensure its own common defense. The historical record should make for skepticism.

As I have argued elsewhere, the history of Western Europe's integrationist efforts in fact suggests the opposite—a curious twist on alliance theory.[10] Conventional alliance theory holds that states coalesce in order to ensure their security. But in the case of postwar Western Europe, the states coalesced because their security was already ensured—by a powerful outsider, the United States, which delivered an external shield as well as internal order, acted as protector and pacifier, and safeguarded the half-continent against others as well as against itself.

America's benign empire in Western Europe was the precondition of alliance and integration, and thus security came first and cooperation came second. France accepted the Federal Republic's admission to NATO only after Britain and the United States had delivered tangible guarantees against its former foe, notably the Anglo-American commitment to station sizable forces on the Continent. With two extracontinental balances anchored in the system, the rules of state behavior changed from rivalry to cooperation. In contrast to the interwar period, when the fears of the victors and the resentments of the vanquished made for a vicious cycle of repression and revanchism, France and Germany could join hands in the alliance and the European Community because a third nation—the United States—more powerful than either would ensure them both against the perilous consequences of their credulity. The smaller nations of Western Europe, especially the wary Dutch, could swallow integration with the large because they did not need to fear domination. Even Great Britain ultimately joined in the continental venture because America's presence blunted the hard edge of this traditional rivalry with France and Germany.

To argue thus is to invite the twin charge of historicism and faint-heartedness. Perhaps the habits of cooperation are now so deeply etched into the collective West European mind that they will endure even in the absence of a powerful American guardian. Might not Western Europe have tran-scended its grim history of mutual rivalry and slaughter? But even assuming transcendence, which one cannot, how would the West Europeans ensure their independence against the other superpower, which will not, and could not, withdraw from Europe because it is, at least one-fifth, in Europe?

This is the key question raised by the idea of devolution, and there is no satisfactory practical answer in the face of nuclear weapons. There are, of course, two theoretical answers. The first is a West European superstate like the United States, which would subsume the half-continent's enormous resources, including a single nuclear deterrent, under one soverign will. But it would be fanciful to assume such an outcome; the nation-state is alive and well in Western Europe, and there is nothing—neither Hobbesian fear nor a great unifier (analogous to Piedmont in Italy or Prussia in Germany)—to force the twelve into a single sovereign entity.

The second theoretical alternative is the obverse of the first: a Europe of fully sovereign states with nuclear weapons for each and all, including the Germans. But as one high French official once put it in half-jest only: "That would be the occasion of an all-European declaration of war against Ger-many." At least in this generation, West German nuclear weapons would act as a pernicious solvent of European security and not as its glue.

With "one Europe, one bomb" and "one Europe, many bombs" outside the realm of the politically possible, what about the third alternative: "one Europe, two bombs"? This is in fact what the devolutionists have in mind: a nuclear umbrella for Western Europe carried jointly by the two indigenous nuclear powers, France and Britain. The reason that this vision is hardly more plausible than the two preceding ones has been reiterated ad infinitum by French leaders and strategists; the more discreet British would surely concur if they were pressed: nuclear weapons protect their possessors only. Hence, "deterrence is exclusively national" and "the nuclear risk cannot be shared."[11] Nor "can the decision [to launch] be shared."[12]

To be sure, French policy keeps evolving ever so slowly, but it stops well short of what devolution would require. There are recurrent allusions to a *sanctuaire élargi*, which might encompass France's neighbor across the Rhine, as well as to the vaunted FAR, the French Rapid Action Force, which might rush to the inter-German border to aid in the "forward battle."[13] Former Prime Minister Pierre Mauroy ventured that France's vital interests extend beyond the borders of the "Hexagon to their approaches. Aggression against France does not begin when an enemy invades the nation's territory."[14]

But even as the military clauses of the Franco-German Friendship Treaty (1963) were rescued from oblivion twenty-five years later, even as West Germans and French formed a joint Defense Council and cobbled together a joint brigade, the first principle of French strategy remained in place: "Autonomous in the commitment of its forces, France does not intend to suffer the consequences of conflicts that are not its own."[15] In his most recent statement on basics (October 1988), Mitterrand virtually used the same language. Mutual assistance in case of an attack on allies was possible, "yet our decision depends on us, and on us only." When he spoke about "solidarity with our alliance partners," he pointedly mentioned only "conventional forces."[16]

Epigrams such as these do not bode well for cordial ententes. And there is not only continuity to them but also logic. Since nuclear weapons, if ever launched, threaten swift, complete, and mutual destruction, they render all vows and pledges null and void when the existential crunch arrives. Since nations cannot share control over the nuclear weapons, nonnuclear states could not rely on the nuclear shield of their allies. Yet mutual control and mutual assistance is the very stuff of alliance—whence it follows that nuclear alliances are impossible. Even if ever uttered, a French guarantee must perforce be a hollow one because, as Mitterrand and countless others have said: "Our decision depends on us, and on us only."

The idea of devolution thus seems to lack a basis in both logic and policy pronouncement. Yet if true, this would also reduce to sheer pretense extended deterrence *à l'américaine* that is supposedly the very linchpin of the Atlantic alliance—at least since the late 1950s when the Soviets had acquired a rudimentary bomber force capable of striking the American heartland. At that point, massive retaliation began to loom as two-way threat, and with it, America's pledge to launch nuclear weapons on behalf of its allies was bound to turn brittle.

Does "NATO at 40" then rest on a historic hoax? The answer must be that superpowers can more easily fudge the irreducible dilemmas of extended deterrence; they are in a different class of guarantors for at least two reasons.

Threatening nuclear strikes on behalf of allies requires a counterforce potential buttressed by numerical redundancies. Only weapons capable of hitting their targets with high precision and low collateral damage can demonstrate commitment or weaken an aggressor without necessarily provoking the apocalypse. The French and the British do not now possess such weapons; their arsenals essentially are to serve a countervalue strategy, and they are minimum deterrents, to boot. "For technical reasons alone, " said French defense minister Charles Hernu, "our deterrent cannot serve to cover Europe or even France and the Federal Republic."[17] Nor is counterforce the motto of the 1990s. "This modernization . . . of our potential," said Prime Minister Mauroy in outlining his country's future plans, "does not imply a transformation of [our] anti-cities strategy. It remains the . . . indisputable foundation of deterrence by the weak against the strong."[18]

For a superpower like the United States, equipped with thousands of strategic weapons, great numbers confer options short of Armageddon. A first volley would not be the last, nor would an initial breach of deterrence signify its complete collapse because large nuclear reserves should still make for intrawar deterrence. It is the possession of abundant assets that raises the probability of an American first use above zero, which may well be enough. And it is the prospect of unlimited damage at the end of the day—no matter how low the probability of going first—that instills caution in those contemplating aggression against American allies.

Having far fewer weapons denies such extended deterrence options to small nuclear powers like France. The ability to mutilate a superpower ("to tear off an arm") is not enough to protect allies. France's first strike will also be its last, and hence it follows that threatening such action on behalf of allies would be justly seen as an empty bluff. Indeed, the French and the British umbrellas cannot substitute for a U.S. guarantee because they depend on the larger American umbrella. The weak can deter the strong because the strong deter each other, and we have the French chief of staff, Jeannou Lacaze, to make the point. What situation, he asks, would the aggressor face after a French strike that "destroyed a non-negligible part of his cities *while the other great nuclear powers would still have their intact military and economic potential?* This argument seems fundamental to me, and it indicates how advisable it is to view our strategy of the weak deterring the strong within the global geopolitical context."[19]

Still, in an age of "peril parity," even a superpower guarantee may rest on feet of clay. The problem common to all alliances, before and after the Bomb, has always been the fear of abandonment. Nuclear weapons merely have exacerbated the problem because they place the very existence of guarantors in jeopardy. So why has NATO endured? To ensure allies against abandonment, protectors must tie their own hands. The United States did so by placing several hundred thousand of its own troops in the path of the potential invader—even before massive retaliation became the strategy of the day—and their message to friends as well as foes is twofold.

First, large numbers of soldiers as hostages signal that an attack on Western Europe threatens values almost as precious as American core security. Hostage armies make for partial congruence between otherwise distinct national territories, thus softening the harshly divisive logic of nuclear weapons. The French are surely right in proclaiming that nations will not commit suicide for another. But the deterrent threat gains credibility when it is wielded for the sake of not just, say, West Germany but of hundreds of thousands of American nationals stationed on West German soil. The United States might not put Chicago at risk for Hamburg, but the aggressor (in whose mind deterrence takes place) will feel far less ready to test the commitment if it also happens to cover a city-sized American contingent on German territory.

Second, large numbers of nuclear weapons in a forward position signal that there may be no sanctuaries: that war may expand to engulf principals as well as junior partners; that an attack on America's ultima ratio in Europe is an attack on the United States itself. As long as they are in place, nuclear weapons may be used, and once even the smallest weapon explodes, there may be no firebreaks or pauses short of Moscow and Washington. Here, too, the quantity of forces and the quality of destruction dramatizes the difference between superpower protectors and middle-power would-be guarantors. In the nuclear age, hostage forces must be more than symbolic; to be credible, they must force the aggressor to attack assets that cannot be written off lightly.

This is something France does not intend to provide. France's 50,000 troops in Germany are tucked away in the southwest, close to the French rather than the East German border. Hence, theirs is not a hostage function; rather they underline the opposite—a nonbelligerency option that American forces in Germany lack. While American nuclear weapons are stationed up front, thus dramatizing the link between a local and a wider war, French nuclear weapons are based at home. The vaunted FAR may join the forward battle, but then it may not. Indeed, while the FAR was touted as reassurance to allies, what was given was simultaneously taken away. And so the FAR's tactical nuclear weapons were separated from the conventional forces to make sure that any eastward engagement does not compromise France's ability to stay out of a nuclear war. "The use of tactical nuclear weapons," said the French chief of staff, "will no longer . . . be necessarily linked to the maneuver of our ground forces."[20]

Nor are such antihostage strategies destined to disappear over time. Or as Mitterand put it: "The Atlantic Alliance is not about to be replaced by a European Alliance. The reason is that no [European] military power can substitute for the American arsenal. France, at any rate, will use its nuclear strike force for its own deterrence strategy only." To be sure, France keeps intensifying its military cooperation with Britain and Germany and, in the Mediterranean, with Spain and Italy. Yet it has "never hidden from its allies that, apart from protecting its national sanctuary and related vital interests, it cannot take charge of Europe's security."[21] There is a good reason that Prime Minister Chirac deplored "sterile debates on the eventual extension of our nuclear guarantee."[22] France cannot extend such a guarantee.

The "maturation of [France's] nuclear efforts" in the 1990s is designed to multiply options, not obligations—to allow France to "explore in *complete independence* ways and means of reinforcing deterrence in Europe."[23] Power and security that depend on imported leverage cannot replace the weight supplied by the American provider. Nor can more and better French weapons unhinge the dominant power relationships in the contemporary international system. At best, a French "force on loan" would merely replicate on a smaller scale the age-old conundra of extended deterrence, and it would be less credible than even the fraying American umbrella. Why then would a country like West Germany place greater faith in the puny nuclear force of a middle power ally across the Rhine (or the Channel) than in the massive arsenal of its American protector? And why would Bonn want to subordinate itself to a close neighbor and potential inferior like France, which is less profitable and certainly less honorable than dependence on a faraway superpower? Although the idea of a European defense seems both plausible and logical, these (decisive) political questions are too frequently ignored by devolutionists.

Devolution, as forced upon the West Europeans by the United States, is not likely to work because America's allies cannot jump over the long shadow cast by nuclear weapons, the ultimate currency of safety in the post-Hiroshima world. Nor can it be assumed that the withdrawal of the free gift that is America's security guarantee will make for more cohesion in Europe. That gift has spared the West Europeans the necessity of an autonomous defense policy—historically and logically the most divisive force in international relations. With America the pacifier no longer in the system, the West Europeans will worry more about each other, thus allocating fewer resources to the collective good of a common defense and more to their own separate purposes. An American withdrawal is more likely to renationalize than to denationalize Western Europe.

If so, it should not be assumed that the supply of security will rise. More likely, key West European nations, above all West Germany, which cannot opt for a national deterrent, will want to reduce their demand for security in order to restore equilibrium in the wake of Atlantis lost. A nasty word for a demand-reduction strategy used to be *appeasement*. Today it is captured by labels such as *Ostpolitik* and *détente*, which are policies of partial propitiation directed against Western Europe's natural adversary, the Soviet Union.[24] A nation can always reduce the threat to itself by reducing through accommodation its adversary's incentives for pressure and hostility. In so doing, a propitiator would yield peacefully what its foe would otherwise want to gain by force and intimidation: nonconfrontational behavior, diplomatic cooperation, military deescalation, and side payments in the form of economic and technological transfers. The watchword would be *interdependence* with the East rather than a common defense with the West.

This is, after all, the dream of the demand siders on the German national left quoted previously. A far more modest version, which pays due respect and respectful dues to West Germany's Atlantic and West European ties, is already being implemented by contemporary German Ostpolitik. Bonn is in the avantgarde of disarmament in Europe; it has gone further than France or Britain in crediting Mikhail Gorbachev with both good intentions and political longevity. The thrust of Ostpolitik is the subtle subversion of bipolarity in Europe: maintaining the Western security tie as a kind of background factor while shaping Europe's evolution in such a way as to render that insurance dispensable in the very long run.

Transcending ideological cleavages at home, the logic of that policy is simple enough. Less demand for security spells less dependence, less dependence spells less bipolarity, less bipolarity spells greater freedom of movement. That is the underlying incentive for the one nation in Western Europe that was the product and profiteer of bipolarity in the 1940s and that continues to pay the highest price for the maintenance of the postwar system—in terms of options forgone and burdens assumed. Conversely, the subtle subversion of bipolarity—above all, through the progressive demilitarization and "deblocization" of East-West relations in Europe—will devalue the currency of military power (where West Germany cannot hold its own), revalue the currency of economic power (where West Germany commands the biggest reserves) and dismantle barriers on the road to the reassociation of the two Germanies.

This is the logic; its effects will be sharpened by a European security equation where the American factor is either withdrawn or significantly weakened. To make up for the deficit, West Germany will have to choose between a devolutionist or accommodationist Western Europe. Implying greater defense efforts within a tighter West European entity, devolution will collide squarely with the larger purpose of German Ostpolitik, which is the transcendence of blocs and the progressive fusion of Eastern and Western Europe. Nor is it likely that the Soviet Union—with or without Gorbachev—will spare the West Germans the necessity of choice. Access to Eastern Europe and reassociation with East Germany are items where Bonn is the *demandeur* and Moscow has something to offer.

Which way is Bonn likely to turn? At best, it will seek to straddle the issue; at worst, it will choose evolution over devolution. If so, France and Britain will once more worry, "Whither Germany?" In the process, they might seek either to outflank Bonn in Moscow or to fashion supplementary alliances, with Britain turning once more to the tried and true special relationship with the United States and France perhaps playing with Mediterranean props and options in Italy and Spain. Alternatively, the two indigenous nuclear powers might seek greater solace (and solitude) in their independent deterrents. In neither case, however, will West European integration flourish, which is the key condition of devolution. West European politics will be renationalized, and in that kind of system, the Soviet Union will be the paramount power willy-nilly.

To be sure, the relationship between the Soviet Union and the rest of Europe circa 2000 will not resemble what Stalin might have had in mind in 1948. The point is that the Soviet Union would not have to conquer or intimidate Western Europe to assert its dominance. Power is, when you do not have to threaten. Dominance would come organically and naturally, as a consequence of coexistence between one very powerful nation and many smaller nations whose superior demographic and economic resources would not be harnessed to a common purpose. Coexistence might even be benign, with multifarious cooperation softening the hard edge of irreducible power differentials. Perhaps evolution might even reach the point where the lesser nations could move around freely in a common European home because the Soviet Union could confidently count on its commanding position as building inspector and supervisor.

Such a Europe might even overcome those divisions that bipolarity has wrought. It would not, however, be the kind of Europe that American policy could contemplate with assurance. Europe does represent the most important weight in the global balance apart from the United States and the Soviet Union. Even a continent linked organically to the Soviet Union would still be the kind of Europe the United States has labored hard to prevent in two world wars and the cold war. It is not in the American interest that Western Europe should evolve into a Soviet sphere of influence—no matter how benevolently that influence might be exercised under Gorbachev and beyond. And so, if an evolutionist Europe is more likely to lead to an accommodationist than an autonomous Europe, then there is no escape from alliance and its burdens.

But what if only trial and error can determine the real outcome? Even then the bet should not be placed lightly because the consequences of a wrong wager could no longer be so quickly undone as after 1917 and 1944. A third rebalancing effort would have to be undertaken in the shadow of nuclear weapons and the enormous price they threaten to exact. Against these perils, the insurance premium currently paid by the United States must necessarily pale. The premium, admittedly, is not negligible; there are some, albeit rather abstract, nuclear risks in extending deterrence as there are the very real and hefty disbursements that finance the U.S. conventional commitment. Yet to lose Europe would be more costly still, and to regain it for a third time would exceed even a superpower's ability to pay.

Notes

1. CENTO, an anti-Soviet alliance in the Middle East, revolving around Britain, was sponsored by John Foster Dulles in the 1950s but did not include the United States as a formal member.

2. George F. Kennan, "The Sources of Soviet Conduct," *Foreign Affairs* (July 1947), reprinted in Hamilton Fish Armstrong, ed., *Fifty Years of Foreign Affairs* (New York: Praeger, 1972), p. 205.

3. For the most exhaustive statement, see David P. Calleo, *Beyond American Hegemony: The Future of the Western Alliance* (New York: Basic Books, 1987).

4. Ibid., pp. 124, 125.

5. Irving Kristol, "Foreign Policy in an Age of Ideology," *National Interest,* no. 1 (Fall 1985): 14.

6. Gerhard Heimann (a Social Democratic member of the German Bundestag), "Vor einer Renaissance des europäischen Staatensystems? Chancen für eine zweite Stufe der Ostpolitik," in Michael Müller et al., *Gorbatschows Reformen—Chancen für Europe* (Berlin and Bonn: Dietz, 1987), p. 155.

7. Ibid., p. 156.

8. Ibid., p. 157.

9. George F. Kennan, *Memoirs, 1925–1950* (Boston: Little, Brown, 1967), p. 464.

10. Josef Joffe, *The Limited Partnership: Europe, the United States, and the Burdens of Alliance* (Cambridge: Ballinger, 1987), chap. 5.

11. This classic statement is still valid today. See Ministère de la défense, *Livre blanc sur la défense nationale* (Paris: Ministère de la Défense, 1972), 1:8.

12. Thus responded French president Mitterrand when asked at a press conference in Baden-Baden on January 16, 1986. With regard to the "employment of prestrategic weapons" (a French shibboleth for tactical nuclear weapons), Mitterrand said that France might be willing to consult with the Federal Republic. "But I repeat, the very nature of this type of combat means that the decision cannot be shared." As quoted in Ministère des Rélations Extérieures, *La Politique Étrangère de la France: Textes et Documents* (January–February 1986): 26.

13. Defense Minister Charles Hernu, quoted in "Le Débat sur la loi programmation militaire," *Le Monde,* December 7, 1982, p. 14.

14. Pierre Mauroy, address before the Institut des Hautes Études de Défense Nationale (IHEDN), September 14, 1981, in *Textes et Documents* (September–October 1981): 17.

15. Prime Minister Pierre Mauroy, "Vers un nouveau modèle d'armée" (address before the IHEDN, September 20, 1982), reprinted in *Défense Nationale* (November 1982): 18.

16. Address to IHEDN, October 11, 1988 (typed transcript), p. 13.

17. Quoted in "Wir können Amerika nicht ersetzen" (interview with Charles Hernu), *Der Spiegel,* June 26, 1983, p. 110.

18. Mauroy, "Vers un nouveau modèle d'armée," pp. 12–13.

19. Jeannou Lacaze, "Concept de défense et sécurité en Europe" (address to the IHEDN, May 19, 1984), reprinted in *Défense Nationale* (January 1985): 22 (emphasis added).

20. Lacaze, "Concept de la défense," p. 20.

21. President Mitterrand, as quoted in Ministère des Rélations Extérieures, *Visite officielle aux Pays-Bas de Monsieur François Mitterand,* February 6–7, 1984, p. 18.

22. Jacques Chirac, "La Politique de défense de la France" (address before the IHEDN, September 12, 1986), reprinted in *Défense Nationale* (November 1986): 12.

23. Ibid., p. 11 (emphasis added).

24. For a theoretical discussion of the appeasement impulse residing in all alliances, to which I am indebted, see Glenn H. Snyder, "The Security Dilemma in Alliance Politics," *World Politics,* no. 4 (1984).

6
U.S. Disengagement and European Defense Cooperation

David Garnham

Astronomers accurately predict some cosmological events far into the future. Political analysts cannot predict discrete events with equivalent precision; we do well to beat the simple statistical odds. It is possible, however, to discern underlying trends and to forecast their eventual consequences. For example, by the early 1960s, one could foresee that eventually America would acknowledge that Beijing (not Taipei) governed more than 20 percent of the world's population. And it was long obvious that the Arab states, and the Palestine Liberation Organization (PLO), must eventually concede Israel's permanence. Conversely, it is clear (despite Israeli hopes) that the Palestinians will not fade into Jordan or other Arab populations. In one of its final decisions, the Reagan administration acknowledged this by abandoning the sterile policy of attempting to influence Middle Eastern politics while refusing contacts with PLO representatives.

This analysis of political relations within the Atlantic alliance is similarly concerned with long-term trends rather than short-term predictions. Two trends in Western security predominate: American disengagement from Europe and closer bilateral and multilateral cooperation among the NATO-European countries. Although these processes remain inchoate, they reflect a deep structural transformation, which events are unlikely to reverse. In the near future, the principal random factor is how revolutionary changes in Soviet policies will affect these trends, for Mikhail Gorbachev's initiatives have weakened alliance cohesion by appearing to diminish the common threat. New rifts are opened, especially between Bonn and Washington, as with the Lance modernization controversy. If current Soviet policies continue, American disengagement will become even more probable, but Gorbachev's impact on European cooperation remains more complex and uncertain.

American Disengagement

No one foresaw a permanent obligation when the United States first committed troops to Europe in the 1950s. It was a temporary measure until

Western Europe recovered from wartime devastation. Since assuming this commitment, the United States has experienced a striking decline in relative power. There are numerous indicators to this decline. Between 1950 and 1987 America's relative share of gross national product (GNP)–gross domestic product (GDP) among the Group of Seven Western industrial countries (United States, Japan, West Germany, France, United Kingdom, Italy, and Canada) fell from more than 70 percent to 43 percent.[1] As recently as 1981, America was the world's largest creditor nation; foreign assets owned by Americans exceeded U.S. assets owned by foreigners by $141 billion. Now the United States is the single largest debtor country, with an external debt equal to approximately $500 billion.[2] There are also gargantuan budget deficits, which rose from 2.6 percent of GNP in 1981 to 6.3 percent in 1983. Although the budget deficit declined to 3.8 percent of GNP in 1988, among the Group of Seven countries, only Italy recorded a larger deficit, and Great Britain actually achieved a small surplus.[3]

Early in his presidency, President Reagan cautioned that before the budget could be contained, the federal debt might exceed $1 trillion, "a figure that's literally beyond our comprehension." But when Reagan left office, the national debt was not a paltry $1 trillion; it surpassed $2.6 trillion. Moreover, the accumulated national debt rose from 27 percent of annual GNP in 1980 to 46 percent of GNP,[4] and the annual interest required to finance the debt now exceeds one-half of the Pentagon's annual budget.

There is broad agreement that some combination of spending reductions (especially for defense and entitlement programs) and increased taxes is essential to moderate these deficits. Although some conservative economists reject this opinion, Federal Reserve chairman Alan Greenspan told the National Economic Commission that "the deficit has already begun to eat away at the foundations of our economic strength."[5]

America's trade deficits also soared during the Reagan years. Although the trade deficit declined from $170 billion in 1987 to $137 billion in 1988, large deficits are structural and will not be erased in the foreseeable future. This situation is worrisome, for as Michael Boskin (chairperson of the Council of Economic Advisers) wrote, "Each year that we import such large amounts of foreign capital will force us to become a larger and larger net exporter in the future, requiring the pendulum of large trade deficits to large trade surpluses to swing still further."[6]

The United States is also bedeviled by an extremely low savings rate. Compared to other NATO countries and Japan, it had the fourth lowest gross annual savings rate for the period 1980–1984, and total net savings declined from an average of 7.5 percent in the 1960s and 6.1 percent in the 1970s to only 2.9 percent between 1981 and 1986.[7] Investment also declined, and since 1986, foreigners have financed more than 50 percent of American investment.

America's manufacturing base is deteriorating. In the second quarter of 1988, the services sector (which includes earnings on foreign investments, airline fares, fees and royalties, and other "invisibles") was in deficit for the first time in thirty years. This is one direct consequence of being a debtor rather than a creditor country. Still more shocking and disturbing, in 1986 and 1987 the United States imported more high-technology goods than it exported. Even America's lead in supercomputers is under siege from Japanese competitors, and in early 1989 a presidential advisory committee warned that the United States might fall behind Japan in applying new technologies for high-temperature superconductors.

Although by early 1989 this deteriorating economic position led 58 percent of Americans to name Japan as the world's leading economic power (while only 29 percent cited the United States),[8] the adjustment of burdens within the Western alliance has lagged behind these new realities. In 1988, the United States allocated 6.1 percent of GDP to defense, while the NATO-European countries averaged 3.3 percent,[9] and Japan's defense expenditures remained frozen at 1 percent. A generation earlier the United States was richer than its allies and could afford to spend a significantly larger proportion of its resources on defense. But Japan and the principal Western European allies now enjoy levels of affluence equivalent to those of the United States. In 1987, American per capita GDP ($13,564) barely exceeded the NATO average ($11,278) and was inferior to the level of Norway, Denmark, Luxembourg, and the Federal Republic of Germany (FRG) and approximately equivalent to France's. Yet all of these countries devoted substantially lower percentages of GDP to defense than did the United States.[10]

This situation is inequitable and unsustainable considering America's economic problems. For this reason, the burden-sharing issue has received renewed congressional attention. The report of the Defense Burdensharing Panel of the House Committee on Armed Services is a notable recent example. According to the committee:

> Many Americans feel that we are competing 100 percent militarily with the Soviets and 100 percent economically with our defense allies. Some have said that the United States has incurred all the burdens of empire and few, if any, of the benefits.[11]

Senator Bennett Johnston (D–Louisiana) was less tactful; he described the current allocation as "astonishingly unfair," and chairman Sam Nunn (D–Georgia) of the Senate Armed Services Committee wrote that "despite the shift in relative economic power to our allies, the cost of defense has remained disproportionately on American shoulders. Adjustments are long overdue."[12]

Even the executive branch, the traditional defender of the alliance status quo, has begun to respond. In late 1988, the secretaries of state and defense issued a report expressing their conviction that "a more equitable sharing of the roles, risks and responsibilities for the common defense is needed and is achievable."[13] Deputy Defense Secretary William Howard Taft IV conveyed this message directly to the allies. In July 1988 he told French leaders that "without a European effort it would be more and more difficult to make military expenditures in Europe politically acceptable in the United States."[14]

Americans are no longer wealthier than their allies, and they are slipping behind in international economic competition. Consequently they are dismayed by evidence that Americans continue to spend more to defend Europe than Europeans spend to defend themselves.

Since President Reagan's first term, when inflation-adjusted defense spending rose by 50 percent, the domestic politics of defense spending have fundamentally changed. In 1980, 60 percent of the public believed that military spending was "too little," and only 12 percent considered it "too much." By 1985, only 15 percent considered it "too little," and 42 percent considered it "too much."[15] In April 1989, Defense Secretary Richard Cheney announced that the fiscal year 1990 defense budget would decline by 1 percent in constant dollars, the fifth consecutive year of reduced military spending. Given the budget deficit, a lower perception of Soviet threat, and perceived Pentagon waste and corruption, this trend will continue. Henry Kaufman, the influential Wall Street economist, advocates reducing military spending from 6.1 percent of GNP to 4 percent.[16] This would be the lowest level in the postwar era, even below the Carter administration level when Department of Defense (DOD) spending dipped to 5.1 percent of GNP during fiscal year (FY) 1978 and FY 1979.

Further reductions in defense spending will almost certainly require cuts in divisional strength, naval forces, and/or air forces. This is true, in part, because only half of the DOD budget is spent during the same year that it is appropriated. Military pay and operating funds are spent quickly; research and development funds are expended more slowly, and less than 15 percent of procurement and military construction funds is spent during the first year. Therefore, to reduce defense expenditures rapidly, one must cut force structure and readiness. Moreover, Secretary Cheney (like Secretary Frank Carlucci before him) explicitly chose "to reduce our force structure, rather than risk deterioration in its effectiveness and capability."[17]

Reportedly even former Navy Secretary John Lehman, the principal proponent of a 600-ship navy, now concedes that thirteen (rather than fifteen) carrier battle groups might suffice if European allies and Japan assumed more naval responsibility in the Persian Gulf.[18] Lehman also advocates a massive shift of forces from the active to the reserve component of all four military services. Specifically, he recommends that active forces constitute one-third of the army and Marine Corps, one-half the air force, and three-quarters of the navy. Senator John McCain (R–Arizona) urges the United States to prepare for the "most likely scenario," which is "low-intensity conflict, outside of Central Europe," and mentions the possibility of retaining "one squadron out of every wing in West Germany, with the other two in reserve."[19]

Moreover, the U.S. Army has considered the option of six-month tours for European battalions rather than continuing permanent deployments. Returning the 200,000 dependents now residing in Europe to the United States might trim annual troop costs by $2 billion.[20] For September 1989, the annual Reforger (Return of Forces to Germany) exercise, which has involved 95,000 NATO troops including 17,000 soldiers airlifted from the United States, was replaced by an exercise two-thirds smaller without an airlift. This responded to Gorbachev's peace initiatives and German objections to training maneuvers, while also reducing spending.[21]

Despite this pressure for change, there is deep-seated resistance to altering well-established U.S. policy. The opening in 1989 of Vienna talks on Conventional Armed Forces in Europe (CFE) may also postpone substantial troop withdrawals. In a reprise of 1973, when the Mutual and Balanced Force Reductions talks derailed the Mansfield amendment's momentum, there is reluctance to undercut NATO's bargaining position by pressing for unilateral reductions as new conventional arms talks begin. However, the continuing deterioration of America's relative capabilities and unilateral disarmament initiatives by the Soviet Union and other Warsaw Treaty Organization (WTO) countries make this obstacle to American disengagement less influential than it was previously. Indeed, Defense Secretary Cheney announced in April 1989 that 4,000 army troops formerly assigned to the Pershing II missiles in the FRG will be withdrawn from Europe and demobilized.

European Cooperation

Europeans are increasingly aware that the status quo is changing.[22] The *Economist* wrote in 1987 that "an America which is no longer much richer than Europe is unlikely to go on for ever spending 7% of its GNP on defence, of which it uses a third or more for Europe's benefit, when most European countries spend only 3–4% of theirs."[23] This is one factor that encourages regional solutions to Europe's security needs. A second is the widespread perception that America's commitment, and especially the nuclear guarantee, is increasingly dubious. A series of American actions, extending back at least to the transition from massive retaliation to flexible response during the Kennedy administration, have had a cumulative effect. And recent events including the Strategic Defense Initiative (SDI), the 1986 Reykjavik summit, and the INF (intermediate nuclear forces) treaty, have reinforced the inference that America seeks to escape nuclear risks. According to retired French general Pierre Gallois, "the installation of the Pershing II [was] an aberrant point on the curve representing American nuclear disengagement."[24]

Although America's option of nuclear first use against Warsaw Pact military targets never required the INF deployments, European specialists realize that withdrawing the Pershing II and cruise missiles reinforces a president's option to renege on the nuclear guarantee. There is, finally, a widening sentiment that defense, foreign policy, and armaments cooperation are essential components of any effort to construct a more integrated Europe and vital for successful technological competition with America and Japan.

The 1980s have witnessed substantial progress in forging a more cohesive European approach to defense issues. This is especially true of the Franco-German partnership. The defense component of the Elysée Treaty (1963) was finally implemented in 1982. Since then, Socialist president François Mitterrand (and former conservative prime minister Jacques Chirac) revolutionized French defense policy by repudiating the Gaullist doctrine of national autonomy and committing France unambiguously to the forward defense of the FRG. In December 1987, Chirac asserted:

> France now possesses means which permit the affirmation of the European dimension of her security. . . . *Were West Germany to be the victim of an aggression, who can now doubt that France's commitment would be immediate and wholehearted? There cannot be a battle of Germany and a battle of France.*[25]

President Mitterrand shares this view, and France's political climate has changed so radically that during the 1988 presidential campaign, Mitterrand and Chirac each competed to appear more "European" than his opponent.

Although the former taboo of nonbelligerency was shattered, France still confronts the issue of extended nuclear deterrence. Laurent Fabius, the former Socialist prime minister and current president of the National Assembly, said, "It is now necessary to consider the extension of our strategic nuclear guarantee to German security."[26] And Defense Minister Jean-Pierre Chevènement expressed his hope "that the French and British nuclear forces could someday constitute the embryo of the European deterrent."[27] Former French defense minister André Giraud implied a similar view by observing, at the 1988 *Wehrkunde* conference, that France's deterrent was intended to protect vital interests and these are partially based upon France's political, economic, and cultural ties with its neighbors: "Thus, a threat can intervene in front of our borders, and likewise our own nuclear deterrent can be concerned in these same circumstances."[28] Moreover, 50 percent of the French public favors using French nuclear weapons to defend the Federal Republic.[29] Mitterrand still rebuffs the possibility of an explicit nuclear commitment. This, he says, is a question for the Atlantic alliance rather than France.[30] However, he has promised, time permitting, to consult with Bonn prior to using French tactical weapons from or on German territory.[31]

In concert, France and Germany established the Defense Council, which first met in April 1989, to harmonize their national military policies and operational plans. They also formed a bilateral brigade, which by 1990 will consist of 4,200 soldiers stationed in Baden-Württemberg serving under rotating French or German commanders. Franco-German arms cooperation has also rebounded, paced by the multibillion-dollar program to produce new combat helicopters in the mid- to late 1990s. Bonn and Paris expanded joint military exercises, and during the Bold Sparrow operation (1987), troops of the France's *Force d'action rapide* served under German command deep within German territory.

Franco-German cooperation is often disparaged, especially by the British, as consisting of dramatic but ultimately empty gestures. It is indisputable, as *The Economist* editorialized concerning the brigade and the Defense Council, that "so far they will not add a man or a franc to Europe's defense."[32] These accomplishments are significant, nonetheless, and until very recently they were unimaginable. Although the United States remains the ultimate guarantor of Germany's security, Bonn and Paris have constructed the essential foundation for a new European-based security system. In recent years, former socialist chancellor Helmut Schmidt has repeatedly advocated a Franco-German defense community, which would unite the two militaries (including the French nuclear deterrent force) under the French president.[33] This remains a distant goal, but nearly 70 percent of the French population accepts the principle of common Franco-German defense,[34] and former Christian Democratic Union defense minister (and current NATO secretary-general) Manfred Wörner did foresee "the possibility that one day there would be a common army."[35] When combined, France and Germany constitute 9.5 percent of the global product (close to the Soviet Union with 13 percent and Japan with 11 percent), which is sufficient to construct a significant military capability.[36]

Great Britain and France have also attempted to strengthen bilateral defense cooperation, especially with respect to arms procurement. Historically, both countries have pursued quite autarkic policies. Britain, for example, spends 75 percent of its equipment budget in Britain on noncollaborative projects.[37] But in 1986 Britain and France coordinated their negotiations with Boeing for Airborne Warning and Control System (AWACS) purchases, and in September 1987 the first in a series of conferences between British and French government officials and businessmen was held to remove barriers to bilateral military procurement. Britain subsequently announced a general policy requiring all British firms awarded major defense contracts to share a portion of the work with NATO-European firms. London obviously hopes, and apparently expects, that its European allies will reciprocate.[38]

There is also talk of Anglo-French nuclear weapons cooperation. In France, former prime ministers Raymond Barre and Laurent Fabius advocated Anglo-French coordination of their nuclear submarine fleets and joint development of nuclear weapons.[39] Frequent and cordial meetings between former British defense minister George Younger and former French defense minister Giraud improved prospects for all forms of defense cooperation. In response to the scheduled withdrawal of American Pershing II and cruise missiles, they discussed potential joint development of a new medium-range nuclear missile and an air-to-surface missile derived from France's ASMP (*airsol à moyenne portée*). Deployed on Tornado aircraft, this missile would replace Britain's WE-177 gravity bombs around the year 2000.[40] There was also agreement for French nuclear submarines to visit British ports, for joint maneuvers, and serious discussions on joint patrolling.[41] Although some of the earlier optimism has faded and Younger excluded joint decisions concerning nuclear operations,[42] overall prospects for Anglo-French nuclear cooperation have markedly improved in recent years.

Multilaterally, the most significant recent development is the revitalization of the Western European Union (WEU). Composed, until its recent expansion, of Britain, France, Germany, Italy, Belgium, Luxembourg, and the Netherlands, the WEU was effectively moribund from 1973 until 1984. In the early 1980s, the INF deployment controversy and fears of U.S. abandonment catalyzed a renewed cooperative effort, and after overcoming some members' reluctance (especially Britain), the WEU eventually emerged as the appropriate forum. In October 1984 the WEU Council met at the level of defense and foreign ministers for the first time in many years and agreed to semiannual meetings at the foreign ministerial level. The revival received a further stimulus from the 1986 superpower summit in Reykjavik, the double-zero option, and renewed fears of U.S. decoupling. Suddenly many Europeans lamented the absence of a European voice on security issues. This was especially true in France, where top political leaders decried the absence of a European defense consensus.

London's interest also rekindled. In March 1987, before the Royal Institute of International Relations (Brussels), former British foreign secretary Sir Geoffrey Howe traced the WEU's revitalization to "a growing perception that a European forum was needed in which we Europeans could consult one another about our common fundamental security needs." Sir Geoffrey observed that events like Reykjavik and double-zero "underline the need for the European countries to consult more closely among themselves about their defense interests as well as with the Americans."[43]

Since its revival, the WEU has taken two particularly significant steps. First, it managed a loosely coordinated European naval response to attacks on Persian Gulf oil tankers during the Iran-Iraq War. This was a landmark: the first successful coordination of a nonregional security policy issue. During

1987, five members of the WEU (Belgium, Britain, France, Italy, and the Netherlands) deployed military vessels to the gulf. The FRG, which interprets its Basic Law as prohibiting military operations outside the North Atlantic area, also reassigned ships to NATO's standby force in the Mediterranean and called this "a contribution to support those allies who are protecting shipping in the gulf region."[44]

Eventually the second initiative may prove even more significant. In October 1987 the WEU approved a common Platform on European Security Interests. Following the Reykjavik summit, Prime Minister Jacques Chirac observed that the superpowers were making decisions affecting vital European interests without any Western European participation. According to Chirac, Europe's voice would be heard only when its position was elaborated and articulated, so a "charter" was needed to define a common European position on principal security questions.

The approved platform included the following major points:

1. European integration will remain incomplete until a security dimension is added.

2. Because Europe is divided and exposed to the Warsaw Pact's superior conventional, chemical, and nuclear forces, Western European security "can only be ensured in close association with our North American allies." American conventional and nuclear forces play "an irreplaceable part in the defense of Europe."

3. A credible European defense policy must combine conventional and nuclear capabilities, for "only the nuclear element . . . can confront a potential aggressor with an unacceptable risk."[45]

4. Arms control and disarmament policy are integral parts of overall Western security policy.

5. WEU member states intend to reinforce the European pillar of the alliance, to enlarge their defense cooperation by all practical measures, to improve their conventional forces, and to pursue European integration (including security). Britain and France will maintain the credibility of their nuclear forces.

This was a consensus document. France saw its essence as the affirmation that nuclear deterrence is central to European security. Both France and Britain were pleased by specific recognition that their nuclear forces "contribute to overall deterrence and security" and the implicit endorsement of their nuclear modernization programs. The FRG appreciated both the pledge that members would defend an ally "at its borders" and explicit recognition that détente, especially arms control, complements rather than contradicts

Western security. The Germans and British applauded explicit references to America's indispensable role.

Following the WEU's revival, several additional states sought membership. Portugal and Spain joined in 1988, and Norway, Turkey, Greece, and Denmark have expressed interest. Prospects for the WEU's long-term success will probably be strengthened if the organization remains relatively small and homogeneous. As the debate over the WEU's common security platform illustrated, it is difficult to resolve divergent military doctrines or weapons requirements, even among the current members. It would be substantially more difficult if the membership included Denmark, Greece, Norway, and Turkey.

The Independent European Programme Group (IEPG) is a second important multilateral institution; it combines thirteen NATO-European states.[46] The Rome Resolution (1976) defined the IEPG's objectives as strengthening the European identity, and the industrial and technological foundation for Western defense, by promoting standardization, interoperability, and efficient use of resources for weapons design and procurement.[47] Inadequate arms collaboration squanders scarce resources and creates a serious lack of standardization and interoperability on the battlefield. It also undermines Europe's technological competitiveness in relation to the United States and Japan. According to the 1987 British *White Paper:*

> A more cohesive European effort will strengthen the Alliance in a number of important ways: *politically,* by demonstrating our ability to work closely together; *militarily,* by reducing the inefficiency that comes from having different and incompatible versions of the same equipment on the battlefield; and *industrially,* by helping to produce a more competitive European industrial base.[48]

Until 1984, the group's work was relegated to the members' armament directors, and the organization was relatively inconspicuous and torpid. But the WEU revival spilled over to the IEPG, and the group convened its first annual defense ministerial meeting in November 1984.

The IEPG assumes that collaborative ventures are more cost-effective than national weapons programs. This is true only under ideal conditions; in the real world joint projects often cost more than national programs. A general rule of thumb states that unit costs for a given production run increase by the square root of the number of partners: 40 percent more for two partners and 100 percent higher for four partners. Therefore, joint ventures become more cost-effective only if economies of scale from larger production runs and research and development savings are sufficient to offset these inefficiencies.

Like the WEU, the IEPG confronts the issue of Europe's proper relationship to the United States. Most WEU members fear that the WEU could divide Western Europe from Washington and might offer a cover for

American disengagement. The IEPG is independent because France insisted on separation from NATO,[49] and many Europeans agree that "it is vital that on the European side of the ocean we should speak with a single voice, representing the whole IEPG, as has already begun to happen."[50] Nonetheless, close contacts exist between the IEPG and NATO. The IEPG has two faces; the Atlantic face emphasizes transatlantic cooperation, but the regional face stresses improved European competitiveness against U.S. defense contractors. The American armaments market is two and a half times larger than Western Europe's, with research and development spending approximately five times greater than Europe's.[51] Successful European competition in the international arms market of the twenty-first century is unlikely without substantial progress in achieving European security cooperation.

Historically, much of the impetus for European defense cooperation has been negative: anti-German when the WEU was first established and anti-Soviet in NATO's case. This pattern persists; all of the principal participants are reacting to various negative stimuli, including American withdrawal (Germany), German neutralism (France), and regional isolation if they "miss the bus" a second time (Britain). But these countries are strongly cross-pressured. For example, Germany values the Franco-German relationship as a hedge against U.S. abandonment but hopes to avoid American disengagement. The Germans will not jump into French arms until pushed from the American nest. In this way, fears of U.S. abandonment catalyze European integration. The dilemma is how to create a genuine European pillar without destroying the alliance in the process. As André Giraud said, "We're facing a house of cards that we have to rearrange without collapsing the original structure."[52]

The Gorbachev Effect

Gorbachev's ascent to the Soviet leadership ended a historical era. There is now, as British foreign secretary Sir Geoffrey Howe said, "a real sense of hope that we can put the 40 years Cold War behind us." Even most hard-liners concede that Gorbachev's initiatives markedly reduce the Soviet threat. But can the Western alliance survive confrontation from a less fearsome adversary?

"Gorby fever" infects both mass and elite public opinion in every NATO country. The FRG is particularly responsive to Gorbachev's "new thinking." In late 1987 (table 6–1) surveys found substantially higher perceptions of increased Soviet "trustworthiness" in the West Germany (73 percent) compared to Britain (65 percent) and especially France (54 percent) and the United States (55 percent). In 1981, 55 percent of German respondents (compared to 45 percent) said they "worried about the threat from the East." By February 1989, this threat worried only 20 percent (versus 79 percent).[53]

This diminished perception of Soviet threat will probably erode Ameri-

Table 6–1
Increased Soviet Trustworthiness
(in percentage)

	United States	France	United Kingdom	FRG
Shows more trustworthiness	55	54	65	73
Does not	40	29	23	16
Not sure	5	17	12	11

Source: World Opinion Update 12, no. 1 (January 1988): 3.

Notes: The Harris Research Centre carried out the survey in the United Kingdom (N = 1,005); the Louis Harris France Survey in France (N = 901); the Emnid Institute in the FRG (N = 1,000); and the Harris Poll in the United States (N = 1,250). All surveys were conducted December 1–15, 1987.

The following question was asked: "It is reported that political, economic, and social reforms have been rapidly taking place in the Soviet Union since Gorbachev took office. The fact that the summit took place seems to be a sign of those changes. Do you think it shows that the Soviet Union is becoming a more trustworthy nation, or not?"

cans' perceived need to remain in Europe, at least in current members, and they may become even less tolerant of spending more to defend rich allies than Europeans spend to defend themselves. It could also undermine the Europeans' conviction that American guarantees are essential to their security, and Germany may seize the opportunity to shed the largely hidden costs of living on the front line. These include 900,000 soldiers stationed in a country the size of Oregon, 5,000 military exercises each year, which cause nearly $100 million dollars in damage, and 580,000 military flights annually, over 100,000 at low altitude.[54]

The Lance modernization controversy is illustrative. Although Chancellor Kohl was a self-described "decisive opponent of a third zero option," his governing coalition postponed its decision concerning modernization of nuclear weapons with a range less than 500 kilometers until after the 1990 German election and embraced Foreign Minister Genscher's position that arms control talks should emcompass short-range nuclear weapons.

Gorbachev's impact on European cooperation is less predictable. Even as the perceived threat ebbs and Atlantic cohesion declines, European defense cooperation could continue to expand for two reasons. First, the principal impetus for European integration is economic rather than military, and Europe's economic and technological competitors remain America and Japan, not the Soviet Union. Therefore, the Gorbachev effect is somewhat isolated from issues such as 1992 (implementation of the Single European Act) or the possible creation of a single European currency or central bank. There is, furthermore, synergy between economic and security cooperation; the IEPG, the European Space Agency, and Eureka all illustrate the spillover between civilian and military technologies. These incentives for closer defense cooperation remain despite a diminished security threat, and many Europeans believe, in the words of the WEU's Platform on European Security, that "the construction of an integrated Europe will remain incomplete as long as it does not include security and defense."

A second consideration is a deep concern, especially in France, that Germany could drift free from its Western mooring. Détente intensifies this danger. One obvious response is to intensify German ties to Western Europe. Historically Bonn has preferred an American to a French guarantee, but Gregory Treverton suggests that "with the need to buy insurance declining, Germans might become less finicky about the insurer. Some form of French (or even British) nuclear pledge might be enough."[55]

Conclusion

Trends toward American disengagement and European defense cooperation appear inexorable. While the United States maintains a sizable conventional troop presence in Europe and threatens, however incredibly, to defend Europe with nuclear arms, Germany (and Britain) will cling to the alliance. But as America's commitment inevitably recedes, European governments will increasingly turn toward regional alternatives. NATO's first forty years were remarkably stable. It is inconceivable that the alliance will escape fundamental restructuring for another four decades or even during the 1990s. In the near future, successful arms control negotiations are the most likely catalyst for sizable American troop withdrawals from Europe. But if the CFE talks break down, America's relative decline will reemerge as a major factor. In either event, Western Europe possesses both the material and institutional means to construct a substantial European defense.

Notes

1. See Mark E. Rupert and David P. Rapkin, "The Erosion of U.S. Leadership Capabilities," in Paul M. Johnson and William R. Thompson, eds., *Rhythms in Politics and Economics* (New York: Praeger, 1985), p. 163, and Central Intelligence Agency, *The World Factbook 1988* (Washington, D.C.: U.S. Government Printing Office, 1988).

I discuss this issue more fully in "The United States in Decline?" in Christopher Coker, ed., *Shifting into Neutral: The Burden-Sharing Debate in the Western Alliance,* (London: Brassey's Defence Publishers, forthcoming).

2. See Clyde H. Farnsworth, "Money Loss Grows for Poorer Lands, World Bank Finds," *New York Times,* December 19, 1988, p. 1. However, there is controversy concerning whether the Commerce Department's methodology (based on acquisition costs rather than current market value) exaggerates American indebtedness. For

contrasting views, see David Binder and Clyde H. Farnsworth, "Pauper or Prince?" *New York Times,* October 25, 1988, p. 12, and Benjamin M. Friedman, *Day of Reckoning: The Consequences of American Economic Policy under Reagan and After* (New York: Random House, 1988), pp. 229–30.

3. The 1988 estimates are: Canada (−3.1 percent), France (−1.5 percent), Great Britain, (0.6 percent), Italy (−11.5 percent), Japan (−2.4 percent), West Germany (−1.7 percent), and the United States (−3.8 percent). See "Le Tableau de bord de l'économie du groupe des Sept," *Le Monde,* February 4, 1989, p. 23.

4. Friedman, *Day of Reckoning,* p. 91, 115.

5. Quoted in Peter T. Kilborn, "U.S. Budget Deficit Must Be Cut Soon, Greenspan Warns," *New York Times,* November 17, 1988, p. 10. Greenspan's predecessor at the Federal Reserve, Paul Volcker, expressed similar views. When chief executive officers of 225 of the largest U.S. corporations were surveyed in December 1988, 68 percent thought that "taxes or user fees should be increased to reduce the budget deficit," and 62 percent thought that defense spending should be decreased (compared to 34 percent who said it would remain constant). See David Kirkpatrick, "CEOs to Bush: Raise Taxes Now," *Fortune,* January 16, 1989, pp. 95–96; N equaled 225 CEOs of Fortune 500 and Service 500 companies. The survey was conducted December 5–15, 1988.

6. Michael J. Boskin, *Reagan and the Economy: The Successes, Failures and Unfinished Agenda* (San Francisco: Institute for Contemporary Studies, 1987), p. 189.

7. Calculated from data in Leonard Sullivan, Jr., and Jack A. LeCuyer, *Comprehensive Security and Western Prosperity* (Lanham, Md.: University Press of America, 1988), p. 143, and Boskin, *Reagan and the Economy,* p. 186.

8. The Gallup survey was conducted between January 27 and February 5, 1989, among 2,048 adult respondents. See E.J. Dionne, Jr., "Public Backs Deep Cuts for Military, Poll Finds," *New York Times,* March 13, 1989, p. 12.

9. See NATO Press Service, *Financial and Economic Data Relating to NATO Defense,* M–DPC–2(88)74 (Brussels: NATO, December 1, 1988), p. 4.

10. See ibid., pp. 4, 5.

11. Defense Burdensharing Panel, *Report of the Defense Burdensharing Panel* (Washington, D.C.: Committee on Armed Services, U.S. House of Representatives, August 1988), p. 12. For example, a February 1988 survey of 1,000 registered voters by the Daniel Yankelovich Group found that "six in 10 said they believe that 'the expense of defending so many countries is a serious threat to our national security,' and 8 in 10 'strongly' or 'somewhat' agree that we 'cannot afford to defend so many nations. . . . 6 in 10 'strongly agree' (and 8 in 10 'strongly' to 'somewhat' agree) that 'economic is as important as military power' in today's world." Jack Beatty, " 'Burden-Sharing,' Jolted," *New York Times,* April 3, 1988.

12. Sam Nunn, "Our Allies Have to Do More," *New York Times,* July 10, 1988, p. 31.

13. Quoted in Richard Halloran, "U.S. Report Prods the Allies to Increase Military Outlays," *New York Times,* December 29, 1988, p. 7.

14. Quoted in "Le Secrétaire adjoint américain à la défense appelle les Européens à un effort budgétaire," *Le Monde,* July 22, 1988, p. 4.

15. See Ted Goertzel, "Public Opinion Concerning Military Spending in the

United States: 1937–1985," *Journal of Political and Military Sociology* 15, no. 1 (Spring 1987): 63. A Gallup survey conducted between January 27 and February 5, 1989, showed substantial public support for reduced defense spending. See Dionne, "Public Backs Deep Cuts," p. 120.

16. See Henry Kaufman, "Memo to the Next President," *New York Times Magazine,* October 9, 1988, p. 36.

17. Secretary Dick Cheney, letter to *New York Times,* May 10, 1989, p. 26.

18. See John H. Cushman, Jr., "Ex-Insider Who Elects to Remain on Outside," *New York Times,* January 6, 1989, p. 11. However, in his recent book, Lehman wrote that "the navy will soon have 15 carrier battle groups." John F. Lehman, Jr., *Command of the Seas* (New York: Charles Scribner's Sons, 1988), p. 427.

19. "Whether and Where to Cut the Military Budget," *New York Times.* February 5, 1989, p. E3.

20. See Richard Halloran, "Army Weighs Shorter Troop Tours," *New York Times,* December 18, 1988, p. 18.

21. See George C. Wilson, "U.S. Plans Smaller NATO Exercises," *Manchester Guardian Weekly,* February 12, 1989, p. 19, and "Les Manoeuvres de l'OTAN en RFA seront réduites," *Le Monde,* February 3, 1989, p. 5.

22. I discuss this more fully in David Garnham, *The Politics of European Defense Cooperation: Germany, France, Britain, and America* (Cambridge, Mass.: Ballinger, 1988).

23. "Europe's Braver Colours," *The Economist,* July 11, 1987, p. 12.

24. Pierre Gallois, *La Guerre de cents secondes: Les Etats-Unis, l'Europe et la guerre des étoiles* (Paris: Fayard, 1985), p. 115.

25. Jacques Chirac, "La France et les enjeux de la sécurité européenne: Allocution du premier ministre le 12 décembre 1987, devant les auditeurs de l'Institut des hautes études de défense nationale," *Défense Nationale* 44 (February 1988): 15–16 (emphasis in original).

26. "M. Fabius propose d'étendre à la RFA la 'garantie nucléaire' de la France," *Le Monde,* June 17, 1987, p. 8. A similar but less explicit proposal is contained in Laurent Fabius, "La Défense de la France à l'aube du XXIe siècle," *Défense Nationale,* 43 (November 1987): 22.

27. "M. Chevénement voit un 'embryon de dissuasion européenne dans les forces nucléaires française et britannique'," *Le Monde,* February 18, 1989, p. 13.

28. Quoted in "Washington met en garde l'Europe contre une dénucléarisation totale," *Le Monde,* February 9, 1988, p. 3.

29. See "Un Français sur deux est partisan d'une garantie nucléaire à l'Allemagne fédérale," *Le Monde,* February 9, 1988, p. 15. The survey ($N = 1,000$) was conducted January 11–20, 1988, by IPSOS for *Le Journal du Dimanche.*

30. See François Mitterrand, "La Stratégie de la France," *Le Nouvel Observateur,* December 18–24, 1987, p. 26. and "Allocution de M. François Mitterrand président de la république devant les auditeurs de l'institut des hautes études de défense nationale le 11 octobre 1988," *Défense Nationale* 44 (November 1988): 26.

31. See *Le Monde,* March 2–3, 1986, p. 4.

32. "It Takes Two to Decouple,"*The Economist,* November 28, 1987. p. 14.

33. See Helmut Schmidt, "Europe muss sich selbst behaupten," *Die Zeit,*

November 21, 1986, p. 3 (trans. in *German Tribune,* November 30, 1986, p. 5, December 7, 1986, pp. 6–7); "L'Equation Allemande: Entretien avec Helmut Schmidt," *Politique Internationale,* no. 27 (Spring 1985): 147–59; Helmut Schmidt, "La France, l'Allemagne et la défense européenne," *Commentaire,* no. 27 (1984): 411–17.

34. See Luc Ferry, "Comprendre la RFA," *L'Express,* February 24, 1989, p. 21. Moreover, in February 1989, French respondents were evenly split (47 percent yes and 45 percent no) on whether France should "abandon all or part of its power in defense policy matters in favor of a European government." See Jean LeClerc du Sablon, "XXIe siècle: l'Europe au défi," *L'Express,* March 17, 1989, p. 59.

35. Quoted in James M. Markham, "Paris and Bonn Set Up Military Link," *New York Times,* January 23, 1988, p. 3.

36. See *Le Point,* January 11, 1988, p. 45.

37. See *Statement on the Defense Estimates 1989* (London: Her Majesty's Stationery Office, 1989), 1: 29.

38. See Michael Evans, "Britain Must Share Contracts," *Times* (London), January 18, 1989, p. 1.

39. See "La France et l'Allemagne fédérale doivent étudier l'organisation d'un espace stratégique commun suggère M. Raymond Barre," *Le Monde,* November 10, 1987, p. 11, and Fabius, "La Défense de la France," p. 21.

40. See *News from France,* October 15, 1987, p. 6, and Michael Evans, "France May Join UK over Missile," *Times* (London), December 1, 1987, p. 2.

41. See Dominique Dhombres, "Paris et Londres veulent construire un missile nucléaire," *Le Monde,* December 16, 1987, pp. 1, 3; "Nuclear Franglais," *Times* (London), December 16, 1987, p. 15; Howell Raines, "Britain and France Stay at Odds on Economic and Defense Policy," *New York Times,* January 30, 1988, p. 3, and Edward A. Kolodziej, "British-French Nuclearization and European Denuclearization: Implications for U.S. Policy," in Philippe G. Le Prestre, ed., *French Security Policy in a Disarming World: Domestic Challenges and International Constraints* (Boulder, Colo.: Lynne Rienner Publishers, 1989), pp. 132–33.

42. See "UK and France in Arms Link," *Manchester Guardian Weekly,* March 12, 1989, p. 4.

43. Sir Geoffrey Howe, "The Atlantic Alliance and the Security of Europe," *NATO Review* 35, no. 2 (April 1987): 8.

44. Quoted in Serge Schmemann, "Bonn, Citing Gulf Effort, Will Aid a NATO Fleet," *New York Times,* October 9, 1987, p. 8.

45. *Platform on European Security Interests* (The Hague: Western European Union, October 27, 1987).

46. The IEPG members are Belgium, Denmark, France, Greece, Italy, Luxembourg, the Netherlands, Norway, Portugal, Spain, Turkey, the United Kingdom, and West Germany.

47. See Eduardo Serra Rexach, "The Independent European Programme Group—On the Right Path," *NATO Review* 34, no. 5 (October 1986): 25.

48. *Statement on the Defense Estimates 1987,* 1: 46.

49. See Trevor Taylor, *Defense, Technology and International Integration* (London: Frances Pinter, 1982), p. 30.

50. Serra Rexach, "The Independent European Programme Group," p. 31.

51. According to European Defence Industry Study Team, *Towards a Stronger Europe* (Brussels: Independent European Programme Group, 1987), 1: 1, "The internal European market for armaments [is] 40% of the size of that of the US."

52. Quoted in Tim Carrington, "Kohl Stance on Nuclear Arms Intensifies Allied Concern about European Defense," *Wall Street Journal,* February 8, 1988, p. 18.

53. Surveys by Emnid Institute. *Der Spiegel,* February 27, 1989, p. 51. In a fall 1988 Emnid survey, 75 percent of respondents said the "communist threat" was "not so great" or "not to be taken seriously." In addition, defense of West Germany ranked last when asked which of seventeen governmental objectives were most important. See Matthias Nass, "Trauer muss die Truppe tragen," *Die Zeit,* February 17, 1989, p. 3.

54. Government of the Federal Republic of Germany, *The German Contribution to the Common Defense* (Bonn: Press and Information Offices of the Federal Republic of Germany and the Federal Ministry of Defense, 1986), p. 21.

55. Gregory Treverton, "West Germany and the Soviet Union," in Michael Mandelbaum, ed., *Western Approaches to the Soviet Union* (New York: Council on Foreign Relations, 1988), pp. 17–18.

7
The Economics of NATO

Alan Tonelson

As long as Americans viewed Western Europe's security as a vital interest, the economics of NATO understandably attracted only fleeting attention in the United States. After all, discussing the economics of anything implies that at some level its cost can be excessive—that it can be greater than any possible benefit. Where truly vital interests are concerned, this conclusion cannot rationally be drawn. Survival, by definition, is worth any expense, as well as anything except suicidal military efforts. But the case for placing America's NATO commitment in this category has been weakening steadily for many years. As a result, the economics of NATO has assumed greater and greater importance.

The introduction of highly accurate intercontinental nuclear weapons has greatly reduced America's vulnerability to a military invasion launched even by an aspiring conqueror with control of the Old World's vast industrial-military potential and manpower. Such nuclear weapons have not only given the United States the capability of devastating the attacker's homeland at rather modest expense; they have also enabled the United States to destroy the armada in one fell swoop. As early as the mid-1950s, President Eisenhower recognized that nuclear weapons would soon bring to an end the days of fighting great power wars by sending vast armies around the world.[1]

Once nuclear weapons achieved intercontinental range, the United States no longer needed strategic nuclear bases in Europe, or anywhere else outside its own borders, in order to maintain deterrence. The shorter-range U.S. nuclear weapons still deployed in Western Europe and the Far East are for the defense of those countries, not the United States; in theory, they are intended for battlefield use and to couple Western European security to the U.S.-based strategic nuclear arsenal.

Another important security benefit that the United States has derived from NATO is receding as well: the use of Western European bases for projecting American power into the Third World. The facilities still exist, but

The author gratefully acknowledges the invaluable research assistance of Rosemary Fiscarelli of the Cato Institute.

U.S. access can no longer be taken for granted. Many NATO allies refused to permit America to use bases on their soil in the effort to resupply Israel during the October 1973 Middle East war. And, in 1986, France refused to grant overflight rights to U.S. bombers en route to attacking Libya. In fact, in 1988, President Reagan's prestigious Commission on Integrated Long-Term Strategy characterized U.S. access to Western European bases in the event of a Persian Gulf crisis as "uncertain."[2]

This is not to say that NATO is worth no expenditures at all from a security standpoint—an extreme position into which the alliance's defenders keep trying to shoehorn all critics. U.S. involvement in European defense may help prevent the West Europeans from plunging into another round of wars into which America could be drawn.[3] And the American nuclear umbrella undoubtedly inhibits the growth of Western Europe's existing nuclear arsenals and encourages other powers—like West Germany—to forswear the nuclear option. Yet both these results should be obtainable for much less than $160 billion annually, the estimated cost of the U.S. NATO commitment.

America's relative economic decline has also put the economics of NATO on the front burner. America's ability to finance its entire range of global defense commitments soundly, and without significant domestic costs or sacrifices, clearly is decreasing. This problem has been exacerbated by the transformation of many of the countries protected by the United States, in NATO and elsewhere, into formidable commercial competitors whose responsibilities for the common defense of the West have not grown commensurately with their economic power.

Many Americans today complain that the NATO allies and others continue to free or cheap ride on a U.S. security guarantee and to spend resources on boosting economic competitiveness instead of defense while sharply restricting America's access to their markets. These actions, it is believed, destroy American jobs, add to the trade deficit, and threaten the future of American manufacturing.

Most such complaints emphasize the harm to America of continuing the Atlantic alliance in its present form. But these trends should worry even those who believe that preserving this status quo, or something like it, should come before domestic concerns. The continued weakening of the U.S. economy may compromise America's ability to remain a military superpower and an alliance mainstay even with the kinds of domestic sacrifices that democracies rarely make in peacetime. But whatever their precise effects, these changes in relative economic power have created new realities that are not reflected in U.S. NATO policy.

Finally, the economics of NATO has been brought to the fore by the diminution of the Soviet threat in the eyes of American and West European publics. Suddenly the costs of countering Moscow loom ever larger, as do the conflicting economic interests that naturally divide countries producing many of the same kinds of products for the same markets.

NATO's Direct Costs

Although the practice of talking about the economics of NATO is still a matter of controversy, the actual scale of U.S. NATO expenditures is not. By any standard it is enormous. According to the Department of Defense, roughly 60 percent of the country's annual military budget is attributable to the NATO commitment—a figure currently equal to between $160 billion and $170 billion per year.[4] According to defense analyst Earl Ravenal, NATO cost the United States between $1.5 trillion and $2 trillion during the first thirty-four years of its existence. In 1985, Ravenal estimated that if current trends continue, NATO's additional costs to the United States could total $2.2 trillion through 1995.[5]

In line with these figures, the bulk of America's armed forces are dedicated to combat in Europe. The primary mission of an estimated two-thirds of the country's standing army is the defense of Western Europe. Some 37 percent of the army's units are stationed on the Continent, along with 42 percent of the air force's tactical strength.[6] These numbers actually understate the U.S. contribution. They do not include the more than $40 billion annual cost of the American military units assigned to protect the Persian Gulf, on whose oil Western Europe relies so much more heavily than does the United States. Nor do they include the costs of America's central strategic deterrent forces, much of whose size and structure is dictated by the requirements of extended deterrence in Western Europe and elsewhere.[7]

At a time when politically available resources for various domestic and foreign policy programs are scarcer than has typically been the case since NATO's birth and when intensified international economic competition has made the efficient use of these resources imperative, it becomes critical to assess the impact this vast current and cumulative NATO-related spending must have on America's economic performance. Such analysis is doubly important considering that America's prime economic competitors do not incur remotely comparable costs.

Thus, the economics of NATO involves not only toting up the alliance's direct military costs but measuring the entirety of its impact on economic activities or policies that add to or subtract from America's economic strength. This means that the economics of NATO is inseparable from the economics of defense spending in general. And a strong case can be made that NATO no longer pays and is unlikely to pay in the foreseeable future.

NATO's Hidden Costs

Even when they discuss economics, NATO supporters tend to use arguments that define costs out of existence. For example, many contend that whatever NATO's costs, the costs to the United States in terms of lost markets and other business opportunities would be far greater if Western Europe was sub-jugated or Finlandized by the Soviets. Leaving aside the questions of whether the Soviets still want to or could dominate Western Europe for any length of time and whether they would shut out American business if they achieved such dominance, the argument fails on several grounds.

First, since 1984, America has been running substantial trade deficits with its leading West European allies. From 1985 to 1987, U.S. imports from Western Europe exceeded U.S. sales to the region by an average of more than $25 billion. In 1988 the deficit dropped to $12.5 billion, but much of this decline stemmed from the declining value of the dollar, which also greatly increased the expense to America of stationing military forces abroad, con-tributed to inflationary pressures, and exacted other economic costs.[8] These figures look much worse when U.S. trade with NATO-ally Canada is factored in. But in this case the link between alliance expenses and economic perfor-mance is much harder to draw because the U.S. military forces devoted to Canadian defense are almost indistinguishable from those defending the American homeland.

Further, Western Europe's importance to the U.S. trade picture has been declining steadily, especially in comparison with East Asia. In 1984, U.S. two-way trade with East Asia and the Pacific surpassed U.S. trade with Western Europe for the first time. By 1986, total two-way U.S. trade with East Asia and the Pacific exceeded $212 billion. The comparable figure for Western Europe was $151.2 billion.[9] Therefore, even if one agrees that, trade deficits notwithstanding, America is better off economically with access to Western Europe than without it, the costs of losing such access are decreasing. Western Europe, moreover, is a region that trades primarily with itself. In 1986, for example, acccording to the State Department, nearly 70 percent of Western Europe's imports and exports stayed within Western Europe, and the trend has been up.[10] Moreover, the Continent's move toward economic integration is likely to boost intra-European trade still further.

Perhaps most disturbing, the argument that the high cost of defending Western Europe must be borne because the cost of pulling out would be much higher appears to condemn the United States to an indefinite hemorrhaging of national economic strength. Such a development is deeply disturbing on its own terms. No nation can afford to accept its own weakening with a shrug. At the very least, it will never fly politically in a democracy. At the worst, if the erosion of American economic strength is not arrested, U.S. national security may suffer tremendously—that is, unless NATO's supporters are confident that Western Europe or Japan would help America in its time of need as much as America helped them. But a debilitated America would also be bad for NATO and its other alliances, for such a country would not be able to uphold the arrangements with which its partners are understandably so satisfied.

Atlanticists insist that America's role in Western Europe's defense gives the United States valuable economic leverage over the NATO allies. An America that abandoned Western Europe would have much less clout and, presumably, trade even less effectively with the Europeans than today.[11]

Yet these arguments are unsatisfactory from America's standpoint as well. America's defense of Western Europe may indeed enable Washington to extract trade concessions in return—that is, to follow an essentially imperialist strategy. But are these concessions sufficient to justify the military expenses? More important, is this the best way for America to maintain or improve upon its trade and economic performance? Conceivably, continuing or even intensifying such an "imperial" strategy could prevent America's trade balance from substantially worsening.[12] But the resulting balances would have less and less to do with relative economic strength and more and more to do with U.S. coercion. In addition, American business would have much less incentive to retool and regain the ability to compete on its own; indeed, the more resources needed to finance the military effort required by the imperial strategy, the fewer would be available for such restructuring.

Nor is it clear that an imperial strategy can be sustained over time. America's NATO allies already resent compensating the United States for its defense efforts through trade concessions. The higher the price America demands—and it is likely to continue rising the longer American business goes without sufficient incentives to retool—the greater European resentment will grow. If these tensions lead to a political rupture, the United States could be left (at least in the short run) with another worst-of-all-possible-worlds situation: lacking imperial access to Western European markets and lacking the economic strength to compete in these markets on its own.

Those doubting that such a scenario could unfold should remember the 1960s and 1970s. Washington antagonized the allies by financing its outsized military expenditures and resulting balance of payments deficits first by inflating its economy and by exporting its inflation primarily to the allies. The dollar, after all, was the noncommunist world's principal reserve currency. Thus, foreign holders of dollars saw their purchasing power decrease as they saw no choice but to hold on to the growing number of dollars of continually declining value that were pouring into the world economy. The inflation strategy was eventually thwarted in 1971, when the West Europeans led a flight from the dollar that forced President Richard Nixon to suspend dollar-gold convertibility and bring an end to the Bretton Woods international economic system.

For most of the 1970s, the United States combined continued inflation with dollar devaluations and "benign neglect" of the currency. Due to the shocks caused by the Organization of Petroleum Exporting Countries (OPEC), and other factors, the allies were at first too weak to respond effectively. But they finally put an end to the second strategy in 1979, when resentment of President Jimmy Carter's expansionary and inflationary economic policies led the West Europeans to threaten to abandon the dollar altogether and prompted Federal Reserve Board chairman Paul Volcker to rein in inflation by engineering a deep recession. By then, an America that was relatively much weaker economically had little choice but to swallow this medicine.[13]

It is true that these imperial policies brought the American public twenty years of relative prosperity and rising living standards. Yet these policies could do no more than buy time and hold the line. By themselves they could not hope to improve the trade picture significantly or economic fundamentals in general. And indeed, they left the U.S. economy much less sound than it was at the beginning of the 1960s. Surely the United States would be much better off today had it concentrated on maintaining and augmenting real economic strength and maintaining a sound economy rather than strong-arming its allies into financing its profligacy. And surely it would be well advised today to capture and hold markets with real economic strength created by the wise use of resources currently consumed by alliance commitments rather than through the coercion apparently advocated by the Atlanticists. Such a strategy, however, is inconceivable politically without massive cuts in a military budget largely devoted to West European defense.

Finally, the Atlanticists' economic case for NATO ignores the fact that U.S. support for NATO has always been strongly related to economic conditions historically much more favorable than they are today. When NATO was founded in 1949, not only did the United States produce 40 percent of the world's total goods and services but was running enormous trade surpluses with the rest of the world.

America's leading trade partners desperately needed American products and credit to rebuild war-devastated industries, resume exporting, and thus begin to finance recovery. Without recovery, U.S. leaders also realized, Western Europe and Japan would never develop into power centers capable of resisting Soviet expansionism more or less on their own. And the United States would have to assume virtually all of this staggering burden indefinitely. Consequently Washington provided these regions with great amounts of foreign aid, opened its markets wide to their exports, and permitted their still-struggling economies to discriminate against American goods. The United States also extended military protection to these countries until they could defend themselves.

What permitted these policies to work—that is, to achieve their aims at a cost that the American people were willing to pay—was U.S. military and economic predominance. Washington could contain the Soviet Union and protect its allies at reasonable cost because of the massive nuclear edge it enjoyed through the late 1960s. In addition, between 1945 and 1965, the United States had to implement containment by fighting a large, costly conventional war only once, in Korea. Further, trade and investment surpluses not only helped finance global containment but permitted the United States to tolerate allied protectionism.

As the makers and supporters of this strategy never tire of observing, post–World War II U.S. foreign policy aimed at ending this predominance and restoring normality to world affairs. But they seem to have forgotten that a relative decline of U.S. strength could serve the country's interests only if its revitalized partners picked up some of the military and economic leadership load. By the mid-1960s, the United States had settled into a pattern of continuing to bear the lion's share of these leadership costs even as the material bases of its predominance had begun to erode. Worse, by hewing to policies that it could no longer afford and relying on the imperial strategy to maintain a deceptive prosperity at home, America accelerated the erosion of its economic strength. In other words, the costs of defense commitments such as NATO and Vietnam, and of the high military budgets they required, became increasingly apparent.

Defense Spending and Competitiveness

The relationship between military spending and national economic performance is anything but clear-cut.[14] Nevertheless, the feeling seems to be growing in Congress, in the foreign policy and defense community, and among the public at large that current levels of U.S. military spending—the highest among the major Western industrialized countries—are hampering America in the economic competition with these same countries. And a close association can be demonstrated between a country's defense effort and various determinants of international economic competitiveness.

A good way to begin is by comparing trade statistics with defense spending statistics. America's trade with Western Europe swung deeply into deficit during the 1980s, averaging some $25 billion between 1985 and 1987. In 1986, the last year for which comparative figures are available, the United States spent 6.7 percent of its gross domestic product (GDP) on defense. Its NATO allies spent an average of 3.3 percent. In fact, America's defense burden has exceeded that of its NATO allies for the entire decade, and the ratio has widened from the 5.3:3.6 figure recorded in 1980.[15]

The apparent relationship between military spending and economic performance is particularly striking in the case of America's most powerful West European economic competitor, West Germany. The Federal Republic's defense burden has been one of the lowest of any other major NATO country, remaining in the 3.2 to 3.4 percent range throughout the 1980s.[16] And from 1980 to 1985, the U.S. trade deficit with West Germany ballooned from $700 million to $14.5 billion.[17] The disparity between American and

Japanese defense spending during this period has been even greater, as have the American trade deficits with Japan.

It is true that the U.S. trade balance with almost every part of the world plunged deeply into the red during the 1980s. Nor can unfair foreign trade practices—a serious problem—explain the shift, for the rest of the world has not become notably more protectionist during this decade. More persuasive are the widely made arguments that the shift in trading patterns has coincided with a great appreciation in the value of the dollar as well as with U.S. economic growth rates that far exceeded industrialized world averages.

At the same time, it would be equally wrong to view these developments as completely unrelated to U.S. military spending—as the product of one president's peculiar economic theories. In making their defense spending and economic calculations, the leaders of democracies, for better or for worse, must think of more than the country's foreign interests, international threats, and the dictates of pure economic rationality. They have to take into account the public's understandable desires for a certain amount of public services, a certain level of material welfare, and a minimal tax burden as well as the demands of powerful interest groups. Reaganomics—and particularly its toleration of huge budget deficits that had to be financed by foreign borrowing—is best understood as an attempt to strike a balance between ultimately inconsistent foreign policy and domestic goals. The unusual extent to which it departed from mainstream economic wisdom largely reflected the administration's need to compensate for the domestic economic impact of its unusually large defense buildup, much of which went to NATO and other alliance commitments. Heavy defense spending also tightly intertwined with the domestic roots of America's international economic competitiveness problems—chiefly relatively low rates of productivity growth and low levels of savings and investment.

It is true that U.S. defense spending has been much higher than that of its allied economic competitors throughout the postwar era, whereas huge trade deficits and other serious signs of competitiveness problems first appeared only during the Reagan years. Yet this does not confirm that Reaganomics has been the main problem. It is at least as likely that the main economic costs of relatively heavy defense spending take time to accumulate and that the true impact of America's long-standing, outsized defense burden has just started to become apparent. Worse, the toll of outsized defense budgets may grow faster over time.[18]

Again, though cause and effect are difficult to prove, key economic statistics support the case for a trade-off between economic performance and high defense spending. Take the growth rates of the world's four primary centers of industrial strength: the United States, the Soviet Union, Japan, and the European Community (EC). From 1966 through 1987, the gross national products (GNPs) of the most militarized of these four economies grew the most sluggishly—an average of 2.85 percent for the United States during this period and even less for the Soviet Union. The figures for much less militarized Japan and Western Europe were 5.96 and 3.01 percent, respectively.

A look behind the simple numbers strengthens the case. America's periods of fastest economic growth since 1966 have been characterized by some combination of inflation and heavy deficit spending: 1976–1980, when average annual real growth rates peaked at 3.3 percent; 1981–1985, when they stood at 3 percent; and 1987, when 2.9 percent growth was achieved. Moscow's performance weakened steadily as its great military buildup took off, with average annual real growth rates plunging from 5.1 percent in the 1966–1970 period to 3.1 percent in 1971-1975 and to 0.5 percent in 1987.

Although no other industrialized nation was more dependent on OPEC oil when the price jumped, the Japanese economy outperformed America's throughout the 1970s. And EC growth rates have been comparable to America's since 1971 despite both the oil shocks and the vigorous expansion of already generous welfare states that are almost universally considered drags on growth.[19]

To be sure, some countries have generated explosive economic growth despite heavy military spending—notably South Korea and Taiwan. But both countries are still in economic stages in which significant growth is relatively easy to achieve. Both have also been autocracies, able to dampen private consumption and levels of welfare spending to degrees inconceivable in Japan, let alone the industrialized West.

What is known about the prime determinants of healthy economic growth also suggests that high military spending can disadvantage an economy, particularly in a democracy. For most of the post–World War II era, nations that have skimped on the military have achieved higher productivity growth rates than those that have splurged. Between 1972 and 1986, the United States registered the lowest level of manufacturing productivity growth of all the other Group-of-Seven industrialized countries (Canada, France, Italy, Japan, the United Kingdom, and West Germany are the other members of the group).[20]

Despite the Reagan military buildup, U.S. productivity growth during the 1980s has actually improved over the levels of the late 1970s, a period of relatively low U.S. military spending. But this development does not prove that democracies can achieve high productivity growth and high military spending simultaneously, at least not for long. The 1.9 percent average annual productivity increases achieved between September 1982 and September 1987 exceeded the 1.3 percent rate registered during the 1975–1980 recovery, but they represented a drop from the 2.6 percent average for all postwar U.S. recoveries.[21]

America's poor savings and investment performance also seems closely related to relatively high levels of military spending. For the 1980–1984 period, the U.S. annual gross savings rate surpassed only Canada's, Denmark's, and Belgium's.[22] Perhaps Americans are, as many have charged, naturally less frugal than West Europeans and Japanese. But the governments of democracies with high military budgets and modest welfare states face more pressure to encourage consumption—and keep voters happy in the all-important short run—than democracies with either low military budgets, generous welfare states, or both.

U.S. investment levels have also lagged behind those of the countries it protects. And the United States has typically channeled much more of its research-and-development (R&D) funds into the military sector than its allies. Between 1981 and 1987, according to the National Science Foundation, nondefense R&D expenditures as a portion of GNP increased from 1.9 to 2.8 percent in Japan, from 2 to 2.6 percent in West Germany, and from 1.5 to 1.8 percent in France. In the United States, these figures increased only from 1.7 to 1.8 percent. The disparity between the United States and its leading allies is even greater in connection with government R&D expenditures.[23]

America's relatively poor investment performance in turn appears to be eroding the technological edge that it has traditionally enjoyed over its economic rivals. U.S. performance is considered particularly unsatisfactory in turning advances in basic research into commercially successful products. In part, the problem is undoubtedly a matter of business management and corporate culture, particularly the short-term horizons that appear to dominate the planning activities of American businesses. But the United States is clearly losing ground as well in the manufacturing and process technologies that enable corporations to bring new products to the market efficiently.[24]

As a result, the U.S. trade balance in high-technology products deteriorated from a $26.7 billion surplus in 1980 to a $2.6 billion deficit in 1986. In 1987 a tiny $600 million surplus was registered—and this only after a major dollar devaluation. America's share of the world merchant semiconductor market, the building blocks of the new information technologies, dwindled from 60 percent in 1975 to roughly 45 percent in 1986—just under the market share held by Japanese manufacturers.[25]

The international technological competition appears to be entering a critical phase. Laboratory breakthroughs in areas such as superconductivity, biotechnology, materials science, and microelectronics promise to revolutionize industry, create enormous new markets for a wide array of new products, and confer enormous economic and political power on those countries that exploit the new technologies most rapidly and most effectively. So far Japan shapes up as America's prime competitor. Nonetheless it is clear that the NATO commitment is one of the greatest consumers of American resources that could otherwise be devoted to economic and technological revitalization.

The Impact of Domestic Politics

The United States could continue to compete effectively in international economics without excessive domestic sacrifices had it retained the international economic preponderance it enjoyed at the outset of the cold war and had the American people's domestic expectations of their government remained the same. Unfortunately, neither circumstance applies anymore.

When NATO was formed, the United States dominated the world economy as had no other country since mid-nineteenth-century Britain, accounting for 40.3 percent of world GNP and nearly 60 percent of the noncommunist industrialized world's GNP in 1950. By 1980, these figures had shrunk to 21.8 percent and 33.5 percent, respectively, rising to 24.1 percent and 40.4 percent by 1983, primarily because of recession in Western Europe.

Yet there has been much less change in America's share of world military spending and the military spending of the industrialized West. In 1950, the United States accounted for 29.5 percent of world military spending and 58.6 percent of the industrialized West's military spending. In 1983, the former figure was exactly the same, and the latter declined to only 56.7 percent.[26]

During the first two-and-one-half decades of the post–World War II era, economic predominance was undoubtedly the key to America's ability economically and politically to support defense spending levels considerably higher even than those during the peak of the Reagan buildup: 10 percent in 1955, 8.9 percent in 1960, 7.4 percent in 1965, and 7.7 percent in 1970.[27] This declining relative defense effort leads Atlanticists and many others to argue that military and alliance spending has little to do with our current economic ills and that the U.S. economy can easily support today's levels of military spending and current defense commitments like NATO.[28]

What they forget is that the United States is not the same country politically that it was during the early cold war years. Given the worldwide defense responsibilities that America assumed, total public spending and the taxes needed to pay for it could be held below economically harmful levels during this period only if the American people accepted the barest skeleton of a welfare state or if public spending was financed through borrowing. Once domestic social services began to expand—and the American welfare state is still much less extensive than its West European counterparts—and the public's enthusiasm for paying higher taxes waned, economic trouble was sure to follow.

In 1949, when NATO was founded, total federal outlays represented 14.7 percent of GNP.[29] Defense (which, of course, is not the sum total of

U.S. foreign policy expenditures) represented 5 percent of national output, human resources (including spending on education, training, employment, social services, health, income security, social security, and veterans benefits) represented 4.1 percent, and net interest on the federal debt 1.7 percent. As percentages of the federal budget, defense spending stood at 33.9 percent, human resources spending at 27.8 percent, and net interest at 11.6 percent.

By the end of President Eisenhower's first term in 1956, with federal outlays up to 16.9 percent of GNP, defense spending had more than doubled, to 10.2 percent of national output, human resources spending had declined to 3.8 percent, and net interest on the debt had sunk to 1.2 percent. That year, defense spending accounted for more than 60 percent of all federal spending, human resources for only 22.7, and net interest for only 7.2.

By 1988, the federal budget had risen to 22.3 percent of national output. Defense spending had fallen to 6.1 percent of GNP and 27.3 percent of the budget. But even at the end of the Reagan military buildup and nearly a decade of relatively slow growth in federal nondefense spending, civilian spending was much greater than in the period of relatively high defense budgets. Since 1956, for example, human resources spending has nearly tripled as a percentage of GNP and more than doubled as a share of the budget (to 50.1 percent). And net interest on the federal debt has nearly tripled as a percentage of GNP and nearly doubled as a percentage of the budget.

Unquestionably the United States today has the economic capability of financing greater defense spending. But politics renders this argument utterly meaningless. These figures and trends represent a sweeping national consensus on spending priorities that has been affirmed repeatedly by voters for thirty years. A return to the defense effort of yesteryear is possible only through a reordering of priorities that would fill American streets with protesters, an increase in taxes that would have a similar effect and undoubtedly slash economic growth rates, or a new binge of deficit spending that could also cripple the economy. In theory, faster economic and productivity growth could provide the extra resources; however, the required improvements greatly exceed those forecast by any reputable economist.

As the fiscal 1990 defense budget request indicates, the Bush administration will have to struggle to prevent defense spending from declining further, both relatively and absolutely, and this struggle will intensify as the bills for long-neglected domestic needs come due—such as the savings-and-loan industry bailout, the cleanup of nuclear weapons plants and toxic waste dumps, and the repair of transportation infrastructure. NATO was affordable in the only meaningful sense in a democracy—the political—during a special moment in history. That moment is long since past.

Burden Sharing and Other Pipedreams

The United States could also better afford a substantial (albeit significantly reduced) commitment to Western Europe's defense if its European allies assumed greater responsibilities for defending themselves. Unfortunately, they show no such interest. As the U.S. burden-sharing debate has intensified, Atlanticists and the allies themselves have trotted out a set of facts and figures showing that the allies "as a group are bearing roughly their fair share of the NATO . . . defense burden," to quote former U.S. Secretary of Defense Caspar Weinberger. In fact, in 1986 the Eurogroup, an informal organization containing most NATO members, suggested that the allies are "contributing more than their fair share to the Alliance."[30]

The principal figures used to make this case concern allied military forces stationed in Europe in peacetime. According to the Eurogroup, of the total NATO servicemen and weapons deployed in Western Europe today, the West Europeans provide 90 percent of the manpower, 95 percent of the divisions, 85 percent of the tanks, 95 percent of the artillery, and 80 percent of the combat aircraft.[31]

Yet as the Eurogroup report notes, unlike the United States, the European NATO members have no major defense responsibilities outside Western Europe. Their military efforts center almost exclusively on homeland defense. Given their economic strength, it is only to be expected that they contribute most of the military forces deployed in their neighborhood. Second, the most important standard for assessing the allies' defense efforts is not how they stack up against U.S. forces in Europe but against the enemy's forces. After all, the allies presumably field their forces not to convince the United States that they are pulling their weight but to counter the Soviets. The levels of U.S. forces stationed in Europe indicate clearly that the West European armies alone are too meager even to maintain deterrence. And the NATO military strategy that they have all endorsed depends heavily on the use of nuclear weapons and conventional reinforcements from the United States.

When the spending side is examined, West European footdragging becomes even more obvious. From 1960 to 1986, the U.S. GDP as a share of the NATO countries' total fluctuated between 52.3 percent and 55.6 percent (and stood at 53.6 percent in 1986). But U.S. defense spending as a share of alliance totals during this period has always been significantly higher—ranging from just under 62 percent to just over 70 percent and standing at 68.64 percent in 1986. Even adjusting the totals to reflect America's non-European defense responsibilities (many of which directly or indirectly benefit Western Europe), the United States has still consistently spent more on Western Europe's defense than the West Europeans.[32]

Additional evidence that the European allies have shirked their defense responsibilities for many years is provided by comparisons of U.S. and West European budgetary priorities. According to the U.S. Arms Control and Disarmament Agency, between 1975 and 1985, the European NATO members' military expenditures as a portion of central government expenditures actually fell from 9.8 percent to 8.8 percent. The comparable U.S. figure rose from 26.2 percent to 26.5 percent.[33] In other words, the European NATO allies are not strapped for public funds. They simply do not want to spend these monies on defense.

Of course, military spending as a percentage of the U.S. budget has been dropping steadily for most of the post–World War II period and will probably continue to drop for the foreseeable future. The allies and the United States evidently face the same kinds of political constraints on defense spending. But America is not asking for Western Europe's help to defend its own territory.

Even these figures, however, tend to obscure the most important burden-sharing reality. If America still needs to spend at least $160 billion to help protect so wealthy a region, then that region's defense efforts are sorely inadequate.

Beyond the Imperial Strategy

Although the U.S. foreign policy community continues to be uncomfortable discussing the economics of NATO, economics as well as the Gorbachev revolution in Soviet foreign policy have brought transatlantic relations to a fateful juncture. If the United States wishes to persist in the imperial strategy followed over the last thirty years and maintain its dominant role in Western Europe's defense, several options are available.

The United States could decide that its foreign creditors simply cannot afford to withdraw their support for the American economy and that allied financing of the budget and trade deficits represents a marvelous way of taxing these countries for the military protection provided by America. Washington could also continue on its present, slightly different, course, counting on a combination of domestic spending restraint, frozen military budgets, unspecified sources of revenue, and vigorous economic expansion to permit the U.S. economy to grow out of its deficits, and on a crazy quilt of public and private measures and ad hoc protectionism to improve the trade balance and restore an adequate measure of economic competitiveness—especially in high-tech industries.

If Americans decide that more of just about the same will not do, the United States might still decide to contain the exorbitant costs of its alliance policies through more systematic, more comprehensive trade protectionism, such as a series of sweeping managed trade agreements with its allies or a coordinated international effort to manipulate currencies to benefit American exports and cut imports.

Alternatively, the United States could conclude that these versions of imperialism yield too much control over America's future to foreign actors. It could decide that continuing to provide the crutch of protectionism, in whatever form, only postpones the day when troubled American industries can stand on their own two feet—and in fact accelerates the erosion of the economic power on which the imperialist strategy ultimately rests.

Rather than try to compensate for U.S. economic and industrial inadequacies by pressuring allies into tolerating international economic rule breaking and subsidizing American indiscipline, the United States could seek security and prosperity through a policy of increasing its own economic competitiveness and building its own real economic strength—for example, by straightening out its public finances, using public policy to create a macroeconomic climate that encourages productive investment and a longer-term planning horizon in American business, retooling its factories, improving its failing schools, and repairing its crumbling transportation infrastructure.

Given political realities and the entirely understandable budget priorities of the American people, it is difficult to see how the resources can be freed up for the tax relief or additional public programs required for this effort without a major cut in the military budgets that support major alliance commitments, especially NATO. And given the cumulative economic costs to the American economy of thirty years of imperialism, it is equally difficult to see how the United States can avoid such admittedly drastic measures—and the overhaul of alliance policy they would require—much longer.

Notes

1. John Lewis Gaddis, *Strategies of Containment: A Critical Appraisal of Postwar American National Security Policy* (New York: Oxford University Press, 1982), p. 166.

2. *Discriminate Deterrence: Report of the Commission on Integrated Long-term Strategy* (Washington, D.C.: U.S. Government Printing Office, 1988), pp. 24–25.

3. For a compelling statement of this argument, see Josef Joffe, "Europe's American Pacifier," *Foreign Policy* 54 (Spring 1984).

4. U.S. House, Armed Services Committee (ASC), Interim Report of the Defense Burdensharing Panel, 100th Cong., 2d sess. (August 1988): 12.

5. Statement by Earl C. Ravenal Before the Senate Foreign Relations Subcommittee on European Affairs, September 19, 1986, p. 39; "Should the U.S. Stay in NATO?" *Harper's* (April 1984): 38.

6. Statement by David P. Calleo before the Senate Foreign Relations Subcommittee on European Affairs, October 3, 1985, p. 254; "The High Cost of NATO," *Newsweek,* March 7, 1988, p. 54.

7. Earl C. Ravenal, "Europe without America: The Erosion of NATO," *Foreign Affairs* 63 (Summer 1985).

8. "U.S. Exports, General Imports and Merchandise Trade Balance: 1974 to Present," Press Release and Publications Preparation Section, Foreign Trade Division, Bureau of the Census, U.S. Department of Commerce.

9. U.S. Department of Commerce, *Statistical Abstract of the United States 1988* (Washington, D.C.: U.S. Government Printing Office, 1989), p. 772.

10. *Trade Patterns of the West, 1986,* Intelligence Research Report No. 133 (Washington, D.C.: Department of State, 1987), p. 2.

11. See, for example, statement by Richard N. Cooper before the Senate Foreign Relations Subcommittee on European Affairs, 99th Cong., 1st sess., October 3, 1985, pp. 195–97.

12. For the definitive discussion of the imperial strategy, see David P. Calleo, *The Imperious Economy* (Cambridge: Harvard University Press, 1982).

13. See ibid. for a fuller discussion of the Nixon-Ford and Carter policies.

14. For an excellent review of the theoretical and empirical issues, see Steve Chan, "The Impact of Defense Spending on Economic Performance: A Survey of Evidence and Problems," *Orbis* 29 (Summer 1985).

15. "Interim Report of the Defense Burdensharing Panel," p. 22.

16. Ibid.

17. *Statistical Abstract of the United States, 1988,* p. 770.

18. The basic arguments are summarized in Chan, "Impact of Defense Spending on Economic Performance."

19. For the economic growth figures, see Karen Elliot House, "For All Its Difficulties, U.S. Stands to Retain Its Global Leadership," *Wall Street Journal,* January 23, 1989.

20. *Competitiveness Index* (Washington, D.C.: Council on Competitiveness, 1988), p. 7.

21. Robert J. Samuelson, "The Republican Economy," *Washington Post,* September 9, 1987.

22. See chapter 4.

23. *International Science and Technology Data Update 1988,* Special Report NSF 89–307 (Washington, D.C.: National Science Foundation, 1988), pp. 8, 11.

24. For key facts and statistics, see Charles H. Ferguson, "America's High-Tech Decline," *Foreign Policy* 74 (Spring 1989): 134–35.

25. *International Science and Technology Data Update 1988,* p. 88.

26. Masahiro Sakamoto, "The Hegemonic Structure and Cost Sharing in the Pax Americana in Comparison with Those in the Pax Britannica" (unpublished paper, June 1986), p. 39.

27. "Interim Report of the Defense Burdensharing Panel," p. 22.

28. See, for example, Joseph S. Nye, Jr., "Understating U.S. Strength," *Foreign Policy* 72 (Fall 1988): 113–16; Samuel P. Huntington, "The U.S.—Decline or Renewal?" *Foreign Affairs* 67 (Winter 1988–1989); and Francis Bator, "Must We Retrench?" *Foreign Affairs* 68 (Spring 1989).

29. All budget statistics are from *Historical Tables: Budget of the United States*

Government Fiscal Year 1990 (Washington, D.C.: U.S. Government Printing Office, 1989).

30. Quoted in *Western Defense: The European Role in NATO* (Brussels: Eurogroup, 1986), p. 13.

31. Ibid., pp. 6, 13.

32. Gordon Adams and Eric Munz, *Fair Shares: Bearing the Burden of the NATO Alliance* (Washington, D.C.: Center on Budget and Policy Priorities, 1988), pp. 42–43, 74–75.

33. *World Military Expenditures and Arms Transfers 1987* (Washington, D.C.: U.S. Arms Control and Disarmament Agency, 1988), pp. 43ff.

III
Implications of a Changing Strategic Environment

8

The Future of the U.S. Military Presence in Europe

Jeffrey Record

D uring the past forty years, every president of the United States has declared Europe to be America's first line of defense, a judgment manifest in U.S. defense spending, force planning, and force deployments. According to Defense Department estimates, the NATO commitment consumes at least one-half of annual U.S. defense expenditure.[1] The NATO commitment also remains, the emergence of new threats to American security outside Europe notwithstanding, the principal determinant of the size and structure of U.S. conventional forces, especially the U.S. Army. In terms of force deployments, the approximately 350,000 U.S. soldiers, sailors, and airmen currently deployed in the European theater account for two of every three U.S. servicemen stationed overseas. Five of the U.S. Army's eighteen divisions are stationed in the Federal Republic of Germany (FRG), with five additional divisions earmarked for Europe's rapid reinforcement.

The Truman administration's decision in 1949 to enter NATO was prompted by a belated recognition, based on the painful lessons of World War I and especially World War II, that a Europe dominated by a single hostile power—whether the Second Reich, Third Reich, or Soviet Union—constituted a fundamental threat to American security. Europe's critical geostrategic importance to the United States has been recognized by every subsequent American administration, all of which have sought by one means or another to contain Soviet military and political expansion on the Eurasian landmass.

The future of the American commitment to Europe's defense, at least as expressed in the number of U.S. troops routinely stationed there, can and should no longer be taken for granted. There is, of course, nothing in the NATO treaty of 1949 that obligates the United States to deploy a single infantry platoon or fighter squadron in Europe. The political commitment of the United States to Europe's defense has never been synonymous with or formally tied to a specific troop level. In fact, since the outbreak of the Korean War, which prompted the first peacetime dispatch of sizable U.S. combat forces to Europe, U.S. force levels have fluctuated substantially, from a high of 427,000 in 1953 to a low of 291,000 in 1970.

Looming over the alliance today, however, is the prospect of a major contraction in the scope of the U.S. military commitment to Europe's defense. Although there is no definitive number of U.S. troops in Europe, since the early 1950s there has existed a consensus on both sides of the Atlantic that a major American force presence on the order of several U.S. Army divisions and a dozen or so tactical air wings is indispensable to both deterrence and defense in Europe as well as to the credibility of the U.S. nuclear guarantee. All American presidents, most congressional leaders, and many opinion makers have shared this view, successfully beating back occasional attempts by congressional dissidents to legislate unilateral U.S. troop withdrawal from Europe.

Today, however, a unique set of factors appears to be converging toward a new consensus. A sizable diminution in the scope of the American military commitment to Europe's defense now seems likely to occur well before the end of this century—perhaps during the next few years. New factors are at play within both NATO and the Warsaw Pact that call into question not only the strategic validity but also the political sustainability of continuing to maintain a large U.S. military presence in Europe.

An Altered Transatlantic Balance of Power

There is, first, the obvious: the balance of both economic and military power within NATO has shifted radically since the creation of the alliance in 1949. In 1949 NATO Europe was economically prostrate. Germany had no military forces, and French, British, Dutch, and Belgian military forces potentially available for Europe's defense were for the most part involved in futile colonial holding actions outside Europe. NATO Europe, however, has long since recovered from World War II and shed its imperial burdens and today has a collective gross national product (GNP), industrial base, skilled work force, and military forces larger than that of the United States. The United States remains *primus inter pares* within NATO, but its power has declined sharply in relation to the economic and potential military power of its European allies. Continued disproportionate U.S. contributions to the common defense would not be politically sustainable within the United States even if a convincing case could be made that the Soviet military threat to Europe today was as clear and imminent as it appeared in 1949.

A Receding Soviet Threat

The second factor bearing on the future of the U.S. military presence in Europe is the sharp and continuing decline in public and parliamentary perceptions on both sides of the Atlantic of the Soviet military threat to Europe, coupled with prospective unilateral Soviet force reductions in Europe that in fact will significantly reduce military instability on the Continent. Even before Mikhail Gorbachev's stunning declarations before the United Nations on December 7, 1988, the absence of war in Europe for over forty years, combined with perceptions of a new, relatively young, and dynamic Soviet leadership committed to fundamental liberalization at home and a lessening of East-West tensions abroad, had significantly affected West European and American perceptions of the Soviet threat.

Open, effusive praise had already been heaped on both Gorbachev the man and Gorbachev the reformer by a conservative American president who once called the Soviet Union an evil empire. Such talk reinforced the conviction, especially widespread in Western Europe, that the Soviet Union posed little more of a threat to peace on the Continent than the United States. Indeed, during the Reagan administration's "Soviet-bashing" years, public opinion in Western Europe tended increasingly to see the United States and the Soviet Union as roughly equal threats to European security, a development that gave rise to the concept of equidistance—the postulation of a Europe trapped in the competition between the equally dangerous defense policies of the two superpowers.

Gorbachev remains far more popular in Europe than any recent American president, and his announced unilateral Soviet force cuts in Eastern Europe and the Soviet Union's western military districts could portend the beginning of the end of the massive East-West military confrontation on the Continent that has overshadowed European politics since the end of World War II. This assumes, of course, that Gorbachev will remain in power, an assumption that some respected Sovietologists do not share.

Gorbachev's initiative, which promotes a declared objective of "depriving the United States of the enemy," strikes at the very heart of NATO's raison d'être and is highly significant for a number of reasons. Aside from the fact that the announced cuts are to be taken unilaterally, Gorbachev's December 7 speech and the nature of the forces to be cut constitute an implicit official Soviet recognition for the first time that Soviet forces deployed in Eastern Europe (especially Germany) are, as NATO has long claimed, positioned and structured for lightning offensive operations deep into NATO territory. To be sure, as a percentage of total Soviet military power, the announced cuts appear modest. Yet their real significance becomes apparent when one looks at exactly what is being cut and where.

It has long been declared by NATO force planners that the greatest source of military instability in the military balance in Europe is the Soviet concentration opposite the inter-German and FRG-Czech border of massive tank-heavy and other offensively structured forces. However, it is precisely upon this concentration that the heaviest of Gorbachev's force cuts falls. In Eastern Europe alone, he is eliminating six of fourteen deployed tank divisions (a reduction of 43 percent) and 5,000 to 10,600 main battle tanks (a cut of 47 percent). Four of the six tank divisions slated for removal are to be taken from the crack Group of Soviet Forces Germany. Moreover, in addition to the approximately 2,000 main battle tanks that will come out with the six divisions, another 3,000 will be stripped from Soviet tank and motorized rifle divisions remaining behind in Eastern Europe as part of Gorbachev's declared intention to restructure those divisions toward a less operationally provocative, more defensive posture.[2]

Implementation of these cuts will still leave NATO facing a roughly one-to-two numerical disadvantage against Warsaw Pact forces in the Central Region, as compared to the approximately one-to-three disadvantage it now faces. However, implementation of the Gorbachev cuts will significantly reduce the initial offensive striking power of Soviet forces deployed in Eastern Europe, and the sustainability of any major Soviet offensive operations will suffer heavily from the announced main battle tank and other weapons cuts in forces stationed in the Soviet Union's western military districts.[3]

Moreover, additional if not unilateral Soviet force reductions in Europe after 1990 may be anticipated. On March 9, 1989, the Soviet delegation to the Vienna negotiations on conventional force reductions tabled an opening proposal that was remarkable for the degree to which it endorsed several long-standing NATO demands. Among other things the Soviets accepted the need for major force reductions, equal limits on the size of postreduction force deployments, and comprehensive verification measures.[4] Though the Soviet proposal contains several features that are objectionable to NATO (such as limits on tactical aircraft and armed helicopters and the creation of special semidemilitarized zones along the East-West border), it forms the basis for serious negotiations that could lead to force reductions on both sides to a level up to 15 percent below those deployed by NATO today.

Of momentous significance, however, was the Soviet side's acceptance of postreduction numerical parity in tanks and other major weapons categories. Parity in armor would eliminate any remaining confidence that Soviet ground forces in Europe could successfully exploit an initial breach in NATO's forward defenses. Indeed, the Shevardnadze speech may be interpreted, from the standpoint of long-standing Soviet operational doctrine, as a renunciation of the principle that the best defense is a good offense.

In sum, even if the Soviet military threat to Europe is measured solely in terms of capabilities, a significant recession of it is in the offing.

Allied Defense Performance

A third factor is allied defense performance. The political sustainability of a major U.S. force presence in Europe depends not only on perceptions of the

Soviet threat but also on perceptions of whether the allies are bearing their fair share of the common defense burden. The allies have not fared well in the eyes of U.S. public and congressional opinion in recent years, and there are strong indications that allied defense performance in the future will be worse rather than better. This will make it increasingly difficult for any U.S. administration to maintain the political constituency necessary to continue a robust U.S. military presence on the Continent.

Many allied military expenditures and national force contributions are already declining. In recent years defense budgets have not kept pace with inflation in many NATO countries, and in some nations budgets have declined in real terms. Of NATO's sixteen nations, only Italy, Luxembourg, Norway, and Turkey registered real defense spending increases in 1988. Indeed, during the period 1984–1986 defense expenditures as a percentage of GNP registered an increase in only three NATO countries: Norway, Turkey, and the United States.

Demographic trends throughout NATO are also militarily adverse. The most unsettling are in the FRG, which has the lowest fertility rates in the world and whose 495,000 men under arms form the core of the alliance's forward defenses. There is virtually no possibility that the Bundeswehr can maintain its present strength beyond the early 1990s. The size of Germany's male population of military age (women are barred by law from bearing arms) has been dropping for years and will continue to do so for the remainder of the century. The German army requires an annual replenishment pool of 225,000 new conscripts; only 125,000 will be available by the early 1990s. By 1995 the Bundeswehr could shrivel to a force two-thirds its present strength (to 335,000).

The German government, beset by political pressures from both left and right, has abandoned some proposed remedial measures, such as an extension of the first term of service from fifteen to eighteen months. Ministry of Defense officials privately concede that within the next decade, the Bundeswehr is almost certain to decline to a force of 400,000 to 420,000 men. A smaller Bundeswehr will weaken the defense of the critical Central Front and could provide a perverse excuse for other NATO countries to cut their own forces.

There may in fact be demographically mandated reductions in other national force contributions, which could be handily excused as permitted by unilateral Soviet force reductions in Eastern Europe. Over the next twelve years, the draft cohort—those 18 to 22 years old—will shrink by 40 percent in Holland, 30 percent in Great Britain, 20 percent in Belgium, and 15 percent in France. Budgetary pressures are serving to reinforce the consequences of demographic trends. Canada has already announced that it will no longer honor its brigade-sized commitment to Norway's defense. There are no prospects for Belgian or Dutch force expansion; indeed, Belgium, which in 1986 met only 38 percent of the key force goals NATO annually establishes for each member, is considering a reduction in the poorly equipped 30,000-man force it deploys in Germany. French defense nuclear programs, which have long starved French conventional forces of timely modernization, are likely to account for an even larger share of the defense budget than they have in the past.

Nor can a robust British Army of the Rhine (BAOR) any longer be taken for granted. British defense expenditure is declining in real terms, and for the first time in decades, defense expenditure as a percentage of GNP is headed downward. These trends, coupled with the Thatcher government's determination to modernize Britain's nuclear deterrent by acquiring the costly Trident, could make a reduction in the 56,000-man BAOR unavoidable. Some German Ministry of Defense officials believe that at least one of the BAOR's three divisions will be withdrawn from Germany by the year 2000.

Justified or not, reduced allied force contributions will hardly play well in Washington, D.C., to say nothing of Peoria.

The American Scene

The relative decline in U.S. power in relation to that of its NATO allies, mounting perceptions of a receding Soviet threat to Europe, unilateral Soviet force reductions in Eastern Europe, worsening allied defense performance, and the passage of forty-four years of peace in Europe will unavoidably influence American perceptions as to what is required in the future in the way of U.S. military forces allocated to Europe's defense. Any decision to alter significantly the size and composition of the U.S. military presence in Europe will be an American one, and it will be based more on developments in the United States than on developments in Europe of the alliance as a whole.

Developments in the United States, however, as those elsewhere in the alliance, are also working in favor of a substantially diminished military commitment to Europe's defense, at least in terms of money and forces. First, an unprecedented federal budgetary crisis has led to declining real annual defense expenditure for the last four years, a trend almost certain to continue well into the 1990s. Although the crisis has yet to affect U.S. force levels in Europe, it has already dictated significant cuts in forces based in the United States. For example, cuts totaling $33 billion in the fiscal year 1989 defense budget will result in a reduction of 36,000 active-duty military personnel, cancellation of eighteen procurement programs, and deactivation of sixteen U.S. Navy warships and three U.S. Air Force tactical air wings. Far larger cuts in the defense budget are anticipated over the next several years. Secretary of Defense Dick Cheney has submitted a budget for fiscal year 1990 that clearly reveals a preference for taking budget cuts in the form of active-duty force structure rather than by canceling procurement programs.[5] This means the elimination or transfer to reserve status of additional tactical air wings, ground force units, and possibly warships. Edward C. "Shy" Meyer, former chief of staff of the army (the service whose interests would be most adversely affected by a reduction in the U.S. military presence in Europe), has stated that U.S. troop cuts in Europe are inevitable and could be safely undertaken under conditions of expanded warning time afforded by Soviet force cuts and exploitation of new verification technologies and procedures.[6]

Reinforcing the defense budget crunch are militarily adverse demographic trends in the United States that call into question the All-Volunteer Force's (AVF) ability to recruit and retain sufficient numbers of qualified people over the next decade. Although the demographic outlook in the United States is far less bleak than that in Germany, the price of military manpower is greater. Even to maintain current force levels, the AVF will probably have to allocate an increasing real percentage of its available funds to preserve its current manpower quality. However, the opportunity cost of meeting this challenge, especially in an environment of declining total defense budgets, will be comparatively less investment in weapons, sustainability, and operations and maintenance.

Growing demands on U.S. armed forces outside the NATO area, demands that have yet to be attended by requisite increases in military capabilities, constitute another factor working on behalf of a reduced force presence in Europe. Actual intervention in the Persian Gulf and possible intervention elsewhere in the Third World have drawn the steadily increasing attention of U.S. force planners in recent years. In addition, the armed services have been called upon to play a major role in combating international terrorism and the international drug trade. These are daunting and relatively new tasks for a military that counts over 500,000 fewer people on active duty today than it had in 1964, the last year preceding U.S. combat intervention in Vietnam.

Calls for a fundamental reassessment of the current strategic allocation of U.S. forces overseas (and of forces withheld in the United States for various regional contingencies) have already been sounded within the U.S. government. In January 1988, for example, Secretary of the Navy James Webb made a speech before the National Press Club in which he sharply questioned the level of U.S. investment in Europe's defense. That same month, President Reagan received a report prepared by the Commission on Integrated Long-Term Strategy.[7] The commission, whose members included Albert Wohlstetter, Fred Iklé, Henry Kissinger, and Zbigniew Brzezinski, concluded that the possibility of a large-scale Soviet attack in Central Europe was becoming increasingly remote (a conclusion subsequently reinforced by Gorbachev's announced unilateral Soviet force cuts) and therefore should no longer dominate U.S. strategic planning. The report called instead for increased attention to meeting threats posed by low-intensity conflicts and regional instabilities outside Europe, along with appropriate reallocations of U.S. defense budgetary resources.

More than a few Europeans also have come to regard an open-ended major U.S. force presence in Europe as undesirable, politically unsustainable, or both. Political opposition parties in Germany, Britain, and other key NATO countries have declared themselves against a continued U.S. nuclear presence of any kind on their national territory and have made it abundantly clear that they would shed no tears over a smaller U.S. ground force presence in Europe. In Germany, rising public outcry over damage to property and occasional loss of civilian lives caused by large-scale U.S. and allied ground force manuevers and low-level training fights has prompted the Kohl government to impose severe restrictions on the latter and a fifty-percent cut in the former.[8]

Former German chancellor Helmut Schmidt, once a stalwart of the transatlantic military partnership during the 1960s and 1970s, has since concluded:

> Dependency corrupts and corrupts not only the dependent partners, but also the oversized partner who is making decisions almost single-handedly. Most of the European governments rely too much on American nuclear weapons and most of them neglect their own conventional defense. An improved military equilibrium requires that the military equipment of the French reserve troops be increased. It also requires more British reserve troops. We need to strengthen the conventional usable German air force and to provide more conventional munitions for the German army. Under such qualitatively and quantitatively improved conditions, a partial withdrawal of American troops would not necessarily be a misfortune. The Europeans would be playing a role of their own.[9]

American public and congressional sentiment for a reassessment of the U.S. force presence in Europe also appears to be mounting. Perceptions of free-riding allies unwilling to bear their fair share of the common defense burden, rising anger over what is seen as unfair allied trade practices, and understandable concern over runaway federal deficits have contributed to a new sense that the United States is being wrongfully used by its allies, some of whom it defended in World War II and whose postwar recovery and subsequent prosperity were in no small measure (directly or indirectly) financed in the United States.

The mood in the Congress on the matter of defense burden sharing was captured in the June 1988 draft *Report of the Senate Committee on Appropriations on the Department of Defense Appropriation Bill, 1989:*

> The Committee believes that U.S. taxpayers are currently shouldering a disproportionately high percentage of the cost of maintaining security in both

NATO and the Far East. By any measure, the United States is outspending its allies. According to the Secretary of Defense's Report on Allied Contributions to the Common Defense, April 1988, the United States ranks first among the allies in per capita defense spending and defense spending as a percentage of Gross Domestic Product. The United States spends $1,164 on defense for every U.S. citizen, while the Federal Republic of Germany spends $454 for every citizen, and Japan spends only $163 per citizen. The United States spends 6.8 percent of its domestic product for defense, while the Federal Republic of Germany spends 3.1 percent, and Japan ranks last among the allies spending only 1 percent. Further, the United States defense budget supports twice the spending of all other NATO allies combined.

The United States maintains forces permanently ashore in these nations to maintain mutual national security interests. At the end of fiscal year 1987, the Department of Defense supported over 1 million people overseas: 455,954 active duty military, 182,011 civilian employees, and 413,020 dependents. 88 percent of these personnel were stationed in NATO nations, Japan, and South Korea. According to another recent report transmitted by the Secretary of Defense, in 1987 it cost the Department of Defense over $34.5 billion to maintain this presence. Over $13 billion of these funds were lost to the U.S. economy and accounted for 8 percent of the U.S. balance of payments deficit in 1987.

The Committee is concerned that the Department of Defense current burdensharing efforts have been paled by additional costs caused by devaluation of the dollar. Since 1986, the additional cost of stationing U.S. forces overseas caused by the devaluation of the dollar has increased from $3,084,781,000 to $6,775,197,000 with an increased cost of approximately $1,500,000,000 in the past year alone. The Committee believes that these costs should be borne by the taxpayers of NATO nations and Japan, who directly benefit from the security provided by U.S. forces; these additional costs should not be passed on as an additional burden for U.S. taxpayers to carry.

The Committee believes that it is time to take tangible action to more fairly distribute the burden of defense spending. Given the very real pressures caused by the budget deficit and the current trade imbalance with these same allied nations, it is not reasonable to expect U.S. taxpayers to continue to finance such a large percentage of the cost of common defense.[10]

Congressional sentiment for pulling troops out of Europe amounts to more than just talk. In March 1989, Congresswoman Patricia Schroeder, a liberal Democrat from Colorado, and Congressman Andy Ireland, a conservative Republican from Florida, announced their intention to offer an amendment to the fiscal 1990 military procurement bill mandating a unilateral U.S. force cut of 25,000 troops, equal to the number (they claim) associated with the intermediate nuclear force (INF) missile deployments now being eliminated under the provisions of the 1987 INF treaty. It will be difficult to marshal convincing arguments against the Schroeder-Ireland amendment. The proposed reduction is modest, certainly in comparison to Gorbachev's announced uniltateral reductions in Soviet forces in Europe, and pegging the number to manpower slots associated with the INF deployments suggests that passage of the amendment would not materially affect NATO's conventional defenses. Yet the amendment may be a stalking horse for far larger cuts down the road. It is frustration with allied defense performance rather than a desire for technical adjustments in the U.S. force presence in Europe that underlies the amendment. Congressman Ireland has characterized the U.S. investment in Europe's defense as "a virtual entitlement program" for the NATO allies "supplied courtesy of the American taxpayer," adding that "American tax dollars are spent to defend our allies who use the money they save to clobber us in trade wars."[11]

Congressional irritation with European allies, hardly mellowed by France's denial of overflight rights to Libya-bound U.S. F-111s in 1986, Spain's expulsion of U.S. F-16 squadrons in 1988, the probable future loss of U.S. bases in Greece, and a politically desperate Kohl government's abandonment of its pledge to support modernization of NATO's battlefield nuclear weapons (indeed, Bonn's insistence that the United States negotiate their reduction irrespective of the course of East-West negotiations on conventional arms), is shared increasingly by other decision makers. One of the most striking developments within the alliance in recent years—and one that bodes ill for prospects for preserving the current measure of U.S. military power in Europe—has been a growing division within the traditionally Eurocentric American foreign policy establishment over the strategic wisdom and moral validity of continuing to maintain a large force presence in Europe.

Until the 1980s, calls for pulling some or all U.S. troops out of Europe came almost exclusively from liberals, libertarians, and midwestern and Rocky Mountain isolationists, some of whom opposed U.S. admission to NATO in 1949 as unwise. The Mansfield resolutions and amendments of the 1960s and 1970s drew upon this sentiment.

More recently, however, prominent members of America's foreign policy elite have joined the ranks of those who favor a reduction in America's present investment in Europe's defense. Henry Kissinger, condemning Europe's excessive reliance on nuclear deterrence at the expense of needed improvements in conventional defenses, has talked of "a gradual withdrawal of a substantial proportion, perhaps up to one-half, of our present ground forces" in Europe.[12] Zbigniew Brzezinski, bemoaning Europe's continuing status as "an American military protectorate some thirty years after Western Europe's economic recovery" from World War II and wishing to build up U.S. military strength for Persian Gulf contingencies, has called for a withdrawal of up to 100,000 U.S. troops.[13] Neoconservative commentator Irving Kristol, arguing that "NATO subverts Western Europe's will to resist and interferes with America's responsibilities as a global power," has proposed a U.S. "withdrawal from that commitment and the reconstitution of NATO as an all-European organization that would boost the morale of West European nations by affirming their independence and national identity."[14]

A no less radical call for an American withdrawal from NATO comes from Melvyn Krauss in a 1986 book, *How NATO Weakens the West.* Krauss argues that "Europe's detente-as-defense strategy has made U.S. membership in NATO inconsistent with its containment objectives" and concludes that "the military weakness NATO has imposed on the Europeans . . . is in neither Europe's long-term interest nor that of the United States."[15] Approaching America's European commitment from a strategic perspective, Eliot Cohen points to "Europe's relative decline as a strategic stake" for America, and he concludes that "Europe has become . . . a strategic liability."[16] Though historian Paul Kennedy, in his widely discussed 1987 best-seller, *The Rise and Fall of the Great Powers,* believes that Europe is essential to American security, he contends that the United States suffers an acute case of "imperial overstretch"—a dangerous disparity between its economic wealth-generating capacity and its ability to service its heavy global military obligations—that at some point could dictate a major reduction in U.S. defense commitments overseas.[17] Earl Ravenal asserts that "the United States sooner or later must abandon containment and drastically reduce its security commitments." As part of that strategy, he urges "an end of the American undertaking to defend Europe," which he characterizes as "our most expensive commitment by any measure—troops, dollars or risks."[18] David P. Calleo, taking a similar view in his *Beyond American Hegemony,* calls for a devolution of the responsibility for Europe's defense on the shoulders of the European allies.[19] And no less a NATO stalwart than Andrew J. Goodpaster, former Supreme Allied Commander Europe (SACEUR) has proposed bringing half of U.S. forces in Europe back home by the mid-1990s.[20]

A final factor bearing on the fate of the U.S. military presence in Europe is the possibility that a president of the United States would either push for a substantial unilateral contraction in U.S. forces deployed in Europe or at least not vigorously oppose congressional attempts to impose one. Presidential attitudes on this matter are crucial because of the White House's constitutional prerogatives. But the mere fact that all presidents since 1949 have vigorously opposed congressionally inspired unilateral U.S. force reductions in Europe provides no basis for confidence that all future presidents can be counted upon to do the same.

One of the reasons that past legislative initiatives to compel unilateral withdrawals have failed without exception to pass either the Senate or the House, to say nothing of both, is the knowledge that such legislation, even if it cleared both chambers, would face an almost certain presidential veto (which would require a two-thirds majority of senators and congressmen to override). The outcome would be dramatically different in a setting in which the president employed the full weight of his office to support such legislation.

To be sure, neither major party nominee for the presidency in 1988 indicated a view on the matter fundamentally different from presidents past. However, times change, and presidential views on substantive issues have been known to change, especially in response to strong budgetary and political pressures. American public and congressional support for continued membership in NATO remains remarkably strong, as it does for maintaining some kind of force presence in Europe. This support, however, cannot be—and never has been—taken as support for a specific U.S. troop strength in Europe.

Some Parting Thoughts

In 1951 then SACEUR, General Dwight D. Eisenhower, observed to a friend:

> Europe must, as a whole, provide in the long run for its own defense. The U.S. can move in and, by its psychological, intellectual, and material leadership, help to produce arms, units, and the confidence that will allow Europe to solve its problem. In the long run, it is not possible—and most certainly not desirable—that Europe should be an occupied territory defended by legions brought in from abroad, somewhat in the fashion that Rome's territories vainly sought security many hundred years ago.[21]

Almost forty years later there are still as many U.S. troops in Europe as there were in 1951. But NATO can hardly be regarded as a failure. On the contrary, NATO is if anything the victim of its own success. It has succeeded in deterring Soviet aggression in Europe for four decades. Moreover, a successfully contained and now economically desperate Soviet Union appears genuinely interested in substantially dismantling the military components of the cold war in Europe. If this is indeed the case, a lot of fundamental new thinking is required on the NATO side of the rusting iron curtain. Among other things, the need for a large and costly U.S. military presence in Europe deserves reassessment. Even if that presence were politically and budgetarily sustainable, its strategic validity is being undermined by what seems increasingly to be a major reduction in the Soviet military threat that prompted NATO's creation. For the first time, budgetarily unavoidable but otherwise undesirable (at least in the eyes of NATO's old guard) reductions in the U.S. military presence in Europe may now be both strategically and operationally permissible.

Alliances thrive on clear and present external danger. The new Soviet leadership seems to have concluded not only that NATO poses no real military threat to the Warsaw Pact but also that its own forces in Europe can be seen to pose such a threat to NATO. Fortuitously, if coincidentally, Soviet force reduction and other tension-lessening initiatives come at the very time when both the United States and its European allies also seem to be tiring of the burdens imposed by continued heavy investment in Western Europe's defense.

Notes

1. Richard Halloran, "Europe Called Main U.S. Arms Cost," *New York Times,* July 20, 1984. Also see Earl C. Ravenal, *Defining Defense: The 1985 Military Budget* (Washington, D.C.: Cato Institute, 1985), pp. 15–21; and Anthony H. Cordesman, *NATO's Central Region Forces* (New York: Jane's Publishing, 1988), pp. 224–25.

2. For a comprehensive discussion of the Soviet force cuts, see Jack Mendelsohn, "Gorbachev's Preemptive Concession," *Arms Control Today* (March 1989): 10–15.

3. See Phillip A. Karber, "The Military Impact of the Gorbachev Reductions," *Armed Forces Journal* (January 1989): 54–64.

4. Douglas Clarke "NATO and Warsaw Pact Opening Positions in the Conventional Arms Negotiations," *Report on the USSR* (Radio Liberty), March 24, 1989, pp. 12–14.

5. Richard H.P. Sia, "Cheney Considers Reduction of Forces," *Baltimore Sun,* April 13, 1989.

6. George C. Wilson, "U.S. Answer to Soviet Military Cuts Weighed," *Washington Post,* January 8, 1989.

7. *Discriminate Deterrence: Report of the Commission on Integrated Long-Term Strategy* (Washington, D.C.: U.S. Government Printing Office, January 1988).

8. Rolf Soderland, "West German Cut in Maneuvers Only Hints at Changes to Come," *Armed Forces Journal* (January 1989): 33.

9. Helmut Schmidt, "Saving the Western Alliance," *New York Review of Books,* May 31, 1984, p. 25.

10. (Draft) *Report of the U.S. Senate Committee on Appropriations on the Department of Defense Appropriation Bill for Fiscal Year 1989* (Washington, D.C.: Committee Print, June 22, 1988).

11. Andy Ireland, "A Hawk Says: Pull Our Troops Out," *New York Times,* March 7, 1989.

12. Henry Kissinger, "A Plan to Reshape NATO," *Time,* April 5, 1984, p. 24.

13. Zbigniew Brzezinski, *Game Plan: How to Conduct the U.S.-Soviet Contest* (Boston: Atlantic Monthly Press, 1986), pp. 181, 196–97.

14. Irving Kristol, "Should America Quit NATO?" *Time,* April 5, 1984, p. 24.

15. Melvyn Krauss, *How NATO Weakens the West* (New York: Simon and Schuster, 1986), p. 46.

16. Eliot Cohen, "Do We Still Need Europe?" *Commentary* (January 1986): 34.

17. Paul Kennedy, *The Rise and Fall of the Great Powers: Economic Change and Military Conflict from 1500 to 2000* (New York: Random House, 1987).

18. Earl Ravenal, "The Case for a Withdrawal of Our Forces," *New York Times Magazine,* March 6, 1983, pp. 60, 61.

19. David P. Calleo, *Beyond American Hegemony: The Future of the Western Alliance* (New York: Basic Books, 1987).

20. Don Oberdorfer, "U.S. Urged to Cut Force by One-Half in Europe," *Washington Post,* April 6, 1989.

21. Letter to Swede Hazlett, quoted in Blanche Wiesen Cook, *The Declassified Eisenhower: A Divided Legacy of Peace and Political Warfare* (New York: Penguin Books, 1984), p. 106.

9

Conventional Force Reductions in Europe: In Pursuit of Stability

Jed C. Snyder

The European Context for Conventional Force Reductions

For much of the postwar period, arms control initiatives by the superpowers and their allies have focused principally on reducing the dangers of the East-West nuclear competition, referred to by Albert Wohlstetter as the "balance of terror." U.S. and Soviet perceptions of that balance are a key variable in gauging the state of European security. A guarantee by the United States (and its allies) to underwrite that security by extending the deterrent of the U.S. nuclear umbrella to Europe has insured against the possibility of aggression by the Warsaw Pact.

The American nuclear guarantee to Europe is designed to deter the full range of Soviet aggressive options, from the use of conventional forces through intermediate- and intercontinental-range nuclear weapons, by providing a credible capability to respond to Soviet actions in kind at every level of force. The deterrent power of the nuclear promise rests principally in the adversary's calculation that nuclear weapons could be used in response to any attack. The credibility of the Western nuclear threat must be uniform along the spectrum of Soviet attack options.

The Conventional-Nuclear Link

The apocalyptic scenarios of superpower conflict generally center on a nuclear exchange in Europe, presumably resulting from the inability of NATO's forces to repel a conventional assault by the Warsaw Pact across the inter-German border, in short, a failure of deterrence in Europe. The guarantee that NATO would introduce nuclear weapons into the conflict functions, it is hoped, to preclude Warsaw Pact forces from initiating conflict at any level.

The author gratefully acknowledges the very constructive comments by Diego Ruiz-Palmer, Jeffrey Record, and several anonymous officials of the U.S. government who have reviewed this chapter.

The assumption that NATO could not tolerate a conventional failure in Europe presumably serves to deter the Soviet Union and its allies from engaging in a process where the dangers of escalation would (in the Soviet calculus) deter Warsaw Pact aggression of any kind.

The factors that could contribute to a failure of conventional deterrence in Europe were rarely examined until recently. Such faith had been placed in the deterrent capacity of atomic weapons that little serious analytical attention was paid to the character of the conventional balance in Europe. Rather, the level of force was emphasized, by calculating a range of conflict scenarios at various levels of engagement. Significantly, it is generally understood that the Warsaw Pact will retain at least a quantitative advantage in Europe at both the conventional and theater nuclear levels.

NATO's refusal to match Soviet conventional strength in Europe is an enduring geopolitical reality. For much of the postwar period, the U.S. nuclear guarantee served to mask the unwillingness of the European allies to increase their conventional posture substantially. NATO planners postulated that the balance of nuclear weapons (on both sides) would govern whether an East-West conflict would be initiated. In short, it was assumed that neither a NATO nor a Warsaw Pact commander could make his strategic calculations on the basis of the conventional balance alone. Yet it would be the failure of conventional forces to hold the Warsaw Pact in check that would, in all likelihood, begin the process whereby the nuclear forces of the United States and the Soviet Union could be engaged.

With the achievement by the Soviet Union of strategic nuclear parity in the early 1970s, confidence in the capability of the American nuclear umbrella to deter a Warsaw Pact conventional attack against NATO forces began to wither. A series of events focused the attention of the Western nations on addressing NATO's conventional deficiencies. These included an impressive quantitative buildup and qualitative improvement of Warsaw Pact conventional forces facing NATO in Western Europe, and they served to reinforce a desire by Western governments to address seriously whether the complex task of arriving at an East-West conventional reductions regime could be accomplished.

After fifteen years of discussions the Mutual and Balanced Force Reduction (MBFR) talks in Vienna ended with virtually no progress achieved on reducing the size of opposing conventional forces in Central Europe. Indeed, the parties to these discussions acknowledged that it had not been possible even to reach agreement on the level of forces deployed by both sides.

With the signing of the Treaty Eliminating Intermediate–Range and Short–Range Nuclear Forces (INF) in December 1987, a sense of greater urgency now accompanied the twin tasks of bolstering the alliance's conventional capabilities (regarded by most observers as politically and economically quixotic) and designing an arms control regime to reduce the size of the opposing forces. Increasingly these two objectives appeared to be mutually exclusive. The INF imbroglio illustrated the difficulty of pursuing arms control and modernization in tandem. Despite NATO's original pledge to pursue each of the two tracks of deployment and arms control with equal vigor, political reality prevented such an approach. Inevitably the requirements of one policy competed with (and often prevented) the successful implementation of the other.[1] The INF weapons were deployed, but the circumstances of their removal seemed to confirm the maxim that political pressures to accommodate the public's attraction for arms control will probably doom a parallel effort to modernize forces.

Certainly any reasonable reading of NATO's history dictated extreme skepticism that the allied governments could be persuaded to enhance conventional forces even if accompanied by an arms control palliative. It seemed foolish to expect that the alliance would seriously entertain proposals to bolster its ground and air units in Europe. Indeed, NATO's inability (or unwillingness) to reinforce its conventional posture in Europe became axiomatic and central to a range of subsequent policy decisions and choices.

Canonical alliance statements and communiqués notwithstanding, the Western governments have effectively proclaimed the impossibility of substantially altering the conventional balance in NATO's favor through quantitative or qualitative Western force improvements. A series of alliance-wide cooperative force modernization initiatives withered as key national governments refused to contribute additional funds or develop public support among their electorates for greater national commitments to defense spending. From the Long-Term Defense Program (LTDP) adopted in the late 1970's to NATO's current Conventional Defense Improvement program (CDI), the alliance has failed to implement quantitative improvements to its conventional force posture, although qualitative measures have been instituted. The net result is that nuclear weapons will continue to bear the greater burden of deterrence in Europe.

Mikhail Gorbachev has introduced a new variable into the European security equation. There is great debate over the effect that perestroika will have on Soviet foreign policy and whether the changes Gorbachev promises will be more stylistic than substantive. In particular, it remains unclear how and whether Moscow's claims of a shift in Soviet military doctrine toward a more "defensive" posture designed to meet requirements of "reasonable sufficiency" will be effected.

In his landmark December 1988 address to the United Nations, Gorbachev pledged to restructure Soviet military forces worldwide and to make radical cuts in air and ground units deployed in Europe and Asia. Compelling evidence of fundamental changes in Soviet military posture has not yet surfaced, but it is clear that the rhetorical power of promised reforms has already had a considerable effect on alliance policy and is likely to affect a range of NATO decisions on force modernization and arms control planning.

For the first time in the postwar period, a Soviet leader has proposed truly massive reductions in the levels of both Soviet and non-Soviet Warsaw Pact conventional forces. This is perhaps the first tangible (albeit tentative) evidence that Soviet policy toward the Western alliance is at least in transition, if not in the early stages of a fundamental transformation. Nevertheless, both the Central Intelligence Agency and the Defense Intelligence Agency have estimated 3 percent real growth in Soviet defense spending during 1988.[2] The synergistic effect of Gorbachev's call for a "common European home," his pledge to reduce Soviet defense spending by more than 14 percent, and dramatic proposals for conventional and nuclear force reductions have already been politically dramatic. Gorbachev's proposals have emasculated alliance plans to modernize both conventional and theater nuclear forces.

As the May 1989 NATO Summit meeting illustrated, the political and strategic terms of reference for alliance planning and policy have changed. Conventional force issues have already replaced the INF controversy as the nucleus of the East-West dialogue. The negotiations on Conventional Armed Forces in Europe (CFE), inaugurated in March 1989, will dominate the East-West and West-West dialogue for the next several years as NATO struggles to respond to both Western public insistence that Gorbachev's arms control initiatives be "seriously" addressed, while simultaneously struggling to implement the much-heralded "Comprehensive Concept of Arms Control and Disarmament" adopted at the May Brussels Summit.

It is within this climate that the West must begin to formulate a strategic approach to European security and, most particularly, attend to the problem of crafting a longer-term strategy designed to preserve some semblance of conventional force sufficiency in Europe.

A Sketch of the Current CFE Proposals

NATO's initial proposal, tabled in March 1989 in Vienna, focused on the three weapons categories where Warsaw Pact advantages were regarded as of most concern: main battle tanks, artillery, and armored troop carriers (ATC).[3] The NATO position proposed five guidelines governing the deployment of conventional forces in Europe. The Western rationale is to accomplish substantial reductions of systems that are highly mobile or generate high rates of fire. In addition, the Western CFE proposals are designed to limit the capability of any one nation to dominate the order of battle on either side.

Finally, NATO was determined to focus on both the level of deployed armaments and the state of military readiness in those regions where the concentration of force is greatest, in addition to prohibiting redeployment of forces from one region to another. This requires establishing a series of connected sublimits covering ground forces in the theater along with additional limits on all active units.[4]

The first guideline established overall levels for each of the three weapons categories in the Atlantic to the Urals (ATTU) region, of which NATO and the Warsaw Pact could each retain 50 percent: 40,000 main battle tanks, 33,000 artillery pieces, and 56,000 ATC.

The second guideline proposed that no single nation could field more than 30 percent of the total weapons deployed. This would limit each nation to no more than 12,000 main battle tanks, 10,000 artillery pieces, and 16,800 ATC.

The third guideline focused on stationed forces, units deployed by alliance members outside their national territory in active units. This measure is designed principally to limit and reduce the percentage of forces contributed by the Soviet Union to the Warsaw Pact's capability. This would effectively restrict each country from deploying more than 3,200 main battle tanks, 1,700 artillery pieces, and 6,000 ATC outside their own territory.

The fourth guideline establishes a series of four geographic zones, ranging in territorial scope downward from the entire ATTU region—encompassing eleven of the sixteen Soviet military districts, the territory of the Warsaw Treaty Organization (WTO) nations, and the European NATO countries—as the first zone, to three smaller zones, the last of which is the critical Central Region area encompassing Belgium, the Federal Republic of Germany (FRG), Luxembourg, and the Netherlands on the NATO side and Czechoslovakia, the German Democratic Republic, and Poland on the WTO side. In this last (and smallest) zone, each alliance would be limited to 8,000 main battle tanks, 4,500 artillery pieces, and 11,000 ATC. NATO and the WTO are both free to determine how to allocate forces within the zones among the nations, although rigid guidelines on stationing would restrict both sides from moving large numbers of forces at will.

The fifth guideline proposes an annual exchange of data on forces for both the NATO and WTO alliances, disaggregated down to the battalion level. It stipulates that any structural changes in combat units above the battalion level (including increases in personnel strength) will be reported.

Subsequent to the tabling of these proposals, President George Bush announced further reduction proposals at the NATO Summit meeting in Brussels in May 1989. There were three components to these proposals: (1) NATO and WTO negotiators would register their agreement on weapons ceilings already proposed in Vienna in March 1989, (2) there would be a 15 percent reduction to equal ceilings, in current NATO levels of helicopters and land-based combat aircraft in the ATTU zone, and (3) there would be a 20 percent reduction in U.S. stationed combat forces in Europe (the United States currently deploys roughly 150,000 combat troops, so this could represent a reduction of 30,000 U.S. personnel) and a resulting ceiling of 275,000 on U.S. and Soviet stationed ground and air force personnel in the ATTU zone. This would require the Soviet Union to reduce its stationed forces in

Eastern Europe by some 325,000.[5] The Bush proposals were offered in dramatic fashion, including the assertion that the reductions could be agreed to within 6 to 12 months and implemented by 1992–1993.

The Warsaw Pact proposals were announced in July 1988, expanded during Mikhail Gorbachev's December 1988 U.N. address, and formally tabled in Vienna in March 1989. The proposal's structure repeats the three-stage framework offered earlier.

The first stage (to be implemented between 1991 and 1994) would reduce the levels of combat aircraft, tanks, combat helicopters, armored combat vehicles and armored personnel carriers, and artillery pieces to equal alliance ceilings, 10 to 15 percent lower than current levels. Subsequently the WTO has proposed specific ceilings of 20,000 tanks, 28,000 armored troup carriers, and 24,000 artillery pieces. In addition, new proposed ceilings of 1,500 tactical strike aircraft, 1,700 combat helicopters, and 1.35 million personnel for each side were proposed, all to be accomplished by 1997. In addition, the WTO proposed "surprise attack prevention measures," including zones of "reduced levels of armaments" along the inter-German border. The second stage of the Gorbachev reductions (to be implemented by 1997) proposed equal reduction of some 25 percent of total armed forces strength (roughly 500,000 personnel). In the final stage (to be accomplished by 2000) the forces of both alliances would be reduced further and restructured to achieve "a strictly defensive character." Furthermore, ceilings on categories not covered in the earlier phases would be implemented. Force modernization would also be constrained. Finally, the Soviet proposal implies that all short–range nuclear forces (SNF) would be removed.

Subsequent refinements to the Soviet proposals yielded the following goals: a global reduction of 500,000 in Soviet forces by 1991; a reduction of Soviet forces in the ATTU region of 10,000 tanks, 8,500 artillery pieces, and 800 combat aircraft; a reduction of six Soviet tank divisions (2,000 tanks) in Eastern Europe (four to be withdrawn from East Germany, one from Czechoslovakia, and one from Hungary); a withdrawal of 3,000 tanks from the remaining twenty-two Soviet divisions in Eastern Europe; and removal of the remaining 5,000 tanks from the western military districts.

Assessing the Conventional Balance in Europe

Few other issues incite the passions of strategists more effectively than the question of how to measure the conventional balance in Europe. Schools of thought have developed to differentiate competing approaches to this issue. Committed students of the art of net assessment have watched such a debate unfold over the last several years in the respected journal *International Security*.[6]

Weighing the Contributing Factors

Although sharp differences remain among those who attempt to draw conclusions about the numerical asymmetries in NATO–Warsaw Pact forces, a consensus has developed that many previous non–governmental assessments have relied excessively on "static indicators" of military strength in reaching determinations about wartime performance. These analyses were generally "bean counts," relying almost entirely on numerical comparisons of comparable weapons and equipment. Conclusions regarding the prospects for victory or defeat were based principally on judgments of numerical advantage, calculations of force–to–space ratios, and inferiority in key weapons classes.

Calculating the balance, however, is not simply an academic exercise, and such net assessments will grow in importance as both NATO and the Warsaw Pact reduce their theater forces in Europe. As the aggregate air and ground (and possibly naval) forces are cut, the importance of nonnumerical factors will increase. Further, enlightened bean counting will continue to be important in macroassessments since decisions on how to prioritize force reductions will be necessarily affected by evaluations of the balance. Force ratios will be carefully scrutinized to determine whether proposed cuts in key weapons systems or equipment will increase overall vulnerability.

As the debate over how to measure capability continues, greater emphasis will be placed on such qualitative factors as reinforcement capability, mobilization requirements, training, technological trends, logistics, doctrine, and political reliability. All of these factors introduce uncertainty into the calculations of military planners and therefore could affect the outcome of a battle, in particular, a conventional battle.

The personnel mix of the NATO and Warsaw Pact forces provides an example of how critically qualitative factors can affect judgments about capability. Over the last two decades, the NATO nations have in the aggregate decreased the percentage of active-duty units deployed in the Central Region of Europe, choosing instead to rely more heavily on reservists and therefore on time-consuming mobilization in the event of a crisis. The Warsaw Pact, in contrast, has increased its commitment of active forces in this region. Thus, in wartime, NATO could be more dependent on the mobilization of reserve units than would the Warsaw Pact.[7] This reliance would complicate reinforcement planning for the alliance and could affect its ability to defend forward positions early in an engagement.[8]

Reaching a conclusion about comparative advantage solely on the basis of mobilization time, however, ignores another qualitative factor: warning and response. Should NATO react quickly to signals of an impending Soviet attack, the time required to mobilize reserves could be less significant to the outcome. Moreover, there is legitimate debate about how effectively the NATO alert system would operate and how rapidly the alliance would recognize and react to indications of imminent hostilities.[9] Two factors are critical in this regard. First, all of NATO's assets are drawn from the national armed forces of the contributing nations. There is no absolute governing supranational authority in peacetime. In the event that one of the key contributing nations hesitates to transfer national military authority to the NATO Supreme Allied Commander (SACEUR), the alert and mobilization system would ს: immédiately and adversely affected. These hobbling political factors do not constrain Soviet forces to nearly the same extent. First, all WTO commanders are Soviet officers (unlike the alliance practice of distributing senior command billets to allied officers), and Soviet authority over WTO forces in peacetime is unquestioned. A central, permanent supranational authority determines the level and speed of a fully integrated military response. It should be noted that centralized control within the WTO command structure is no longer taken for granted, however. Analysts of the southern tier Warsaw Pact nations have great doubts about the willingness of Hungary and Rumania, for example, to contribute forces to a Warsaw Pact invasion force.[10]

In sum, military balance calculations increasingly will be affected by subjective assessments of intangible but potentially critical factors, which at lower levels of force (such as those envisioned in the CFE framework) could affect both judgments about the wisdom of striking first and the prognosis for success.

NATO–Warsaw Pact Comparisons

Although qualitative factors are critical, numercial comparisons are necessary to establish a data base from which judgments about quantitative advantage can be determined. These in turn would be useful as a guide to establishing milestones in conventional force negotiations. In addition, quantitative comparisons of in-place forces are useful in evaluating the feasibility of a Warsaw Pact standing-start attack, where there would be little or no mobilization. It is this concern to avoid a surprise attack that has motivated much of the East-West confidence–and–security–building measures (CSBMs) initiatives over the last several years.

There are considerable discrepancies between the NATO assessment of the European conventional balance and the calculations made by the Warsaw Pact. For comparison purposes, table 9–1 summarizes NATO and Warsaw Pact estimates of the balance, focusing on six broad categories of weapons and personnel. The two sources used for this comparison are generally regarded as the most authoritative official documents for both NATO and Warsaw Pact deployments. The NATO material is current as of January 1988. The Soviet-supplied figures are current as of July 1988. The estimate covers the ATTU region, the agreed-upon zone of reductions for the CFE negotiations.

Table 9–1
NATO and Warsaw Pact Official Force Estimates for Europe

	Force Deployments for NATO		Force Deployments for Warsaw Pact	
	NATO *Estimates*	WTO *Estimates*	NATO *Estimates*	WTO *Estimates*
Main battle tanks	22,220	30,690	51,500	59,470
Artillery[a]	17,330	57,060	43,400	71,560
Armored troop carriers and infantry fighting vehicles	47,640	46,900	89,100	70,330
Aircraft	4,510	7,130	8,250	7,875
Combat helicopters	2,600	5,270	3,700	2,785
Total military personnel (thousands)	2,215	3,660	3,090	3,575

Sources: NATO: *Conventional Forces in Europe: The Facts* (Brussels: NATO Headquarters, NATO Press Service, January 1988). Warsaw Treaty Organization: *Warsaw Treaty Organization and North Atlantic Treaty Organization: Correlation of Forces in Europe* (Moscow: Military Publishing House, Novosti Press Agency, 1989).
[a] The Soviets include anti–tank guns and small caliber systems (i.e., below 100mm), which NATO excludes from its count.

The differences in Warsaw Pact and NATO estimates are significant and reflect divergent approaches to estimating force levels, due principally to differences in counting rules for specific weapons systems. These differences may become a significant obstacle to an early accord, since complex counting formulas (a contentious issue among the NATO allies) will be required to reach agreement where the disparity in estimates is greatest.

In addition, Soviet methodology in arriving at force balances differs markedly from that employed by Western planners. Generally Soviet planners assume a much wider range of conflict scenarios and a much richer set of assumptions about how the qualitative factors would affect the balance. The effect of training, doctrine, and the extent of surprise contribute to Soviet calculations. Uncertainty about how the Soviets calculate the quantitative balance is compounded because military planners have been careful not to reveal publicly the precise force ratios they use in reaching combat net assessments.

Further, Soviet planners have developed an elaborate system of subdividing the globe (including the European region) into theaters of strategic military action (TVDs) in order to maximize the flexibility of their forces in meeting a range of scenarios. Soviet conceptions of "strategic directions" of attack, for example, could significantly affect Western assumptions about how the Soviets would allocate forces within the European theater.[11] While command-control specialists debate the military operational significance of the TVD concept, it does suggest a more sophisticated approach to military planning than has generally been ascribed to Soviet military thought in the past.[12]

Table 9–1 summarizes total European deployed forces for NATO and the Warsaw Pact in order to provide a context for a comparative assessment. The principal focus of concern for NATO in a crisis, however, would be the Central Region. NATO nations contributing forces to the Central Front are the United States, West Germany, Belgium, Canada, Denmark, France, the Netherlands, and Great Britain. WTO forces are those of the Soviet Union, the German Democratic Republic, Czechoslovakia, and Poland. Table 9–2 lists WTO Category I divisions (those at the highest level of Warsaw Pact force readiness) available for the Central Region; table 9–3 lists NATO divisions available for a Central Region conflict; and table 9–4 estimates the size of fully mobilized forces for both NATO and the Warsaw Pact.

Table 9–2
Warsaw Pact Divisions in the Central Region

Soviet Divisions	Peacetime Location[b]	Strength	Mix[a]
Soviet forces in USSR {	Baltic MD	2	AIR
	Belorussian MD	2	1 MRD, 1 AIR
	Carpathian MD	1	1 TK
	Moscow MD	1	1 AIR
Soviet forces in East Germany		19	11 TK, 8 MRD
Soviet forces in Czechoslovakia		5	2 TK, 3 MRD
Soviet forces in Poland		2	2 TK
Total Soviet divisions		32	16 TK, 12 MRD, 4 AIR
East German forces		6	2 TK, 4 MRD
Czechoslovakian forces		6	3 TK, 3 MRD
Polish forces		8	5 TK, 3 MRD
Total Warsaw Pact divisions		52	26 TK, 22 MRD, 4 AIR

Sources: William P. Mako, *U.S. Ground Forces and the Defense of Central Europe* (Washington, D.C.: Brookings Institution, 1983); *U.S. Ground Forces and the Conventional Balance in Europe* (Washington, D.C.: U.S. Congressional Budget Office, 1988).

Note: Soviet divisions are classified in three categories, depending on their strength and readiness status. This table lists only Category I divisions—those evaluated by NATO as fully equipped and fully manned within twenty-four hours.

[a] The Warsaw Pact deploys three types of divisions: tank (TK), motorized rifle (MRD), and airborne (AIR).

[b] MD = military district. The Soviet Union is divided into sixteen military districts for purposes of administration, training and mobilization.

Table 9–3
NATO Divisions Available for a Central Region Conflict

	In Place[a]	Active Reinforcements[b]	Reserve Reinforcements[c]	Total
United States	5⅓	10	15	30⅓
West Germany	12	0	2	14
Belgium	⅔	⅔	⅔	2
Canada	⅓	0	0	⅓
Denmark	0	1	0	1
France[d]	3	12	0	15
Netherlands	⅓	1⅔	1⅓	3⅓
Great Britain	2⅔	⅔	⅔	4
Total divisions	24⅓	26	19⅔	70

Source: Adapted from *U.S. Ground Forces and the Conventional Balance in Europe* (Washington, D.C.: Congressional Budget Office, 1988).

[a] A portion of the in-place forces would be prepared to engage Warsaw Pact forces immediately, with the balance available 24–72 hours after NATO mobilization commences.

[b] The availability of these forces varies depending on national mobilization plans but are generally expected to be in place within one week. Six of the U.S. active reinforcement divisions are expected to arrive in Europe within ten days, with the remainder following over a period of two weeks. Questions have been raised, however, about the logistical difficulties inherent in such a massive reinforcement operation, aggravated by the paucity of U.S. heavy lift assets for such an operation.

[c] European reserve units are expected to be in place, beginning seven days after mobilization (M + 7). The final U.S. reserve units would not arrive until approximately eleven weeks after mobilization commences.

[d] French armed forces have not been committed to NATO since President de Gaulle's decision in 1966 to withdraw France from the alliance's military framework. A series of bilateral agreements between France and NATO outline the conditions under which French forces would participate in a NATO operation.

Although one cannot produce precise time schedules of either NATO or Warsaw Pact mobilization capabilities, the resource pool from which both alliances would draw its forces is known with some precision. Soviet forces would come principally from the three western military districts (MDs): Baltic, Belorussian and Carpathian. Additional forces could be brought to bear from the Kiev, Odessa, and Leningrad districts. The three MDs supporting the Central Strategic Reserve (Moscow, Urals, and Volga) would add to the mobilization base of the MDs in European Russia. It has been estimated that after a sixty-day mobilization, the nine MDs could provide more than ninety-six divisions.[13] Over the past decade, the Soviets have significantly bolstered their reserve complement, adding more than twelve divisions.[14]

Table 9–4
NATO–Warsaw Pact Balance after Full Mobilization

	NATO Divisions		Warsaw Pact Divisions
United States	30⅓	Soviet Union	90
West Germany	15⅓	East Germany	6
France	15	Czechoslovakia	10
Great Britain	3⅔	Poland	13⅔
Belgium	2		
Netherlands	3⅓		
Canada	⅓		
Total mobilized divisions	70		119⅔

Source: *U.S. Ground Forces and the Conventional Balance in Europe* (Washington, D.C. Congressional Budget Office, 1988).

Note: A condition of full mobilization for both NATO and the Warsaw Pact would not occur until after at least thirty days beyond the initiation.

On the NATO side, Europe's dependence on early reinforcement by American ground forces deployed by air from the continental U.S. (CONUS) has actually grown over time.[15] If one is impressed with declarations by previous SACEURs (and the results of a series of NATO–Warsaw Pact conflict simulations) concluding that NATO's in-theater ground units are so insufficient to repel a Soviet conventional attack that early nuclear release is probable (perhaps as early as D–day plus 10), then the increased allied dependence on early insertion of U.S. ground reinforcements is cause for alarm.

Unless the European allies are able to increase their contribution of ground forces, NATO's reinforcement disadvantage will grow, particularly because U.S. budgetary pressures will likely force a reduction in both the European-deployed and CONUS-based American units as well as cuts in planned air– and sea–lift capabilities. Should NATO be able to increase the European share of early (D + 1–5) ground reinforcements, U.S. reinforcement priorities could shift to accelerating the number of air wing deployments to Europe early enough in the mobilization process to benefit the theater air balance, thus allowing U.S. ground troops to arrive later. This could enable American forces to function essentially as an operational reserve for European ground units.

Responding to adverse demographic trends in Europe that will substantially reduce available manpower over the next two decades, a number of proposals have been offered designed to result in a radical shift in the division of labor between the European and American forces. In a recent issue of *Foreign Affairs,* a former U.S. army chief of staff, General Edward C. Meyer, and

Table 9–5
NATO–Warsaw Pact Force Ratios for the Central Region

	Estimated WTO Assets	Estimated NATO Assets	Force Ratio
Main battle tanks	19,700	7,100	2.77:1
Infantry fighting vehicles	10,700	4,800	2.22:1
Tube artillery	8,200	2,100	3.90:1
Armored personnel carriers	13,400	10,600	1.26:1
Heavy mortars and multiple rocket launchers	4,000	1,300	3.07:1
Air defense guns	3,900	1,300	3.07:1
Surface-to-air missiles	3,200	1,300	3.00:1
Attack helicopters	900	500	2.46:1
Combat aircraft	3,000	1,400	2.14:1
In-place divisions	36	24⅔	1.50:1
Armor division equivalents [a]	25	22	1.10:1

Sources: *The Military Balance, 1987–1988, 1988–1989* (London: International Institute for Strategic Studies); John M. Collins, "NATO–Warsaw Pact Conventional Forces," in *NATO–Warsaw Pact Conventional Force Balance: Papers for U.S. and Soviet Perspectives Workshops* (Washington, D.C.: General Accounting Office, December 1988, report no. GAO/NSIAD-89-23B); and Phillip A. Karber, "The Military Impact of the Gorbachev Reductions," *Armed Forces Journal International* (January 1989).

Note: The Central Region includes the Federal Republic of Germany, Belgium, the Netherlands, Luxembourg, the German Democratic Republic, Poland, and Czechoslovakia.

[a] Armored division equivalents (ADE) are a measure of combat capability developed by the U.S. Army to estimate and compare the performance of heterogeneous forces more precisely.

former State Department official Henry Owen proposed that a greater burden of heavy armor reinforcement be given to the Europeans, allowing the Americans to focus on providing forces that emphasize non–heavy armor technologies, including precision-guided missiles, directed energy weapons, unpiloted aerial and ground vehicles, and the application of low observable technologies to the battlefield.[16]

It is generally accepted that the Warsaw Pact forces enjoy a margin of quantitative superiority over NATO forces in most of the key indicators of static military power. The greatest margins of advantage are in the Central Region, where the bulk of NATO's forward combat elements are concentrated to defend the East-West frontier. In the aggregate, NATO forces are outnumbered by roughly two and a half to one. This figure is not very meaningful, however, until one examines the component force ratios used to arrive at this conclusion. Table 9–5 estimates key NATO–Warsaw Pact force ratios for the Central Region. In each of the eleven categories listed, the Warsaw Pact enjoys some degree of numerical advantage. The asymmetries are most severe in tube artillery, heavy mortars and multiple rocket launchers (MRLs), and surface-to-air missiles (SAMs). The smallest gaps are found in armored personnel carriers (APCs) and armored division equivalents. In the aggregate, the Warsaw Pact advantage appears substantial, regardless of how one defines the terms.

The Soviet conventional advantage in Europe was achieved over more than two decades of a sustained program of investment in military modernization. Ironically, the alliance's preoccupation over the state of the theater nuclear balance was most acute during the height of the Soviet conventional buildup.

CFE's emphasis on the Central European military competition is well placed. Over the last two decades, this region has seen an unprecedented concentration of mechanized, modern weaponry, the vast majority of it contributed by Soviet and non-Soviet Warsaw Pact forces. More than 80 percent of the tank buildup alone in the Central Region is attributable to increases in Soviet inventories. More than 75 percent of the armored infantry vehicle buildup is also due to Soviet modernization. The artillery and MRL inventory has also increased dramatically, with the Soviets responsible for 90 percent of that increase.[17]

The most alarming modernization and quantitative increases in Soviet forces have come in connection with the Western Group of Forces (WGF) in East Germany, where the most modern equipment is deployed to support the most capable Soviet units. The five Soviet WGF armies deploy some 7,000 tanks, predominantly the latest generation T-64 and T-80 models.[18] Of the twenty-six Soviet tank and motorized rifle divisions (MRD) deployed on the territory of its key Warsaw Pact allies, nineteen are located in East Germany, and all are Category I status. The WGF forces would be of the most concern to NATO planners, and therefore any significant reductions in these units would be regarded as serious evidence of Soviet intentions to reduce the potential for a surprise attack.

Force Reductions and the Implications for Stability

The principal concern of alliance military planners is to deploy sufficient forces to deter a Warsaw Pact at any level. Therefore reductions in the forces of either or both sides must not be allowed to increase NATO's vulnerability to an attack but should erode incentives for such action.

Clearly, the reductions Mikhail Gorbachev has proposed would reduce the effectiveness of an unreinforced attack, but it is unclear whether the remaining Soviet force would be insufficient for such an operation. Soviet military and political authorities have said that their post-CFE forces in Europe will be substantially reorganized. Although they deny it, a streamlined force structure could actually improve the Soviet Union's attack capability by removing extraneous support elements. Gorbachev has pledged, however, that post-CFE Warsaw Pact forces would be left with only a "defensive" capability. Further, if President Bush's proposal for a 20-percent reduction in U.S. combat forces is implemented, NATO's post-CFE posture could actually make it less prepared to meet a Soviet standing attack even if faced by a substantially smaller force. Although under both the NATO and Soviet proposals NATO would be removing far fewer personnel, weapons, and equipment, the post-CFE balance would afford the Warsaw Pact some residual and significant advantages. The Soviets could still plan a rapid mobilization attack that would exploit all of NATO's structural and political disadvantages.

NATO planning is founded on the assumption that the Warsaw Pact would require one to three weeks to mobilize its most important forward units and would be prepared to attack after the second week, with most of its divisions in Eastern Europe and in the western military districts of the Soviet Union.[19] NATO's assumptions, however, have not changed, despite a series of Soviet initiatives to reorganize its command structure and to alter its tactical approach to allow the introduction of new operational concepts. These initiatives could reduce the military impact of even large reductions in Soviet front-line forces.

For example, the Soviet high command has reorganized air force and air defense units to give them greater flexibility in defending ground forces and deploying conventionally armed long-range strike aircraft against key NATO targets, including airfields and command–and–control headquarters. The old Soviet mobile group concept has been revised to enable them to penetrate NATO forward positions, possibly preempting NATO early use of theater-nuclear weapons.

In addition, Soviet airborne forces have been modernized, along with the creation of helicopter-borne air assault brigades[20] to enable Warsaw Pact forces to carry out deep strikes against NATO high-value targets.[21] Soviet deep-strike capability has also been strengthened indirectly through the INF treaty, which, although removing the threatening SS-20, SS-23, and SS-12 tactical missiles, allows continued deployment of the SS-21, a system that can carry accurate nuclear, chemical, or conventional warheads. These significantly increase Soviet ability to hold at risk communications, command, control, and intelligence assets, air defense sites, airfields, and key choke points.[22]

Table 9–6 estimates the impact of Soviet-proposed conventional force reductions for both the Central Region and the entire ATTU area. The reductions would be significant and would remove a substantial portion of forward-deployed Warsaw Pact armor and personnel. As the respected analyst Phillip Karber has noted, the size of the force that Gorbachev is proposing to with-

Table 9–6
Estimated Impact of Soviet Conventional Reductions for the Central Region and ATTU Area

	Central Region		ATTU Area	
	Level of Cuts	% Reduction	Level of Cuts	% Reduction
Personnel	50,000	9	240,000	10
Tank divisions	6	20	—	—
Main battle tanks	5,000	50	10,000	20
Artillery	800	10	8,500	20
Combat aircraft	150	? [a]	800	10

Sources: Phillip A. Karber, *Soviet Implementation of the Gorbachev Unilateral Military Reductions: Implications for Conventional Arms Control in Europe,* Briefing Prepared for Committee on Armed Services, U.S. House of Representatives, March 14, 1989; "Documentation, Conventional Arms Control," *Survival* (London: International Institute for Strategic Studies, May–June 1989); author's discussions with U.S. Defense Department officials.

Note: There has been some ambiguity and contradiction in and among statements by Soviet officials regarding the precise geographical breakdown for the proposed reductions. These estimates should be regarded as tentative, pending further clarification at the CFE negotiations in Vienna.

[a] There are significant differences between the Warsaw Pact and NATO counting rules for aircraft, and therefore there is no agreed-upon data base for this category.

draw from Europe is greater than the forces now deployed in Europe by the U.S. 7th Army.[23]

Even after the reductions are implemented, the Soviets would still be left with about a two-to-one advantage in manpower, although the remaining armored divisions would be lighter. In addition, the Warsaw Pact tank margin, at 25,000, would still be considerable.[24] General John Galvin, currently SACEUR, notes that despite the seemingly dramatic impact of the Gorbachev cuts, the Soviet arms industry will still continue to produce 2,700 tanks annually, nearly three times the production level of the alliance, and will still be able to field three new regiments of artillery every month. Galvin estimates that after all the Gorbachev reductions, the Warsaw Pact would still enjoy a 2.5:1 advantage in tanks, a 2.4:1 margin in artillery, and nearly a 2:1 advantage in combat aircraft.[25] A recent net assessment by the U.S. Joint Chiefs of Staff concludes that Warsaw Pact forces will "continue to have numerical superiority over NATO in all categories, although near parity exists in attack helicopters, anti-tank guns, and anti-tank guided munitions (ATGM). This Warsaw Pact advantage would remain if recent Soviet arms reduction proposals are implemented."[26]

It is difficult to draw conclusions about comparative military advantage in Europe with any precision because such judgments are the functions of many factors, all susceptible to bias. In addition, a real net assessment of

NATO and Warsaw Pact capabilities will inevitably raise a debate over the significance of qualitative versus quantitative factors. For example, although Warsaw Pact forces are quantitatively superior in virtually every weapons category examined, their in-place ground forces, according to some analysts, are in a generally lower state of readiness than is the case with NATO's in-place ground units, and therefore one could conclude from that assessment that in a standing-start attack, NATO could fare more favorably than a static analysis would suggest.[27] Still other observers conclude that Warsaw Pact quantitative advantages have been exaggerated and that the actual balance of forces is considerably less gloomy than conventional wisdom suggests.[28]

Force Improvements versus Reductions: Reaching a Balance

Regardless of how one evaluates the current state of the NATO–Warsaw Pact balance in Europe, it is difficult to avoid the conclusion that significant reductions in forces could change assumptions (in Moscow and the NATO capitals) about preserving deterrence in Europe. To a large extent, the CFE negotiations will highlight NATO's refusal to address seriously two decades of military neglect in Europe. Generally U.S. ground force modernization rates in Europe have not been competitive with Soviet rates over the last decade.[29] The same has been the case with allied units. As a result, the reductions asymmetry in WTO-NATO forces must be substantial. A 1987 RAND Corporation study concluded that in order to achieve a meaningful effect on the balance, the reductions would have to approach a five-to-one ratio, which in real terms would mean removing eighteen to twenty-four Warsaw Pact divisions for every three to four NATO divisions.[30]

The cuts NATO proposed would seriously erode the alliance's ability to conduct a forward defense, especially if the combat reductions are centered primarily on U.S. forces. Although the precise details of how U.S. forces would be removed from Europe have not yet been determined, the sheer magnitude of the proposed U.S. cut (30,000 combat personnel) would adversely affect NATO's posture in the Central Army Group (CENTAG) region, where two U.S. corps (V and VII Corps) share defensive responsibility with two West German corps (II and III Corps). A reduction of 30,000 personnel (roughly the equivalent of two divisions) would place enormous pressures on the remaining West German and U.S. forces in the CENTAG region.[31]

Much would depend on the degree of flexibility given to U.S. negotiators to tailor the reduction in order to reduce the strategic impact. It is unclear, for example, whether the reduction will focus exclusively on smaller combat units (brigades and battalions) where the support forces (noncombat personnel) are relatively small or whether entire divisions (with their larger supporting elements) will be removed. Generally the smaller the unit being reduced, the greater the likely impact on combat capability.

Over the past four decades, the U.S. military presence in Europe has developed an unusually large supporting infrastructure. Much of that infrastructure could be removed without a significant erosion of actual combat potential. Considering the magnitude of the proposed Soviet reductions under the Bush plan (some 325,000 stationed Soviet forces), however, it is difficult to imagine that Soviet negotiators would allow the United States to structure the reduction in a way that does not significantly erode the U.S. combat role in the CENTAG region.

This would suggest that NATO adopt a method of reducing the U.S. presence over a greater time than the current proposals would allow for. Although the demographic and political trends in West Germany are quite discouraging, stretching out the implementation period of a CFE agreement might allow the Federal Republic to adjust its conscription laws to compensate partially for the reduction in U.S. combat units.

Quite apart from arguments about the strategic logic of reducing the U.S. combat presence in Europe is the larger issue of whether the Soviet threat to Europe remains as serious today as it clearly was when American forces became part of the European landscape four decades ago. The predominant school of thought is that in order for Mikhail Gorbachev's reforms to succeed, the burden of Soviet defense expenditures must be substantially reduced. This would require the Soviets to focus on those components of military force that would afford the greatest savings if disbanded. Clearly conventional forces offer such savings, and a large proportion of Soviet conventional forces are deployed in Europe. As part of this strategy, and supposedly in accordance with a newly embraced benign policy toward the West, Soviet civilian and military leaders (including Gorbachev) have offered elaborate doctrinal arguments to support radical changes in Soviet political-military thinking.

Although I accept the pragmatic economic necessity for change in Soviet international behavior, I am neither persuaded that Soviet military doctrine is experiencing a radical transformation nor am I yet convinced that a reduction in the Soviet military presence opposite Western Europe will appreciably reduce the threat to the alliance. Nevertheless, it is worthwhile to describe the tenets of Soviet "new thinking" as it applies to European security.

The twin pillars of Soviet claims that doctrine is under revision are the reasonable sufficiency and nonoffensive defense arguments. The sufficiency argument advocates force levels necessary only for deterrence rather than to balance the capabilities of the opposing forces. This, of course, assumes the Soviet Union has no territorial ambitions in Western Europe and therefore does not pose a threat to NATO. The nonoffensive argument focuses on the elimination of those forces most useful for lightning strikes and surprise attacks and supports Gorbachev's thesis that substantially smaller forces (on both sides) would be sufficient for this goal.[32] This argument has also been offered by former Warsaw Pact commander in chief Marshal Victor Kulikov[33] and by Alexei Arbatov, a leading Soviet analyst at the Institute for World Economy and International Relations (IMEMO) in Moscow.[34]

The claims of doctrinal revision and genuine reductions in Soviet defense spending were supported by the extraordinary appearance before the House Committee on Armed Services of Marshal Sergei Akhromeyev, former chief of the Soviet General Staff and now a close adviser to Mikhail Gorbachev. Akhromeyev testified that Soviet weapons production would be reduced by 19.5 percent by the end of 1990 and that tank production would be cut by 40 percent. In addition, he reaffirmed earlier claims by other senior Soviet officials that the current Soviet defense budget totaled only 77.3 billion rubles, or 8.4 percent of estimated Soviet GNP.[35]

It is too early to determine the seriousness of Soviet claims regarding the revision of their military doctrine or the promises to implement radical reductions in conventional arms. It is, however, difficult to imagine that it is simply an elaborate campaign of deception. The question is to what extent the West can afford to alter radically its security strategy and defense commitments simply on the promise of reform.

Conclusion

The current effort at the CFE negotiations in Vienna to reach an East-West accord, significantly reducing the level of conventional arms in Europe, is forcing both the NATO and Warsaw Pact leadership to assess whether an aspect of the cold war has come to an end. For more than four decades, the military component of East-West competition has been symbolized by the sustained presence and continued buildup of conventional and nuclear forces across the East-West frontier.

Concern over the conventional buildup was eclipsed until recently by a preoccupation with limiting nuclear arms, regarded by the Western public and its governing elites as the most immediate threat to peace. To some, the implementation of the 1987 INF treaty marked a desirable watershed in that it represents the settlement of issues that have been marked historically by divergent approaches to contentious East-West nuclear arms control problems. The treaty has also, however, exposed a set of even more technically abstruse and politically complex conventional force issues, which will likely present the alliance with stark choices about the viability of its deterrent mission. Most particularly, the CFE negotiations will unveil a politically painful aspect of the burden-sharing issue.

If the Vienna talks result in significant reductions of American troops stationed in Europe (which appears likely), NATO's leaders will be obliged to move from an essentially existential debate about nuclear deterrence to one that confronts the emerging core question for the alliance in the 1990s: how serious is NATO about conventional defense? How likely is it that the European allies will adopt measures to compensate for the removal of U.S. (or for that matter European) troops? Will the alliance be able to sustain political support to modernize the post-CFE force posture? What will be Western priorities in an environment where perestroika is the guiding concept, and can a reasonable policy of deterrence be developed in such an environment? As with the INF debate, the CFE negotiations will again focus attention on the arms control–force modernization dichotomy.

The struggle to modernize NATO's conventional forces has been a subset of a larger policy problem—that of encouraging the European allies to make more significant contributions to the common defense. Those contributions, however, cannot be measured simply by the amount of resources invested. The Federal Republic of Germany, for example, has arguably made greater strides in improving its forward defense capability than any other European ally, but its defense spending (measured as a percentage of gross domestic product) has actually dropped over the last fifteen years.[36]

Efforts by the United States to establish a baseline for annual defense spending increases among the NATO members (begun in 1978 by the Carter administration) failed to produce the desired result, sometimes referred to as the 3 percent solution. Washington sought a commitment by each of the alliance members to a 3 percent annual real increase in defense expenditures. Instead, the pressure of the 3 percent goal fueled isolationist sentiment in the United States and created a sense of resentment among the allies, who are quick to remind their critics that the bulk of NATO manpower, tanks, artillery, aircraft, and so forth facing a Warsaw Pact attack will be European, not American.[37]

The alliance has failed every year since 1979 to meet the 3 percent goal for a majority of the NATO nations. A special report by the American secretary of defense to the U.S. Congress in March 1988 concluded with diplomatic understatement that a successful burden-sharing program "will require a degree of allied cooperation and integration not yet fully realized in NATO."[38] The annual NATO aggregate increases over the last decade have averaged barely 2.0 percent, a level the United States itself will fail to meet in fiscal year 1990.[39]

To be fair, the alliance has been able to fund selected projects that have contributed to allied defensive capabilities. The NATO air command and control system is an example of successful cooperative efforts on a very large scale. It involved a $20 billion commitment by the allies, including $10 billion in national procurement pledges, to field a European-wide air defense umbrella. In addition, a number of allied cooperative efforts, including the advanced conventional munitions program designed to produce weapons for antiarmor and air-defense missions have been spurred by NATO's follow-on–forces–attack (FOFA) initiative.

FOFA depends heavily on the exploitation of emerging technologies, a dependence urged by former SACEUR General Bernard Rogers. In order to institutionalize this effort, NATO approved the Conceptual Military Framework in May 1985 to establish priorities for research, development, and acquisition of FOFA technologies.[40] To date, neither the CDI nor CMF has produced significant improvements in conventional capability. Concern over the erosion of NATO's conventional posture has produced little more than new bureaucracies tasked to study the problem.

I remain doubtful that conventional force improvements can be made in the current political climate, which is likely to regard force modernization as antithetical to the CFE process. As a West German military analyst has recently observed, "Whether the effort not to allow arms control hopes to impair improvements will be sustainable is doubtful, given the growing resource, demographic and psychological constraints which are already affecting the defense planning of some allies."[41]

There are force enhancement options that could be pursued in tandem with even a radical conventional arms agreement and that could also usefully test whether pledges by Mikhail Gorbachev and senior Soviet military figures to change Soviet military doctrine are genuine. It is unlikely, however, that they will be seriously pursued as long as political accommodation is allowed to dictate alliance strategy.

Gorbachev's dramatic arms control proposals and NATO's response (including President Bush's unprecedented offer to remove U.S. combat forces from Europe) are designed to explore whether the East-West political landscape is in fact becoming such that maintenance of large opposing forces in Europe will be unnecessary or even undesirable. The CFE negotiations will provide a window on the future for both NATO and the Warsaw Pact. George Bush and Mikhail Gorbachev will learn whether their respective alliance partners share their vision of the future. More specifically, both leaders will find out whether they will be allowed to plan for their security on the basis of expectation rather than demonstrated change. In this sense, both Gorbachev and Bush are taking rather large risks, although it appears that Gorbachev's hopes (if unrealized) carry a considerably larger penalty in the near term than do Bush's.

For the Warsaw Pact, the CFE proposals, if implemented, would alter the political foundation of Soviet power in Eastern Europe. There will be increased pressure for Gorbachev to make further reductions in the size of Soviet forces deployed on the territory of satellite nations. At some point, the Soviet leadership will have to face the prospect that the era of enforcing its will through a garrison strategy is no longer credible. This prospect is certainly not lost on the Eastern European leaders who are slowly forming competing and divergent political approaches toward Moscow and who may find WTO membership (and the expensive contributions to that alliance) superfluous. Should the Soviets begin a total withdrawal from their Eastern European allies (a prospect I regard as fanciful in the near term), much of the basis for the current bipolar security paradigm in Europe would vanish.

For the Western alliance, CFE will serve several purposes. First, it will test whether the European allies are willing to accept the possibility that either: (1) an era of East-West relations defined essentially through rigid systems of opposing alliances may be coming to an end, or (2) Mikhail Gorbachev may represent only a political aberration and, once he has left power, the political status quo in Europe will be reinforced and a return to a Brezhnevite Soviet policy could materialize. Alternatively, the alliance may be facing a long period of political uncertainty in the East, which can only fuel the simmering disputes over political-military policy within NATO and perhaps force a premature break in the transatlantic relationship. I regard this alternative possibility as the most likely near-term prospect against which NATO must plan.

Clearly, if Soviet reform results in a significantly reduced military threat to Western Europe, then much of NATO's rationale erodes quickly. In that sense, CFE may be a very effective Soviet Trojan horse, designed to probe for opportunities to split NATO further—along predictable fissures of nuclear allergy and the European public's impatience with an incremental Western negotiating style—while delaying actual implementation of force reductions. That would move NATO along the path of radical change at a greater pace than the Soviet reforms that are supposedly the catalyst for a revision in Western strategy.

Because CFE is a multilateral forum, the ability of Washington to set the pace for these negotiations (preferably by linking implementation of any accord with Soviet actions to reduce the threat of attack in Europe) will be constrained to a greater extent than if the only parties at the table were the Soviet Union and the United States.

For Washington, the most immediate priority should be to establish obstacles to premature action. Considering the budgetary and political climate in the U.S. Congress, a precipitous removal of U.S. forces from NATO or the giddy encouragement of reform before the conditions are clear and favorable to the West could remove the alliance's framework for defense before the threat has receded. That would be fatal perestroika for both American and allied interests.

Notes

1. For a discussion of the INF issue, see Jed C. Snyder, "European Security, East-West Policy, and the INF Debate," *Orbis* 27, no. 4 (Winter 1984).

2. Author's discussions with U.S. government officials.

3. For a detailed description of the various CFE proposals, see "Documentation, Conventional Arms Control," in *Survival* (London: International Institute for Strategic Studies, May–June 1989), pp. 269–81.

4. The western negotiating position (to date) has not included sublimits for aircraft.

5. For the official text, see *Declaration of Heads of State and Government Participating in the Meeting of the North Atlantic Council in Brussels, 29th–30th May 1989* (Brussels: NATO Press Service, 1989)

6. For further discussion, see various *International Security* issues, beginning in 1982 and continuing through 1988–1989. The authors engaged in the debate include Eliot Cohen, John Mearsheimer, Barry Posen, and Joshua Epstein.

7. For further discussion on possible changes in Soviet force structure, see *Soviet Military Power, 1989: Prospects for Change* (Washington, D.C.: U.S. Government Printing Office, September 1989).

8. For an excellent collection of papers on the issue of mobilization and reinforcement, see Jeffrey Simon, ed., *NATO–Warsaw Pact Mobilization* (Washington, D.C.: National Defense University Press, 1988).

9. For an excellent discussion of the problems of warning, see Richard Brody, "The Limits of Warning," *Washington Quarterly* 6, no. 3 (Summer 1983): 40–48.

10. Ivan Volgyes, *The Political Reliability of the Warsaw Pact Armies* (Durham, N.C.: Duke University Press, 1982).

11. See the discussion in *The Voroshilov Lectures: Materials from the Soviet General Staff Academy,* vol. 1: *Issues of Soviet Military Strategy* (Washington, D.C.: National Defense University Press, 1989), pp. 93–96. ˙

12. See *NATO–Warsaw Pact: Conventional Force Balance: Papers for U.S. and Soviet Perspectives Workshops,* GAO/NSIAD-89-23B (Washington, D.C.: General Accounting Office, December 1988), esp. the contributions by John Battilega and Judith Grange, John Hines, and Chris Donnelly.

13. A CFE agreement would reduce this number considerably.

14. John J. Yurechko, "Soviet Reinforcement and Mobilization Issues," in Simon, *NATO–Warsaw Pact Mobilization,* p. 80.

15. Ibid.

16. Henry Owen and Edward C. Meyer, "Central European Security," *Foreign Affairs* 68, no. 3 (Summer 1989): 22–40.

17. Phillip A. Karber, "The Military Impact of the Gorbachev Reductions," *Armed Forces Journal International* (January, 1989): 56.

18. Jane Hamilton-Eddy, "Recent Developments in the Soviet Conventional Threat to Europe," in Uwe Nerlich and James A. Thomson, eds., *Conventional Arms Control and Security in Europe* (Boulder, Colo.: Westview Press, 1988), p. 68.

19. *NATO Central Region Military Balance Study, 1979–1984* (Washington, D.C.: U.S. Department of Defense, July 1979).

20. Gorbachev has proposed disbanding these units as part of a CFE agreement.

21. Dennis M. Gormley, *Double Zero and Soviet Military Strategy* (London: Jane's Information Group, 1988), pp. 30–31.

22. Stephen J. Flanagan, *NATO's Conventional Defenses; Options for the Central Region* (London: Macmillan Press, 1988), p. 123.

23. Karber, "Military Impact" op. cit., p. 59.

24. Frank C. Carlucci, *U.S. Department of Defense Annual Report to the Congress, Fiscal Year 1990* (Washington, D.C.: U.S. Government Printing Office, 1989), p. 19.

25. General John R. Galvin, "Some Thoughts on Conventional Arms Control," *Survival* (March–April 1989): 100.

26. *1989 Joint Military Net Assessment* (Washington, D.C.: Office of the Joint Chiefs of Staff, 1989), pp. 5-3, 5-4.

27. *Soviet Readiness for War: Assessing One of the Major Sources of East-West Instability,* Report of the Defense Policy Panel, Committee on Armed Services, U.S. House of Representatives, 100th Cong., 2d sess., December 5, 1988, p. 9.

28. Carl Levin, *Beyond the Bean Count: Realistically Assessing the Conventional Military Balance in Europe,* Committee on Armed Services, U.S. Senate, January 20, 1988. A revised version of the Levin report concluded that the WTO conventional advantage was significant in certain categories.

29. *United States Military Posture, FY 1989* (Washington, D.C.: Office of the Joint Chiefs of Staff, 1988): p. 57.

30. James A. Thomson and Nanette C. Ganz, *Conventional Arms Control Revisited: Objectives in the New Phase,* N-2697-AF (Santa Monica, Calif.: RAND Corporation, December 1987), p. 13.

31. President Bush's proposal is to reduce total combat personnel by 20 percent. The media has generally misrepresented this, implying that the reductions would be limited to *ground troops*. In fact, the Bush proposal covers *ground* and *air* units deployed in Europe. It is reasonable to assume that the reductions would follow the current force ratios of two army units for each air unit. That could mean roughly the equivalent of two ground divisions for every air wing, or 20,000 ground personnel versus 10,000 airmen.

32. See a discussion of this in Phillip A. Peterson and Notra Trulock III, "Equal Security: Greater Stability at Lower Force Levels," in *Beyond Burdensharing: The Alliance Papers: Proceedings #1* (Brussels: U.S. Mission to NATO, April 1989): 88–90.

33. Victor Kulikov, *The Military Doctrine of the Warsaw Treaty Has a Defensive Character* (Moscow: Novosti Publishing House, 1988).

34. Alexei G. Arbatov, *Lethal Frontiers: A Soviet View of Nuclear Strategy, Weapons, and Negotiations* (New York: Praeger, 1988), pp. 270–71.

35. Michael R. Gordon, "Soviets Cite 40% Cut in Tank Output," *New York Times,* July 22, 1989, p. 6.

36. Anthony H. Cordesman, *NATO's Central Region Forces* (London: Jane's Information Group, 1988): p. 56.

37. For an excellent discussion of the technical intricacies involved in measuring the NATO-Warsaw Pact balance, see Richard L. Kugler, "The Conventional Military Balance in Europe: Strategy, Forces and the Dynamics of War," in *Conventional Arms Control and East-West Security,* edited by Robert D. Blackwell and F. Stephen Larrabee (Durham: Duke University Press for the Institute for East-West Security Studies, 1989): 44–65.

38. Frank C. Carlucci, *Report on Allies Assuming a Greater Share of the Common Defense Burden* (Washington, D.C.: Department of Defense, March 1988), p. 3.

39. Estimate based on my calculation of allied defense spending trends 1979–1988, as documented in the Department of Defense annual *Report on Allied Contributions to the Common Defense,* U.S. Department of Defense, for the years 1979–1989.

40. For a discussion of NATO efforts to implement new conventional force initiatives, see *The Future of Conventional Defense Improvements in NATO,* Proceedings of the Tenth NATO Symposium, 1987 (Washington, D.C.: National Defense University Press, 1988).

41. See Klaus Wittman, "Challenges of Conventional Arms Control," *Adelphi Papers,* no. 239 (London: International Institute for Strategic Studies, Summer, 1989), p. 76.

10
The Changing Nature of Deterrence in Europe

Paul Bracken

I f officials in the United States take seriously the changes occurring in
Europe, then they should act by relating them to U.S. military strategy.
The changes in Soviet foreign policy, the increasing perception of the
implausibility of a bolt-from-the-blue attack, and the proposed cutbacks in
Soviet and Eastern European armed forces signal a long-term transformation
of the European security situation. U.S. political and military strategy must
adapt to this new environment by a broader kind of analysis than has
heretofore been common in its national security policy.

The tendency to read the European strategic situation in terms of a
military balance between two blocs leads to asking who is ahead in this
balance, who would win in a large war, and how particular weapons affect
general deterrence. This focus, however, misses some of the most important
relationships affecting the United States in Europe. The big attack on NATO
is the simplest case and the one that can most easily be studied. Although per-
tinent, discussing the simple case means that the complicated cases are usually
never reached.

The nature of deterrence in Europe is changing, and it is becoming more
important to discuss some of these more complicated relationships. Specifically, military forces have roles that go beyond fighting large wars. First, they
influence the long-term deterrence environment by their deployment and doctrine, preventing certain developments and encouraging others. U.S. military
forces and doctrine can influence the size and scope of European nuclear
forces, the consolidation of European defense efforts, and the rate at which
intra-European bilateral security cooperation advances. All of these clearly
have an important effect on stability and deterrence in Europe.

Second, the role of military forces in crisis management, and especially
in preventing forces withdrawn from Central Europe from coming back,
increases. The business of crisis management changes with a smaller Soviet
presence in Eastern Europe in ways that are quite complex. Similarly, deterrence of reentry or reinforcement into Europe becomes far more important
and represents a different kind of deterrence from that which has shaped

extended deterrence policies aimed at preventing a large-scale attack on NATO.

The ability of military forces to influence the future environment involves the way they can contribute to a transformation of the long-term security environment in Europe. Their ability to cope with certain contingencies, especially for a shifting set of contingencies, involves whether any long-term environment can be reached peacefully, or at least with a minimum of danger. The relationship between these two functions—influencing the future security environment and coping with crisis contingencies—must be taken more seriously than it has in the past.

The problem with much of the discussion in the United States over alternatives in Europe is that the relevant strategic concepts and information are not developed to a degree whereby the overall level of debate is raised. All too often positions are advocated about U.S. policy options without any consideration of the alternatives or of the uncertainties associated with particular outcomes and developments. Concepts too often are excessively stark, posing artificial and extreme choices. Unless a greater appreciation of complexity and subtlety enters its planning strategy, the ability of the United States to shape developments in Europe will be ceded to other nations, both allied and adversary.

Trends

Following a decade and a half of intense rivalry after World War II, the superpower competition in Europe settled down to a stalemate. Sometime between 1962 and 1972, depending on differing interpretations, the political contest peaked. Many people believe the 1962 Cuban crisis signaled the height of confrontation, a crisis where both sides became scared at the prospect of operating with brinkmanship strategic policies.

In the 1960s, NATO changed its military strategy and also emphasized arms control. Formerly NATO strategy was premised on the immediate use of atomic weapons to defeat a Soviet attack. Under the flexible response strategy adopted in 1968, NATO decided to rely on stronger conventional forces, and delaying nuclear use. This change reflected an American recognition that the Soviet Union was unlikely to attack Western Europe in a premeditated manner. The path to war through inadvertent escalation of a crisis in Eastern Europe was one that ought to be managed conventionally, and the new NATO strategy took this into account. Within Europe, there was also a new emphasis on arms control and stability, reflected in the 1967 Harmel report, which called for opening a dialogue on these matters. Such a dialogue was a recognition of the status quo of a divided Europe. The fact that Moscow and Washington were diverted by other problems and competitions away from Europe also reduced tensions there.

All of these factors produced a dramatic series of political events. Willy Brandt's historic meeting in 1970 with Willi Stoph, East Germany's premier, the signing of the 1971 Berlin accords, Bonn's recognition of Polish territorial boundaries, and renunciation of the use of force to change boundaries in Europe greatly defused the main sources of contention between East and West and ratified a new period of declining political tensions in Europe.

A curious effect of that decade of political developments was to institutionalize a military competition that was more and more decoupled from an underlying political competition. This was an unusual development in historical terms. Typically in European history, arms races caused political tension, or alternatively, political tensions caused arms races. Political scientists have studied these alternative models at length to see which way the arrow of causality went.[1] But both alternatives presume some coupling between political and military activity. What is striking about post-1970 Europe is that an arms competition developed without an accompanying effort to change political boundaries or change in other ways the status quo that developed in the aftermath of World War II. After 1970 both superpowers accepted the division of Europe, forswore dangerous meddling in the other side's affairs as occurred in the late 1940s and even agreed to a set of arms control negotiations that for all intents and purposes concertized this relationship.

The remarkable nature of this competition is not readily appreciated. After the mid-1960s, most Soviet challenges to the West in Europe had to do with attempts to block different kinds of military deployments or modernizations. While certainly real, these challenges were nothing like those launched by Moscow in earlier periods. At one time Moscow directly interfered in free elections in France and Italy through front groups and with intelligence operations. The Soviets instigated labor strikes at critical moments to block distribution of Marshall Plan aid through Belgium and France. And the Soviet Union's repeated attempts to sever Berlin from the West nearly led to uncontrollable confrontations. These were all provocative challenges to the West. They were not limp attempts to separate the United States from its allies in Western Europe or feeble efforts to undermine the will to resist. There would have been nothing limp or feeble about the election of a Moscow-oriented communist government in France or Italy or a stunning capitulation of the West in Berlin.

After the peak in political confrontation, the Soviet Union directed its energies toward stopping new generations of NATO arms, especially atomic arms. While this new challenge could at some level be described as an attempt to intimidate the Western democracies, the election of centrist-right governments throughout most of Western Europe around 1980 signaled that even if this were the goal, it would be counterproductive. More fundamentally, the political challenge was of a far lesser magnitude than that of the earlier period.

One consequence of this situation was to produce a kind of ritualistic competition in the 1970s between NATO and the Warsaw Pact. The instruments of competition were the two sides' military programs. NATO was driven by a need to avoid the appearance of falling behind in an arms race with the East. This competition was expensive. It had to be run, however, because not engaging in it would produce subtle but unacceptable consequences and risks. If the military balance in Europe became too one-sided, security could be threatened in some unlikely, unintended, and largely unimaginable contingencies.

Extended deterrence became easy because the Soviet military buildup in Europe did not lead it to take any of the risks and provocations it had taken a generation earlier. In the 1950s, the French strategist Pierre Gallois argued that deterrence had to be directed at preventing a specific threat by utilizing a specific set of capabilities. Yet in Europe during the 1970s, specific believable threats, like the large attack on NATO, degenerated into something murky and ambiguous.

"If It Ain't Broke . . ."

Throughout the 1970s the United States was in a position in Europe of closing doors that the Soviets did not want to open. The Soviets did not mount efforts to change the division of Europe through either political or military means. U.S. policy, however, was designed to resist such initiatives. Almost anything that Washington might have done in the 1970s would have secured the status quo for the simple reason that the Soviet Union had no great desire to change it.

Now it appears that the Soviets may be opening some of these doors. What is clear is that the way the Soviets are going about this was not foreseen in past examinations of deterrence and NATO strategy. Through more benign policies, arms control, and unilateral internal restructuring, Moscow is opening up the European political situation in a truly fundamental way.

The essence of the problem confronting American leadership is whether to continue a holding operation in the face of these developments. A holding operation would attempt to preserve a U.S.-dominated NATO, although there could be many variations even around this objective. An alternative to a holding operation is to embrace this new strategic situation with counteroffers and initiatives, basically accepting an open agenda that could include questions that might be easier to leave unexamined—such as the issues of German reunification, long-term stability in southeastern Europe, and economic viability of the East European states. The problem is that we cannot know in advance if the United States were to join this examination exactly how far Moscow might take it.

Although most U.S. political leaders appear willing to entertain some degree of change to American European policies, there is an understandable caution and conservatism against undertaking major examinations of policy on Europe because these would necessarily bring the fundamental relationship of the United States to the alliance under review.

For four decades NATO and U.S. European policies have performed extremely well. They have blocked the expansion of Soviet influence in Western Europe, contributed to an environment for recovery, reconciled France and Germany—reversing the long historical pattern—and more broadly gone a long way toward creating a viable Europe. Why, then, would any sane country change course, especially if other courses consisted of unexplored territory and unknown dangers and pitfalls where American influence might be considerably less than in the present arrangement?

There is nothing wrong with a holding operation for a great power like the United States, especially when it produces beneficial results.[2] All other things being equal, there is a great deal of wisdom contained in the American saying, "If it ain't broke, don't fix it." There is much to be said for continuing with the devil one knows rather than the devil one does not know. And there is a great deal of difference between a holding operation and a policy of muddling through, where short-term individual and bureaucratic interests push the overall direction of policy. In a holding operation, one is trying to maintain a successful policy. If different groups forget or overlook the successes, then education is the answer, not fundamental policy change.

Exactly this distinction—between a holding action and muddling through—characterizes America's stance today. By slowing down the changes in Western Europe, the United States may appear to get a better deal and at the same time apply economic pressure to the Soviets. This is a policy that has a focus to it. Alternatively, the American security establishment left to its own direction would likely push for a continuation of the military balance approach to Europe, something that is not germane to that situation. The appearance of such an irrelevant policy could itself have many destructive consequences. The United States, for example, might be seen as having a vested interest in a stalemated cold war.

It seems likely that we will increasingly hear calls for a precipitate dismantling of the NATO military apparatus. The prospect of American diplomacy freed from the artificial constraints imposed on it by its allies and of the possibility of swift exploitation of sweeping arms control opportunities, a grand European settlement, and a definitive conclusion to the cold war will be offered.

All of these things should be treated with the greatest care. The cold war is receding and has been at least since 1970. This process is historical, and there is no great reason to incur risks in order to accelerate it beyond its already steady pace. Moreover, there is a possibility, whose likelihood may not be high but with consequences that would be disastrous, that some radical or revitalized successor to the present leadership of the Soviet Union will come to power to revive the military and political threat to Europe. The ability for the United States to reenergize a powerful NATO is worth preserving and might be difficult to achieve if some of the more far-reaching changes being called for are acted upon in haste.

The chief difficulty for a U.S. holding operation is that it can be tested and strained by developments in the Soviet Union and by U.S. allies. If Moscow carries out a substantial military withdrawal from Eastern Europe and a major demobilization of its armed forces or even a significant cutback of its forces deployed against Western Europe, it will compel significant changes in the alliance. It will also lead to political changes and strains in Eastern Europe, and it may lead to military instabilities there as well.

Although precipitous changes in U.S. policy should be resisted, a dispassionate analysis of European policies, and especially of the role of U.S. military forces in the new situation, is long overdue. Ultimately the question will emerge whether NATO is a functional institution, designed for some specific purposes, or whether it exists unto itself as a good, independent of changes in the external situation. If the level of changes under way is an indication of future developments, then a U.S. holding operation cannot succeed in the long term. It is therefore essential to think about changes in the European environment that would benefit long-term stability there.

The United States should recognize that its military forces can contribute to achieving desirable environments in Europe. It is not destined to respond to whatever the Soviet leadership offers. The range of strategy includes arms control initiatives of its own, but it also includes a wider set of alternative force postures in Europe with their doctrines and weapons. The United States should avoid getting boxed into a narrow game of arms control escalation, where each side increases the number of forces it offers to cut. There is no reason, or even likelihood, to think that this game in and of itself is the most robust path to stability in Europe. Besides, this approach militarizes strategy excessively: it focuses on forces as the source of tension in Europe, something only partly true.

More attention needs to be given to the short-term consequences to stability emerging from Soviet-initiated changes. Increased strains in Eastern Europe, crisis management, deterrence of the reintroduction of withdrawn forces into Central Europe, and countermobilization strategies are all subjects that take on increased importance. Indeed, even armaments once considered to be destabilizing may be important contributors to deterrence in the new environment.

In analytical terms, the strategic problem facing the United States in Europe can be divided into two parts: environmental strategies to reduce and manage the military competition while cultivating new or existing structures for long term stability and hedging strategies to cope with failures in this or other policies.[3]

Using Military Forces to Shape the Security Environment

The classic scenario for first use of U.S. nuclear weapons is to attack Soviet forces as they attempt to invade Western Europe. The United States has guaranteed the defense of Western Europe with these and other forces, promising to defend against any Soviet aggression, whether conventional or nuclear, a pledge that constitutes the extended deterrent that it has provided to its allies for forty years.

While the details of how this is achieved constitute a subject of justifiable importance, there is another dimension to extended deterrence more salient in the current situation. Alternative U.S. policies and forces for extended deterrence can influence the force postures and strategies of other nations, both opponents and allies. Some of these alternatives are more or less desirable from the U.S. viewpoint, and some are better than others for stability in Europe.

Security environments do not just happen by historically deterministic laws. The European security environment cannot be determined by forecasting, if this assumes that the forecaster has little influence on what happens. In order to estimate where current changes in Europe may lead, something more ambitious than forecasting or playing a wait-and-see-game is demanded. The function of strategy is not to cope with change, at least not exclusively. It is to try to nudge the forces of change in certain directions rather than others. If the Soviet military and political threat aimed at Europe declines, this dimension of strategy will become increasingly important.

U.S. military forces, weapons, and doctrine, as well as U.S. arms control efforts, can greatly influence the long-term European security environment. In the past decade, this aspect of strategy has received relatively little attention.

What are needed are more systematic explorations of the dynamics of how military forces can shape the security environment and how different packages of initiative can be designed and integrated into overall strategy. One way to view this is to consider the U.S. role in Europe as managing different kinds of barriers to encourage or discourage certain developments.

Two kinds of barriers merit special attention: entry barriers and exit barriers. Entry barriers are obstacles actors face in trying to expand their activities into certain areas, such as those that restrain the West European states from carrying out more of their own defense. Exit barriers are obstacles to leaving certain activities, such as those faced by the Soviet Union in trying to remove military forces from Eastern Europe.

The United States has been in the business of defending Europe for a long time because the West European states themselves were unable to do this. In the early days of NATO, only the United States had the economic power and technology to enter into the business of defending Europe against a Soviet threat. Now this is changing. Not only has the European economic and technical ability for self-defense increased, but the threat has declined. Consequently the entry barrier for European self-defense is lowered. If an entry barrier for self-defense is lowered, states may or may not seek to enter this business for themselves. The degree to which it is or is not lowered, and the encouragement for European states to enter this business more fully than they have are factors over which the United States has some influence.

Exit barriers are often neglected but constitute a vital feature of any strategic situation. In Europe, even after the political competition peaked in the 1960s, there were many books and articles suggesting that the withdrawal of both superpowers would not be far behind.[4] This did not happen. One of the main reasons that it did not happen is that the exit barriers to withdrawals, particularly for the Soviets, were high. Having never institutionalized a system of political parties in Eastern Europe, the Soviets virtually became an occupation army whose presence was required to prop up the satellite communist regimes.

Exit barriers to major military withdrawals in Europe are now declining. The announcement of a unilateral removal of five divisions made by Mikhail Gorbachev in his December 1988 United Nations speech and later announcements in which he essentially agreed to parity in troops and armaments from the Atlantic to the Urals represent a significant lowering of the exit barrier to Soviet military withdrawal from Central Europe. Prudence and caution must always characterize Western policies. A major new development in the European security situation is the significant Soviet withdrawal from Eastern Europe.

Military forces can shape a security environment through the effects they have on the entry barriers to new European efforts at self-defense and the exit barriers to Soviet military withdrawal from Eastern Europe. Focusing on these particular strategic concepts seems to yield a better management handle for American leaders in the current environment than focusing on the concepts of deterrence, containment, and forward defense.

The United States could lower entry barriers to greater European self-defense by gradually cutting back on the applicable cases where the American nuclear guarantee would apply. This would continue what has been a de facto trend already. Regardless of stated doctrine, a limited U.S. nuclear guarantee applies. If the United States continues to move its central war forces toward a purely second-strike posture, if tactical nuclear weapons continue to be withdrawn from Europe, and if intermediate-range nuclear weapons like the ground-, air-, and sea-launched cruise missiles are given up or greatly constrained in the Strategic Arms Reduction Talks (START), then the number of cases where the United States can credibly employ nuclear weapons in the defense of Europe is greatly limited but not altogether eliminated.

The declared nature of the American guarantee to Europe also could be altered as part of an effort to lower entry barriers to European self-defense. For example, the United States could announce that by the year 2000 the form of its guarantee would change from the threat of first use against aggression to a declaration of war on any aggressor that attacks Western Europe. This, after all, was the mechanism for U.S. involvement in 1917 and 1941, and that very fact normalizes the U.S.-European defense relationship. In war, the United States might decide to use nuclear weapons first, but, then again, it might not. No power can take lightly the prospect of war with the United States, so this would not have the undercutting effects that many no-first-use pledges have on U.S allies. The effect of such a change in policy would encourage European conventional and nuclear force development and would, in turn, more closely approximate the kind of security ties the United States has with other countries.

The level and armament of U.S. troops in Europe can also lower the entry barrier for European defense. A U.S. conventional strategy in Europe that emphasizes its air and naval contributions and deemphasizes its ground force contributions would encourage greater European efforts at self-defense. The size of the ground forces could be determined by different principles, such as making up the shortfall from European contributions or as a forward command and control skeleton to prepare the way for troops from the United States using a reserve and mobilization strategy.

These military postures and doctrines would lower entry barriers and encourage a European defense capability that is more independent but still linked to the United States. They would do this gradually and in a planned way. However, the United States could act in the opposite direction if it chose—that is, by raising entry barriers to European self-defense.

Although many political stresses might follow if this avenue were pursued, in certain respects this is how Washington has been operating over the past few years. The significance of increased Franco-German military cooperation is denigrated and even criticized, U.S. relations to NATO often emphasize bilateral rather than multilateral dealings, the Western European Union is cast as at best irrelevant and at worst as a French trick to advance its narrow national interest within NATO without paying the burden, and the prospect that French nuclear forces contribute any real deterrent (even as French forces build up) is dismissed as naive. All of these actions contribute to the United States' feeling threatened by these developments.

Raising the barriers to an independent European defense capability is not without some advantages for the United States. With a declining threat, the overall defense burden may level off or even decline, so that the unit price of a given level of deterrence may actually decline. The classic reason the United States has been lukewarm toward the idea of a more independent and integrated Europe is that such a Europe may act in ways the United States does not like. However, the forces for a more autonomous and independent Western Europe are quite strong, and the period of the American protectorate over Europe now seems to be drawing to a close. To resist this development will probably create many more stresses and ultimately be unsuccessful.

American military strategy can also influence exit barriers. By agreeing not to exploit conditions in Eastern Europe to the Soviets' disadvantage, Washington can reassure Moscow that it will not use these states as a base for political attacks on the Soviet Union. It may be necessary for the United States to maintain a reduced level of ground forces in Europe for a transition period so that a new, stable system for Eastern Europe may develop. However, by winding down the U.S. role, Washington could encourage the formation of a new, more European-dominated security system for the Continent.

When entry and exit barriers are managed together in a coordinated way, a serious policy to reshape the European security environment can come about; the two are related. Lowering the exit barrier to Soviet military withdrawal should also lower the barrier for European states to mount more of their own defenses. Of course, these are all questions of degree rather than ones of absolute capabilities. But one of the reasons for the European perception that self-defense is utterly impossible has been the magnitude of the Soviet threat. For decades it has been U.S. policy to get Europeans to spend more on their defense, but when the perception that the Soviet exit barrier from Eastern Europe was very high, such expenditures seemed to add little marginal military or political benefit to what was already being spent. If the Soviet threat recedes, greater European self-defense becomes more credible.

Managing exit barriers is a relatively abstract concept, which includes the political notion of the United States facing the question of how best to manage the decline of Soviet power in Central Europe. One answer to this question is to do it gracefully. In that process, however, there is a need to hedge against unanticipated failures and to deter major reversals, such as a reintroduction or reinforcement of Soviet troops back in to Central Europe. Managing these risks depends on Western military forces and strategy.

Using Military Forces to Hedge against Uncertainties

The need to consider hedging strategies will increase across a wide range of alternative security environments in Europe because no one can say with confidence whether the path to a new security arrangement will be peaceful or crisis prone. While the threat of the classic big attack on Europe may be decreasing, other dangers are increasing, certainly in a relative sense.

The thrust of virtually all of the arms control initiatives in Europe is to reduce forces in the Central Region. Doing this may have many positive benefits, but it recreates the classic military conditions for war in Europe that have existed for the past one hundred years. From the race toward the forward mobilization of the infantry armies of 1914, to the remilitarization of the Rhineland in 1936, and to the 1939 partition of Poland, military stability in Europe has been determined less by force balances and more by the ability of quick-reacting forces to advance ahead of an opponent's opening moves. An arms control regime that works toward the goal of a demilitarized Central Europe will necessarily cause military staffs to reconsider the development of rapid deployment mobilization plans.

Another consequence of current arms control initiatives is the assumption that large-scale force reductions can be made without having political consequences. The picture acvanced is one of bringing the military competition into line with the reduced political competition. While this may be possible, it is hard to believe that reductions of the scale being discussed will be the end of the transformation if they are carried out. The proposal by President Bush for 20 percent reductions will lead to further reductions. If the American forces were reduced by 50 percent and the Soviet forces were also reduced to this level in Eastern Europe, strains and tensions in Eastern Europe could, in certain circumstances, necessitate a reintroduction of Soviet forces into the area. A significant mobilization of Soviet armed forces and their forward deployment back into Eastern Europe is something that could not be idly watched in the West. Moreover, a protracted period of turmoil in Eastern Europe may not be likely, but it is a contingency whose management deserves careful attention.

Several military issues arise from these possibilities. If the threat of a short-warning attack recedes because of Soviet withdrawals, then the object of Western deterrence is to prevent these forces from being reintroduced into Central Europe. Several mechanisms can be designed to accomplish this. The American nuclear guarantee could be changed so as to come into effect automatically should Soviet armies cross a particular geographic threshold, say, the Russo-Polish border or some obvious line farther east. Then, if advancing Soviet armies attacked NATO, the West would be free to employ nuclear weapons in defense. This shifts the onus of breaking the nuclear threshold onto the Soviet side and ought to restrain their willingness to move back into Central Europe.

This could be a unilateral American declaration intended to serve notice that reentry of forces would be a grave threat to world peace. For lesser contingencies, such as military operations involving only remaining Soviet forces in Eastern Europe, the United States might consider having a de facto no-first-use policy and posture. With the numbers of forward Soviet forces cut, it should be more than possible for U.S. allies to build adequate defenses.

In order to counter such a reintroduction, the United States would have to acquire a mix of conventional and nuclear systems, and to defeat it, to position them farther from the Federal Republic's border than has been considered in the past. The United States could take military responsibility for handling a big Soviet attack away from Europe in order to protect a nascent European ability to defend itself against whatever Soviet forces might remain in Eastern Europe.

One troubling aspect of this is clear. If the Soviets engage in significant withdrawals back to the motherland, and if an arms control environment dominates the European security arena, then it could be very difficult to muster support for new weapons systems of the kind needed to support the mentioned policies. Funding for new systems would also be hurt by the bureaucratic pressure to maintain the kind of forces the United States already has. As U.S. strategic forces move to a posture that is essentially a second strike against Soviet strategic targets, as distinct from Soviet projection forces, then a significant disjunction could develop between strategy and capability. The evolution of American strategic forces has been under way for over twenty years, save certain initiatives during the Reagan administration, and with the budget cuts of the current era, they are once again evolving in just this direction.

The demands on Western crisis management abilities also become more complex. On one hand, with military reductions in the forward area, the danger that a spark in Eastern Europe will lead to general war should decrease because NATO will not feel as outnumbered. And with a thinning out of tactical nuclear forces, the necessity to take provocative alerting actions, such as dispersing thousands of tactical nuclear weapons from peacetime storage sites and turning them over to military users, declines. Since such actions can themselves trigger counteralerting actions by an opponent and since in crisis management the threat of short-range nuclear attack is unneeded, there would be less danger that these systems would get mixed up in some complicated crisis interaction.[5]

On the other hand, fewer Soviet forces in Eastern Europe, and a shift in the strategic landscape wherein ending the division of Europe becomes a more legitimate subject of discussion, could lead to more frequent and bolder challenges to the remaining Soviet authority there. Crisis management is not the best way to handle such a situation, but depending on the foresight of political leaders, it may be the only way available under those circumstances.

Several desirable features of crisis management in Eastern Europe need greater elucidation. First, it would be desirable to keep nuclear weapons out of crises—certainly when it comes to use but also when it comes to alerts, conventional mobilizations, and implicit or imputed threats. As obvious as this may appear, for the past twenty years, it has not been a feature of the crisis management regime existing in Europe. That is, an East German uprising that necessitated Soviet intervention would also entail a rolling nuclear alert of thousands of weapons from the Netherlands to Turkey. It is imprudent to continue such a policy if we anticipate a greater likelihood of such incidents in the future.

Second, and this is a delicate subject, if the Soviets reduce deeply enough and a crisis should follow in Eastern Europe, then it is conceivable that Moscow could be defeated. The Soviet army has 165 divisions and an almost unlimited number of sophisticated weapons. The conventional argument is that the Soviets would ultimately prevail and that the West would not be drawn into the fray. However, the political use of military force imposes major constraints on its use. If the Soviets can be defeated in Afghanistan and if the United States can be defeated in Vietnam, then Moscow may be more militarily vulnerable than it thinks in Eastern Europe, especially after major troop withdrawals.

Finally, the greatest hedging strategy for crisis management is to maintain U.S. forces on the ground in Europe. Air and naval forces have many uses, but crisis management in Central Europe is not one of them. U.S. forces deter crises because both superpowers have an interest in not rocking the boat in an area as sensitive as Europe. The size and character of the American presence needed to accomplish this mission is difficult to quantify, but the vision of a Europe completely free of a U.S. ground presence is difficult to reconcile with the intense uncertainties surrounding the changing European situation.

While clear guidance on what to do is difficult to specify in advance, the more complicated cases suggest a great need for flexibility. Instead of focusing on the one big attack, a far wider range of messier crises with politically imposed military constraints and a new demand on intelligence and command and control needs to be factored into planning.

Relationship between the Two Uses of Military Forces

The two uses of military forces described are intimately related to one another and together provide a useful management framework for conceptualizing the problems and opportunities facing the United States in Europe. Relying on a one-dimensional conceptualization of strategy ignores too many of the issues that must be considered.

A hedging strategy for military forces is to recognize that alternative long-term security environments can never be fully mapped out. Although certain outcomes and developments seem more likely than others, the actual state of affairs years hence may be quite different from that provided for in any one vision of Europe's future.

Moreover, although military forces can shape a future environment, there is no assurance that this will work in the intended way. It is a common error to conclude that the future environment is totally under American control or that the forces of chance and resistance are so large that nothing done with military postures makes the slightest bit of difference in the long term. The truth lies somewhere in the middle, and thus hedging strategies must be adapted.

Strategies to shape the environment and to hedge against uncertainties often conflict. If, for instance, developing an ability for the nations of Western Europe to defend themselves completely were desired, then maintaining a U.S. ground presence there would be inconsistent with this policy. Conflicts of this kind abound in strategy, and all that can be done is to manage them as well as possible. A good European strategy for the United States will balance the risks of difficulty in coping with a range of adverse contingencies against the risk of defeating its long-term objectives for the shape of the European security environment.

One additional advantage of looking at military forces in these terms is that it does not call into question the cornerstones of past policies. If these are openly reviewed, the tremors to alliance cohesion could be large and counterproductive. As a practical matter, the U.S. government can hardly announce that it is launching a review of whether to continue stationing U.S. troops in Europe. In the past, when Washington has changed significantly its troop levels in Europe, it has always been without an announced policy review, as for example, during the Vietnam War when Europe was used essentially as the cash cow to generate manpower for Southeast Asia. This was acceptable to the allies as long as Washington did not declare the withdrawals to be part of a change in fundamental policy.[6] In the same way, the current environment may not be a good one to announce a NATO study of alternatives to MC 14/3, the doctrine of flexible response.

Yet it is still necessary to reexamine policy toward Europe in ways that take account of the fundamental changes that have begun. Alterations in MC 14/3 may be desirable, and it is certainly desirable to look beyond the military balance when thinking through alternatives in Europe. This will be an especially difficult task for the United States; as a nation, it has been better at ideology and crusade than at subtlety, complexity, and diplomacy. If any broad generalizations can be made, it is that the United States will have to improve in these characteristics if it is to be a significant influence on the changes occurring in Europe. If it is not prepared to think through alternatives, if it rejects complexity in favor of the simple cases, then its interests will be damaged. To attempt to lead Europe and the West on the basis of an allegedly inherent military dependence on the United States in the face of all allegedly stark and overwhelming Soviet military threat is likely to lead to exactly this result.

Notes

1. For example, see Jeffrey S. Milstein and William C. Michell, "Computer Simulation of International Processes: The Vietnam War and the Pre–World War I Naval Race," *Peace Research Society Papers* 12 (1970): 89–141; and the discussion by Peter A. Busch, "Mathematical Models of Arms Races," in Bruce M. Russett, *What Price Vigilance?* (New Haven, Conn.: Yale University Press, 1970).

2. I do not dispute that some legitimate objections can be raised as to the complete success of America's European policy. Some critics point out that a free-rider problem has developed wherein the United States shoulders a disproportionate share of the alliance's burden. Even if this is true, however, this criticism must be viewed as picayune, and certainly if compared to the overall benefits that NATO has contributed to the United States.

3. This conceptualization draws from corporate strategic planning. See William Ascher and William H. Overholt, *Strategic Planning and Forecasting* (New York: Wiley, 1983).

4. See Ronald Steel, *The End of Alliance: America and the Future of Europe* (New York: Viking, 1964); and David P. Calleo, *The Atlantic Fantasy: The U.S., NATO, and Europe* (Baltimore, Md.: Johns Hopkins Press, 1970).

5. For a discussion of this, see my *Command and Control of Nuclear Forces* (New Haven, Conn.: Yale University Press, 1983), chap. 5.

6. I know of no studies that make this point, and this represents something of a gap in the scholarly literature. There have been many studies of troop levels in Europe and of the American buildup in Vietnam; however, the direct relationship between the two has not received the attention it deserves.

11
NATO and Warsaw Pact Forces: A Grand Strategic View

William S. Lind

The usual approach to a topic such as this—prospects for NATO and Warsaw Pact force reductions—is to dive immediately into the arcana of arms control. Force reductions are automatically seen as the result of elaborate, carefully negotiated agreements, the purpose of which is to leave everything the same at a different level of forces.

This is not a satisfactory approach. As Henry Kissinger recently wrote, "The West needs to put arms control into a better perspective. What started as an understandable preoccupation with controlling weapons of mass destruction has turned into a cult administered by a priesthood of esoteric technicians advancing arcane formulas leading to agreements which they rationalize to their parliaments on the astonishing ground that they will leave existing military capabilities unaffected."[1] That is, the game assumes that the larger, strategic situation stays the same, and the agreements must keep it the same.

In one sense, this is correct. The balance of forces in Europe, and a great deal more besides, reflects a certain grand strategic situation. To get at the heart of the question of the balance of forces and changes in that balance, it is necessary to look first at grand strategy. If the grand strategic situation is stable, then force reductions almost certainly will proceed as the priesthood of the arms controllers anticipates, through complex negotiations leading to elaborate agreements. No agreement that results in strategic changes is likely to be acceptable to all parties.

On the other hand, if the grand strategic situation is changing, then force reductions may proceed from entirely different causes, and drastically different balances may be established and accepted. The careful business of arms control may be swept aside by far larger forces and the esoteric technicians replaced by strategists and statesmen.

The available evidence suggests that, in Europe and elsewhere, this is precisely what is about to happen. The current balance of forces in Europe and the division of Europe between NATO and the Warsaw Pact reflect a passing era in grand strategy. The prospect for force reductions in Europe is more—far more—a factor of changes in the world strategic situation than of arms control negotiations. While the reductions that result may formally be proposed in the forum of such negotiations, they will be products of these larger changes, not of arms control as we have come to know it.

The Grand Strategic Situation

To see what these changes might be, we must first look at three aspects of the current grand strategic situation: the grand strategy that lies behind the current balance of forces in Europe, the actual grand strategic situation in today's world and notable trends in it, and the contradiction, if any, between the two. The potential for change in the European force balance, beyond that which might be achieved by the usual arms control process, is a product of the dimensions of that contradiction. The greater the contradiction is, the greater is the potential for change.

What is the grand strategy that lies behind the current balance of forces in Europe? To answer that question, we must first ask, Whose grand strategy? We could answer from the standpoint of a number of nations: the United States, the Soviet Union, West Germany and the European Community, France, and others. From the Soviet standpoint, the grand strategy behind the current balance of forces has arguably been either to bring Western Europe under its control or to defend itself from the capitalist West. From the European standpoint, it has been to prevent another war in Europe. Seen from Paris, it has been the latter plus the restoration of France as an independent great power.

This chapter will look at grand strategy from the standpoint of the United States. What American grand strategy lies behind the current force balance? The answer is multilayered. On the most fundamental level, it is a great power grand strategy. The United States seeks to play the classic great power game, exerting influence around the world through diplomacy backed by military power. It must be emphasized that this is itself a major grand strategic choice. Through most of its history, the United States rejected the role of great power. Only since World War II has it accepted it unreservedly. The current situation in Europe is, first and foremost, a product of that choice.

Within that framework, we have further assumed that the United States is the dominant great power in an essentially bipolar world. The "threat" is the Soviet Union, and while Soviet power is dangerous, the United States has viewed its own as superior. Indeed, most American policymakers have assumed (and still tend to do so) that U.S. power is sufficient to achieve essentially any end. This is often expressed in the sentiment, "we have the capability; the only question is whether we have the will."

Moving up another layer, the United States has followed a strategy of containment. While it has not been precisely clear what is to be contained where, containment has generally meant opposition to any expansion of the Soviet sphere of control. Because the United States has viewed Soviet expansionism as virtually universal, at least in ambition (as it may at one time have been), its opposition has also been universal. All conflicts have been subsumed into this conflict, with the result that the United States has seen virtually everything happening around the world as touching on it and therefore on its vital interests. The outcome has been what might be called a universalistic internationalism.

While the United States has involved itself globally, Europe has generally remained the top priority. American policymakers have felt that if Europe were to fall under Soviet sway, all would be lost for America. This brings us to the next layer: translating containment and "Europe first" into strategy, the United States adopted and still follows a continental strategy; that is, it committed its continued existence to land battles on and for the European continent.[2] It did so through the nuclear guarantee to the European NATO nations, in which it stated that it would if necessary initiate a strategic nuclear war with the Soviet Union in response to Soviet aggression in Europe.

These three choices—to follow a great power grand strategy, containment, and a continental strategy—produced the current grand strategic environment, as seen from the American perspective. They created the current balance of forces in Europe to the extent it was generated by American actions (others, principally the Soviet Union, played at least an equal role; this chapter is not an argument for revisionist theories about the origin of the cold war). Other, more specific decisions, of course, shaped the details of that force balance: the doctrine of flexible response, the inability of NATO to generate adequate conventional military power despite superior resources (a totally unnecessary failure, as Steven Canby, among others, has shown), the unwillingness of allies to specialize their forces, and so forth.[3] But at the grand strategic level, a great power strategy, containment, and a continental strategy were the central factors. They remain so today, as they remain the pillars of American grand strategy.

How does this American grand strategy accord with the grand strategic realities and trends today? To answer this, we need first to look briefly at the world in which the grand strategy arose: the world of the late 1940s. In that world, it was necessary—and easy—for the United States to play the great power game; it was the only real great power. The Soviet Union was the only competitor, and it was far inferior in all measures of power except land forces on the Continent. The other prewar great powers had been battered into a bloody pulp during the war, and most of the rest of the world was just beginning to emerge from colonial status. Soviet intentions were threatening, and Soviet power was attempting to expand wherever it could. It needed to be contained, and the United States was the only nation that could do the containing. In Europe, a massive Red Army could roll almost unhindered to the English Channel; all that could stop it was an American commitment to defend the Continent, a continental strategy based on the nuclear guarantee. At the time when it was devised, America's grand strategy made eminent sense. It was complementary, not contradictory, to the world grand strategic situation. Its creators, particularly George Kennan and Dean Acheson, are to be admired for their handiwork.

But what of today? In the past forty years, the world has changed greatly and in ways that have made hollow each of the three pillars of the grand strategy. The great power game has become highly competitive and difficult. The Soviet Union has become much more powerful relative to the United States than it was in the late 1940s, in a military sense. At the same time, it has become much weaker as an ideological threat; communism is now almost wholly discredited. More important, other nations and forces have entered the game. China is now a great power, as, economically, is Japan. Power has generally become much more diffuse, with some smaller powers (Vietnam, Afghanistan) able to defeat supposed superpowers militarily and others (Korea, Taiwan) able to compete with them economically. Nonnational forces and elements, such as the Palestinian diaspora and Islamic fundamentalism, are now players. America controls only a small fraction of the total sum of world power—military, economic, and cultural—compared to what it had forty years ago.

This change in the nature of the environment in which the great power game must be played, if it still chooses to play, is of special meaning to the United States. Its governmental institutions were never designed to enable it to play the great power role. The fundamental obstacle is the separation of powers mandated by the Constitution. The founders adopted a tripartite government—executive, legislative, and judicial—where each element was in constant tension with the others in order to protect domestic liberty. They wanted a government that would have difficulty making decisions and sticking with them. When Congress hobbles the president, or the action of both is overturned by the courts, the government they established is functioning exactly as the founders intended.

These same tensions make it difficult for the United States to act as a great power. Great powers need to make cold, calculated decisions and stick with them. They need to isolate foreign and military policy, including military action, from public opinion. They need governmental unity. The United States does not, and cannot, have it. This observation would not surprise the founding fathers. They understood it perfectly well. De Tocqueville wrote about it, noting that the new nation would need to be a monarchy to act effectively as a great power. The founders had no such ambitions; they explicitly decided not to play the great power game.

For about twenty years after World War II, Americans could ignore this fundamental contradiction because the country's overwhelming power made playing a great power easy. They can ignore the contradiction no longer. Since the game again became competitive, the United States has not done very well at it. The public is not comfortable with it, and public opinion cannot be isolated from foreign affairs. The Congress expresses it, as it did during the Vietnam War and as it does now in regard to Central America. At some point, some point soon, the United States will have to face the contradiction and think through how to resolve it.

Change has also undermined the policy of containment. Who is to be contained? The world is no longer bipolar; a growing number of challenges do not emanate from Moscow. Indeed, threats of a wholly new nature are arising, not identifiable with nation-states, and potentially equally threatening to both the United States and the Soviet Union; the Islamic revival and the international drug traffic are examples. With them, the very nature of international relations may change, not to speak of alignments of states, and a new generation of warfare may emerge.[4]

At the same time, under Mikhail Gorbachev, the Soviet Union appears to be adopting the status of "satisfied power." This would be a change of historic importance; the cold war would be over and, with it, containment. It is too soon to say with certainty whether it will in fact occur. While it seems to be the policy of the current Soviet government, the stability of that government remains in question.

But even if the Soviet-American rivalry persists, containment is clearly out of date. It fails to account for the real state of world affairs, which no longer revolves around a Washington-Moscow axis, and it fails to consider the great relative decline of American power. The hubris of the "inside the Beltway" crowd notwithstanding, it is not just a matter of will. The United States lacks sufficient power to impose its will even in Central America or Lebanon. In the showdown between the United States and Panama's lilliputian Mussolini, General Manuel Noriega, Noriega is winning. The Soviet Union finds the same problem, not only in its relations with China, Poland, and Rumania, but also in Estonia and Lithuania. Being a great power does not mean what it used to.

The termites have gotten at the third pillar of the grand strategy, the continental strategy, as well. The continental strategy is directed at defending Western Europe from Soviet aggression. But is Soviet aggression in that direction at all likely? Even before the advent of Gorbachev, U.S. military leaders consistently referred to a war in Europe as the least likely contingency. Now it appears the Soviets may be willing to agree to roughly equal levels of conventional armaments in Europe. Especially in view of Soviet military doctrine and characteristics, this would make successful aggression almost impossible.[5] Increasingly, Europeans, especially the West Germans, do not see a Soviet threat.

Even if there is such a threat, Western Europe is quite capable of defending itself against it. In the late 1940s, Europe, exhausted and devastated by war, could not defend itself. Today, it can; in the words of the old jingle, it's got the ships, it's got the men, it's got the money, too. By use of the classic German army reserve system, it can have a viable conventional defense.[6] More important, in the British and French nuclear forces, it has its own strategic deterrent. The French force is particularly important; because of French military doctrine, even a purely conventional attack is likely to bring a strategic nuclear response.[7] While the American defense subsidy is undoubtedly welcome to the Europeans and they will cry endless tears at the thought of losing it, they do not need it. They are entirely capable of defending themselves.

Finally, it must be asked, what does the United States contribute to Europe's defense? It contributes about five divisions of troops, at enormous cost, in view of the price of the rotation base that must sustain them overseas. Incorporated as they are into NATO's unviable cordon defense, their ability to fight a conventional war successfully is doubtful. But as every European knows, that is not their function. Their function is to serve as a trip wire—hostages, really—for the American nuclear deterrent.

Is that deterrent real? This raises the nasty question all the NATO partners like to avoid: would the United States in fact initiate a strategic nuclear war with the Soviet Union in response to a Soviet attack on Western Europe? No definitive answer is possible (which itself contributes to deterrence), but it must be said that if the United States did, it would quite possibly be the most unwise strategic decision in history. For the United States to commit suttee on the pyre of a burning Europe would be the ultimate gesture of pique. That is exactly what it would be because the whole point of the nuclear guarantee is deterrence. If it fails to deter, there is no point whatever in honoring it. Others—Charles de Gaulle was the first—have noted this point, with the result that the deterring effect of the guarantee is clearly not what it was before the Soviet Union gained a real capability to inflict nuclear devastation on the United States. A European nuclear force might have a greater deterrent capability, despite its smaller size, for the reason that it would be significantly more likely to be employed.

Where does all this leave us in terms of the third question we began with: is there a contradiction between America's current grand strategy and the environment in which it must operate? The contradiction is evident, and it is great. The world in which the current grand strategy was born, and to which it was appropriate, has vanished. Its shadows remain, and they often mislead us into thinking they are real. But shadows they are: shadows of a lost American power, shadows of a weak and helpless Europe dependent on America, shadows of Stalin's Russia. The balance of forces in Europe is a shadow too, deterring a war that is not going to happen for reasons larger than the balance of forces. Future events in the Soviet Union could again lend some substance to the shadows, at least for a time. But the world is moving steadily onward, away from the late 1940s. If it stops briefly at some point, it will only be to glance back, not to return.

Some Alternative Grand Strategies

The current U.S. grand strategy is obsolete, reflecting a world gone by. Therefore, we need a new grand strategy. What will it be? No one, of course, can say what it will be. But we can discuss what it might be. We can identify some promising alternatives, with the goal of getting people talking and thinking about them. That is the first step in initiating change.

Variations on a Great Power Grand Strategy

Starting with the least radical alternatives, we can identify two that bring some greater consistency with the world as it is, yet remain within the framework of the great power game. The first is a maritime strategy. Adoption of a maritime strategy would continue both the great power grand strategy and containment but change the nature of the U.S. role in containment, especially in Europe.

A maritime strategy is very different from what the U.S. Navy means by the term. The navy uses it to describe its plans in a war with the Soviet Union—in effect, to describe a campaign plan that is a subset of the larger continental strategy. While in classic usage a continental strategy and a maritime strategy are opposites, the Navy sees the latter as an element of the former. This has led to considerable confusion.[8]

Here I use the term in its classic sense, following Sir Julian Corbett.[9] A nation following a maritime strategy—it must be a nation separated from the European continent by water—makes only a limited commitment on and for the Continent. It may station forces there or send an army in wartime, but it does not commit its national existence to a battle on or for the Continent. If it is driven from Europe, it survives (to return). This was Great Britain's grand strategy from the time of Marlborough up until the formation of the Entente Cordiale. Britain was twice driven from the Continent in modern times, by Napoleon and by Hitler. It survived and returned.

There would be a number of ways a maritime strategy might change the U.S. force posture in Europe. Two elements would be common to all, for without them, there would not be a maritime strategy. The United States would no longer offer Europe a nuclear guarantee, which commits it to a battle on and for the Continent, and, for its own defense, it would maintain an adequate nuclear deterrent and a dominant navy. Beyond those two points, it could vary the strategy in a number of ways. It could still maintain an army in Europe, probably a smaller one. Whether the Europeans would want it after its trip-wire function were taken away is a question. The United States could withdraw all ground forces and keep tactical air forces there. It could keep no forces in Europe in peacetime but be prepared to reinforce in time of war, with ground or air forces or both. The best "cost benefit" would probably come from a promise to reinforce quickly with tactical air power and, more slowly, after a mobilization, with ground forces.

The second alternative is a grand strategy of reuniting the West, including the Soviet Union. This continues the American role as a great power but changes both the continental strategy and containment. Instead of containing the Soviet Union, the objective would be to reintegrate it into the community of Western nations: not détente but entente.

The arguments for this grand strategy are two. First, it seems to be becoming possible. If, as its present leadership has indicated, the Soviet Union is prepared to end the cold war and act as a satisfied power, then it should be possible to reunite the West. The West, it must be remembered, includes Russia. It is Christendom: the culture that has grown up from Jerusalem and Athens, Rome and Constantinople over the last 3,000 or so years. Since the Bolshevik revolution, the Soviet Union has waged war on this culture, at home and abroad. The necessary response of the rest of the West was the cold war. But if the Soviet leadership is now prepared to end its offensive, at home and abroad, the West should be prepared to welcome it back. Where there is no attack, there need be no defense.

Second, the West needs to reunite to face increasing non-Western and anti-Western challenges. Geostrategically, the Soviet Union holds the West's long right flank, from the Black Sea to Vladivostock.[10] Should that flank collapse, we might well again see Islam at the gates of Vienna. Around the world, the axis of conflict is shifting to north-south. It will be very difficult for the West as a whole to meet this shift if it is still warring among itself on an east-west axis. Nor is a military conflict the only consideration. Economically, the West will compete far more effectively if Russia and Eastern Europe are part of it than if they remain Third World economies.

The grand strategy of reuniting the West is, to some extent, prospective. It is consistent with what appear to be current trends in Soviet policy and behavior, but it is not certain those trends will continue. Should the Soviet Union's policy change back to a class basis and thereby revive its attack on Western culture, the cold war would necessarily be revived also. The West would again have to defend against the attack. However, should current trends continue and prove solid—within the Soviet Union as well as in its foreign policy—then reunification of the West would make a sensible, and perhaps a vital, grand strategic goal. Should such a strategy be successful, the question of balance of forces in Europe would be moot.

A Populist Grand Strategy

Unlike the two previous alternatives, this one moves away from the great power game itself, and with it the universalist internationalism the United States has pursued since World War II. To see clearly what it is, we must first set aside a notion that the internationalist foreign policy establishment has made dogma. That is the idea that the United States has only two choices: universal internationalism or isolation. The latter is portrayed in dire terms, usually as a return to the tragic errors of the 1930s—as if this were the world of the 1930s. Isolationism, in this mythology, means Fortress America, in which the country walls itself off from the rest of the world, as Tokugawa Japan did.

Isolation is indeed a strategic error of the first rank.[11] But it is by no means the only alternative to the establishment's desire to play the great power game—a game off which it lives, it should be noted, with a bow to public choice theory.[12] A promising alternative, one of a grand strategic nature, is a populist grand strategy.

What is a populist grand strategy? It is seeking to relate actively to the rest of the world but primarily through commerce and ideas rather than diplomacy and military force. It is relating on a people-to-people basis more than government to government. It is the grand strategy the United States pursued very successfully through most of its history as a nation. It was never "isolated" in the nineteenth century. Quite the contrary, it was a shining beacon of hope, the hope of democracy and opportunity, to peoples from Poland to China. It spoke to those peoples through the ideas it stood for and also through commerce, which was very active.

Can the United States do so again? A world in which diplomatic and military power is much more evenly distributed than it was in the late 1940s should be friendlier to this sort of grand strategy. A world in which the economy is international and where information flows quickly across all borders should be more hospitable than was the world of the nineteenth century. In such a world, a populist grand strategy would play from American strengths—as a great power grand strategy plays from its weaknesses, a government of separated powers, and the public's discomfort with overseas military action.

It does, of course, bring with it a requirement: that the United States gets its house in order at home. Its ability to follow a populist grand strategy in the nineteenth century was a product of what was happening within the United States. Culturally it was sound, not only calling for but on the whole following traditional Western values. Because the culture was sound, the United States was economically productive and, by the end of the century, able to compete internationally. If, in contrast, the United States enters the twenty-first century disintegrating culturally and uncompetitive economically, then a populist grand strategy is unlikely to work. So, however, is any other strategy beyond making certain the United States does not have ambitions that overreach its rapidly falling capabilities.

Should the United States adopt a populist grand strategy, the question of the balance of forces in Europe is irrelevant—or rather, it changes its nature. America would not have military forces stationed in Europe or treaty commitments to defend Europe, but it might well have considerable force there, through its example. How many divisions is the force of example worth? Potentially, quite a few. An example is President Wilson's Fourteen Points proposal in World War I. The Fourteen Points played a significant role in the collapse of the home front in Germany in 1918 because they offered Germany an honorable peace and a better postwar world (an offer that proved, of course, deceptive). Had they been offered by Lloyd George or Clemenceau, it is safe to guess that their credibility would have been doubtful. But they were offered by the American president, and that gave them force with the German people because of what America stood for in their eyes. They may have been worth a great many divisions, in that without the collapse at home, Germany was quite capable militarily of fighting on.

A Cultural Grand Strategy

Normally, when we think of a nation, we think of an outline on a map, a capital, a government, a flag, army, and navy. But in most cases, these are merely superstructure. What defines a nation is its culture.[13]

Cultures can be subject to attack, external and internal. Internal attacks include decline and revolutions. External attacks may be mounted formally by other nations using armies and navies. But sometimes the attacks are quite different from what we normally think of as war. They are attacks on the culture that bypass a nation's national security apparatus. Examples include the spread of religions or ideologies, immigration, or simply information flow.

The United States is currently under at least one direct cultural attack: the drug invasion. The drug trade bypasses its national security apparatus, despite its best efforts. It is supported by a powerful fifth column: American drug users. It has already had a damaging effect on the culture; it has probably done more direct damage in the United States than have the Bolsheviks in all the years since the Russian Revolution.

Other Western nations could point to different attacks on their culture. Together they should raise some questions. Do they portend a major change in the world grand strategic environment, a change potentially far greater than that which has already occurred since World War II? Are they part of the shift from an east-west to a north-south conflict axis? Do they represent at least part of the first serious non-Western threat to the West since the last Turkish siege of Vienna in the seventeenth century? Most of these attacks do not come from a nation-state. Do they represent a movement away from the (Western-conceived) nation-state as the basic actor on the world stage? It is too early to answer these questions, but it is not too early to pose them. At least to the degree the answers are affirmative, they suggest how much of an artifact the whole debate over force levels in Europe is, along with the grand strategy that is focused on those force levels.

If we conclude that cultural attacks represent the wave of the future, what might a response—a cultural grand strategy—look like? Because most cultural attacks will bypass the national security system, a response by that system will probably not have much utility (as it has not in the case of drugs). The response itself will need to be cultural. One approach would be cultural revival: reviving the traditional culture that rejects the invader on the basis of morals and values. In such an effort at revival, education policy would obviously play a major role. So would legal policy. Governmentally, departments other than the defense department would become the first line of defense. Government alone would probably not be sufficient. The support of the media would be of central importance, as it is in the current campaigns against drug use and drunk driving. The goal would be to create a popular movement, like the movement against cocaine use that was developed in response to the cocaine epidemic earlier in this century. The invader would be fought on the highest level of conflict, the moral level.[14]

Conclusion: Are We Asking the Right Question?

I began with the question of prospects for NATO and Warsaw Pact force reductions but have gotten far afield from that question. That is precisely the grand strategic point. When we look at what has happened and what is happening in the world in terms of grand strategic developments and trends and consider what the U.S. response to those might be, the question of the balance of forces between NATO and the Warsaw Pact in Europe fades into insignificance. It suggests Vienna and St. Petersburg in 1914, each thinking only about whether Romanov or Hapsburg will win the coming confrontation, when the world is changing around them in ways that will make that issue wholly irrelevant.

What should we do? We need to change the terms of the debate. We must look beyond the usual minutiae that preoccupy discussions about NATO, discussions that revolve around how to keep everything the same, to preserve NATO like a fly in amber, despite the changes taking place in the surrounding world. Until that changes, until considerations such as those raised here become the subject of official thought and consideration, the world will continue to change more rapidly than the West can adapt to it. That, unfortunately, is a well-traveled road to disaster.

Notes

1. Henry Kissinger, "Dealing with Moscow: A New Balance," *Washington Post,* February 7, 1989, p. A25.

2. In this chapter, the distinction between a continental and a maritime strategy will follow traditional British usage. A continental strategy involves so strong or heavy a commitment to warfare on the Continent that a defeat there can be fatal to the nation. In a maritime strategy, continental commitments are limited, and ultimate security rests on naval superiority.

3. See Steven Canby, *Short (and Long) War Responses: Restructuring, Border Defense, and Reserve Mobilization for Armored Warfare,* DOD paper MA903-76-C-0270 (Washington, D.C.: U.S. Government Printing Office, March 1978).

4. See William S. Lind; Col. Keith Nightengale, U.S.A.; Capt John Schmitt, U.S.M.C.; Col. Joseph W. Sutton, U.S.A.; and Lt. Col. G.I. Wilson, U.S.M.C., "The Changing Face of War: Into the Fourth Generation," publication forthcoming in the *Marine Corps Gazette* and *Military Review.*

5. From a Soviet standpoint, a successful attack requires a large superiority in number of tanks. Soviet tanks are not intended so much to engage the enemy as to flow around it. Equal tank numbers would imply many more engagements, which creates severe problems for the Soviets in view of their level of crew training and reliance operationally on tempo.

6. The classic German reserve system uses a conscript army as a training machine, the primary peacetime object of which is to produce well-trained reserve units. These reserve units can be maintained at low cost in peacetime while yielding a large, trained force upon mobilization. See Canby, *Short (and Long) War Responses,* and other Canby works.

7. Under French doctrine, there is no room for a nonnuclear war in Europe; the French response would be strategic nuclear, with conventional forces and tactical nuclear weapons merely giving warning that a strategic strike would come if the aggression continued.

8. For a more complete discussion of the U.S. Navy's "maritime strategy," see William S. Lind, "The Maritime Strategy—1988: Bad Strategy?" *U.S. Naval Institute Proceedings* (February 1988): 54–61.

9. Sir Julian S. Corbett, *Some Principles of Maritime Strategy* (London: Conway Maritime Press, Ltd., 1972).

10. See Dimitri Cyril Ramesses, "Reflections on the North-South Axis in the Eastern Hemisphere and the Mega Strategic Line Gibraltar-Caucasus-Vladivostok" (unpublished paper, May 1983).

11. See Col. John Boyd, USAF, ret., "The Strategic Game," in *A Discourse on Winning and Losing* (unpublished briefing, August 1987).

12. James M. Buchanan and Robert D. Tollison, eds., *Theory of Public Choice* (Ann Arbor: University of Michigan Press, 1972). Public choice theory says, in brief, that the choices made by public officials are as much determined by incentives—money and power, for example—as choices made in the private sector. The success of the policy is not necessarily one of the incentives.

13. Some nations are multicultural, with the nation defined in terms of boundaries, regime, dynasty, ideology, and so forth. A general twentieth-century trend has

been for such nations to be unstable, often breaking down into new monocultural nation-states.

14. Col. Boyd makes the point that conflicts are fought on three levels: physical, mental, and moral. The moral dominates the mental and the mental the physical. See "Patterns of Conflict."

12
The End of the Soviet Threat?

Stanley H. Kober

Reassessing the Threat of the Soviet Union

The Soviet Union is undergoing a revolutionary transformation. Recognizing the serious economic situation their country was in, Soviet leaders have taken significant steps to reduce the burden of their military expenditures. Not only have they agreed to the INF (intermediate nuclear forces) treaty whose terms were rejected out of hand by the Brezhnev regime, they have pledged to reduce their overall military budget by 14 percent and the production of military equipment and arms by almost 20 percent. Moreover, the Soviet reductions in personnel and equipment, announced by General Secretary Mikhail Gorbachev in a speech to the United Nations in December 1988, have served as an apparent spur to the other members of the Warsaw Pact. In addition to the Soviet troop cut of 500,000 men, the other members of the Warsaw Pact will reduce their forces by 56,300 men. Similarly, they will eliminate almost 2,000 tanks to augment the Soviet pledge to demobilize 10,000.[1]

These actions by the political leadership have had a mixed reaction from the Soviet military establishment, which must see its position in the Soviet policymaking hierarchy threatened.[2] Indeed, the Soviet military has apparently witnessed a steady erosion of its authority since Gorbachev took office. A U.S. State Department expert on Soviet affairs observed in early 1988, "Recent symbolic actions . . . suggest a decreased role for the Soviet military," which "appears to be losing ground in important foreign policy areas."[3] Top Soviet officers are now beginning to express open resentment at the way they are being treated. "In the past 2–3 years the prestige of the Armed Forces has been somewhat undermined," complained the commander in chief of the Soviet navy in February 1989. "Should this not alarm society? And all those who really think about our motherland's security and inviolability?[4]

The admiral's outburst reflects the military's conviction that the West still represents a threat. According to the chief of the General Staff, Colonel General Mikhail Moiseyev, although "confrontation in international relations has begun to give way to cooperation . . . there has been no fundamental

breakthrough in these relations." The United States, he warns, "has not re-
nounced and is not thinking of renouncing a single one of its military-
technical programs. . . . It is not a case of some 'alleged military threat.'"[5]

Moiseyev's statement is nothing short of an open challenge to one of the
basic principles of perestroika (restructuring), for revising the image of the
United States as the implacable enemy of the Soviet Union lies at the heart of
Gorbachev's "new thinking" in foreign affairs. "We certainly do not need an
"enemy image" of America, neither for domestic nor for foreign-policy interests," he writes in *Perestroika*. "An imaginary or real enemy is needed only
if one is bent on maintaining tension, on confrontation with far-reaching and,
I might add, unpredictable consequences. Ours is a different orientation."[6]
Elaborating on this position, an article in *Izvestia* in April 1988 maintained
that the United States has no intention of attacking the Soviet Union:

> The group of Soviet forces in Germany is a guarantee that the past will not
> repeat itself. Could it repeat itself? Could a second Hitler emerge? No,
> history never copies itself exactly. *Do the Americans covet our territory?
> No,* because they ascribe [*sic*] to ideas of maintaining their influence in the
> world by means other than the seizure of territory.[7]

The question must naturally be asked: If history cannot repeat itself, if
the United States does not covet Soviet territory, why does the Soviet Union
need such large military forces? For decades the Soviet people have supported
a backbreaking military burden, generally estimated to be approximately 15
percent of their gross national product, because they felt they were faced with
a serious military threat and because they had no choice in the matter. Now
that this threat appears to be easing and they have been given an effective fran-
chise, they are eager to reduce military spending and to devote the savings to
improving the quality of their lives. In their electoral campaigns, some Soviet
military leaders, like good politicians anywhere else, responded to the yearning of the voters. The newspaper *Rural Life* reported that in a candidates'
debate, First Deputy Defense Minister K.A. Kochetov received the greatest
applause when he declared that "maintaining the Army is costing us an immense amount of money. So would it not be better to cut the army by half
and use the money that is saved for the development of the national
economy?" The newspaper concluded its account by noting that Kochetov
was "the only candidate registered by the okrug electoral commission."[8]

This incident illustrates the extent of the changes occurring in the Soviet
Union. While Western defense analysts have been studying the pro-
nouncements of Soviet military officials about the criteria of "reasonable sufficiency" and the new defensive military doctrine, power has been shifting from
the strategists in their offices to the people in their voting booths.[9] After all,
can anyone seriously believe that Kochetov, in proposing to a cheering crowd
that the army be cut in half, was basing his position on detailed studies by

the General Staff? And if he was not, what importance do such studies have?

In short, there can be no doubt that the nature of the debate on military spending in the Soviet Union has changed significantly. The issue is no longer whether it should be reduced but rather by how much. In a speech in January 1989, Gorbachev described the budget deficit, rather than the Reagan buildup, as the gravest problem he inherited on assuming office. To deal with this threat, "We will also have to take a look at our defense expenditures. A preliminary study shows that we can reduce them without lowering the level of the state's security and defense capabilities."[10] Shortly afterward, an editorial article in *International Affairs,* a journal published by the Soviet Foreign Ministry, observed that "a realistic estimation of security requirements" could lead to "the possibility of further unilateral reductions meeting our interests."[11] Similarly, another article in this journal stressed that the shift in military "doctrine" is not from offensive to defensive orientation of the armed forces but rather from military to political approaches to solving problems of national security:

> Attempts which are still made by our press to link new political thinking with "defense-oriented" conscience are in fact relapses of that "siege" thinking which rejects a weaker emphasis on the role of military force and the disintegration of the "enemy complex," regarding this as a dangerous encroachment on national security. In reality, however, it is a truly new political thinking. . . It will permit, among other things, to avoid an unnecessary waste of funds and forces of our society, to do away with the "militarized" approach to security issues, and to see political solutions which previously were in the "dead zone."[12]

In other words, having decided that the United States and the other Western democracies do not harbor aggressive intentions against the Soviet Union, Gorbachev has decided to refocus Soviet resources on satisfying domestic needs. His foreign minister, Eduard Shevardnadze, has explained, "The goal of diplomacy is the formation of an external environment that is favorable for internal development." This means not only saving money on defense but also avoiding burdens in the Third World and elsewhere. "We must enhance the profitability of our foreign policy," he has stressed, and take care that "relations with other states burden our economy to the least possible extent."[13]

Democracy and Foreign Policy

This reorientation of Soviet foreign and defense policy, while critical to understanding "new thinking," still does not grasp the full dimensions of the changes now under way. Gorbachev himself has stressed, "Soviet foreign policy today is most intimately linked with perestroika, the domestic restructuring of Soviet society."[14] The fundamental nature of this linkage between domestic and foreign policy is made clear in an extraordinary article in *Kommunist* in January 1988. Assessing the military threat from the United States, the authors state that "it is in principle impossible to resolve the problems of capitalism at the end of the 20th century by means of military aggression against socialism. This is one of the main reasons why today there are no politically influential forces in either Western Europe or the U.S. that place such tasks before them." But even if there were such forces, they continue, America's democratic institutions would make such large-scale aggression impossible:

> . . . bourgeois democracy serves as a definite barrier in the path of unleashing such a war. The history of the American intervention in Indochina clearly demonstrated this. . . . the Pentagon now cannot fail to recognize the existence of limits placed on its actions by democratic institutions.[15]

It is remarkable enough to see an article in the leading theoretical journal of the Soviet Communist party praise Western democratic institutions in this fashion, but even more important, the authors pose, albeit only implicitly, an extremely profound question. For if it is the West's democratic institutions that prevent it from unleashing a world war, then, logically, the absence of such institutions in the Soviet Union must make Moscow the only feasible source of such a conflict.

Astonishing as it may seem, this realization is one of the foundations on which perestroika is being built. Again and again, one reads in the Soviet press that the tragic decision to invade Afghanistan and other blunders in Soviet foreign policy were a result of the lack of democratic institutions in the Soviet Union and that this situation must be corrected. In the words of a commentator on the popular nightly news program "Vremya:"

> Taking a critical look at our way of life, we can now see that, in the domain of foreign policy, our state mechanism has not been notable for its democratic nature. Afghanistan is, perhaps, the most dramatic example. Even the Supreme Soviet, the plenipotentiary organ of power, was unaccustomed to meaningful foreign policy discussions. Where, for instance, were its relevant commissions when our intermediate-range missiles were being deployed in ever-increasing numbers? Who stood up and said that was an invitation to bring the Pershings into Western Europe?[16]

What Western observers seem to be missing is that perestroika is, in Gorbachev's own words, "a legal revolution."[17] As Soviet commentators have explained, it is an effort to create a "government of laws not by men," which amounts to "reform or changes of the whole political system."[18] Indeed, the reforms under way in the Soviet Union today are heavily influenced by the constitutional debates that took place in the United States 200 years ago. According to Ambassador Vladimir Lomeiko, "We . . . admit the need to advance towards the ideals of common human democracy, the humanistic ideals adopted back at the time of Ancient Greece and the epoch of the Enlightenment, the ideals of the French, American and Russian revolutions."[19] In the even blunter words of Deputy Foreign Minister Anatolii Adamishin:

> In building a rule-of-law state, it is useful to borrow some "formal" structures of bourgeois democracy. Some important questions we are now working on have been posed within its framework and have been handled in a unique way. They are the correlation between executive and legislative power, the independence of the judiciary, and safeguards of political pluralism.[20]

This principle of the separation of powers, so intimately associated with the American form of government, is one of the main foundations of perestroika. "We must prevent excessive power from being concentrated in the hands of a small group of people," Gorbachev has warned. "We have started dividing responsibility up strictly and consistently between the Party and legislative, executive and judicial authorities."[21] Tatyana Zaslavskaya, a leading proponent of perestroika, has bluntly described this new distribution of power:

> Restructuring may be called a revolution. . . .
>   A revolution signifies a substantive change in the structure of political power.
>   We are now dealing with such a change. The decisions of the 19th Party Conference signify a redistribution of a significant part of existing powers—from Party to state agencies, from executive to representative agencies, from central to republic and local agencies.[22]

The diminution of the role of the Communist party has been acknowledged even in the pages of its central organ, *Pravda*. "The reorganization of the CPSU [Communist party of the Soviet Union] Central Committee apparatus and the apparatus of local party organs . . . must result in a substantial reduction of the total number of workers," it noted in an editorial in August 1988. "The time when the party apparatus, in the conditions created by the administrative edict system, felt entitled to take charge of everything and everybody . . . [is] irretrievably receding into the past."[23]

To be sure, top party officials still pay lip-service to "the strengthening of [the party's] functions as the political vanguard of society," but at the same time they point out that the "new supreme organ of state power" for which elections were held in March 1989 "will determine our country's domestic and foreign policy, direct restructuring, and create a socialist rule-of-law state."[24] Perhaps most striking, the introduction to a recent book on perestroika states that "the 19th Party Conference, held in June 1988, found it necessary . . . to restore the leading role of electoral bodies with respect to the executive and its apparatus."[25] But if electoral bodies are to be restored to their leading role, then that must mean the body that performed this function in the past— the Communist party—will no longer do so.[26]

This diminished role of the party raises questions about the possible emergence of a multiparty system. Party officials still formally dismiss the possibility of a multiparty system in the Soviet Union, but there are interesting rumblings beneath the surface. For example, in a remarkable interview in *Pravda* in April 1988, a history professor argued that Lenin had no objections to a multiparty system in which the Communist party would share or even surrender power:

> Lenin not only did not show intolerance toward the existence of other parties, he also did not rule out cooperation with them in bodies of power, since these parties expressed the opinion of certain strata of society. Lenin was not frightened by the inevitability of diversity, or, as we would say today, by a pluralism of opinion. . . .
>
> Soviet power—and here again we turn to Lenin's words—is higher than parliamentary forms of democracy; "it gives the working people the opportunity, if they are dissatisfied with their party, to elect new delegates, to transfer power to another party and to change the government without the slightest revolution."[27]

The evolution in Soviet attitudes is also reflected in discussions of multiparty systems in Eastern Europe. Whereas just a few years ago indications that Eastern European leaders were thinking of introducing multiparty systems in their countries would have prompted violent denunciations from Moscow, now they are reported objectively and without criticism, and some press accounts even have a favorable tone.[28] Indeed, when Hungary's Communist party chief, Karoly Grosz, met with Gorbachev in March 1989, he reported that the Soviet leader expressed no objections to plans to create a multiparty system.[29] If anything, far from being concerned about these developments in Eastern Europe, Soviet proponents of perestroika appear to be viewing them as a way of introducing such concepts into the Soviet Union in the future. In an interview on Budapest television, a Soviet scholar assessed the implications of the developments in Hungary for his country in these words:

Political pluralism is an indispensable condition of democratic socialism or socialist democracy. However, the concrete form of this political pluralism, coming about either through a multiparty system or the emergence of such social organizations that advocate different alternatives within the framework of one-party rule, is to be determined by given historical conditions. Our party has not put the issue of a multiparty system on the agenda *for the time being*.[30]

Ending the Division of Europe

Soviet tolerance toward developments in Eastern Europe reflects a new view about security concerns also, for when Gorbachev proclaims the need for all countries to have "freedom of choice" to determine their form of government, he is, in effect, repudiating the Brezhnev doctrine. As a Soviet journalist put it while assessing the 1968 invasion of Czechoslovakia on its twentieth anniversary:

> After 1968, the trenchant cliché "the Brezhnev doctrine" began appearing in the Western press. No such "doctrine" existed, of course, in any thought-out and formulated way. Nor can there be a situation in relations between socialist countries where one arrogates the right to decide for the others. This is inadmissible. Respect for this principle is the most reliable guarantee that there will be no repetition of 1968. Those who were involved in those events have drawn the most serious lessons possible from them.[31]

Indeed, one Soviet commentator has gone so far as to chide Western observers for failing to acknowledge the emergence of this new "Gorbachev doctrine.":

> No party has a monopoly of the truth and no one has the right to lay claim to a special position in the socialist world. In March 1988, during M.S. Gorbachev's visit to Yugoslavia, these provisions were supplemented by the thesis on the impermissibility of interference in internal affairs on any pretext whatever. It is of fundamental importance that this approach is . . . proclaimed in the biggest, politically and economically most powerful, socialist country—the Soviet Union. This is not a question of imprecisely formulated statements like Brezhnev's, it is, if you like, a real doctrine, which, for some reason, the Western press is in no hurry to label the "Gorbachev doctrine," continuing, instead, to harp on the notorious "Brezhnev doctrine."[32]

This acceptance of ideological diversity in the Soviet bloc reveals a new attitude in Moscow's views of its own security requirements. Given their revised assessment of the threat from NATO and apparent recognition of the burden of their empire in Eastern Europe, Soviet officials have begun to indicate that they would be willing to remove all their forces from Eastern Europe if the United States would also withdraw its troops to its own territory. In February 1987 Gorbachev called for "dismantling foreign bases and bringing troops stationed there back home," adding pointedly that "we apply this to ourselves too."[33] More recently, when asked by the West German magazine *Der Spiegel* about the "possible withdrawal of all foreign troops from Europe," he replied that "we are for the solution of this issue. . . . We are prepared to consider on a reciprocal basis the issue of our troops on the territory of our allies."[34] Similar sentiments were expressed by Foreign Minister Shevardnadze at a major conference on Soviet foreign policy:

> It is in everyone's, including our own, interests to seek to have the military activity of all countries confined to their national boundaries. This stand has been stated by us and is already being implemented. The withdrawal of Soviet troops from Afghanistan and troops from Mongolia is the most graphic illustration.
>
> The same idea is expressed in the proposals to dismantle military bases on the territory of other countries and also to dissolve opposing military-political alliances.[35]

To be sure, such proposals will evoke skepticism because Soviet forces in the Soviet Union are still on the European continent, while American forces in the United States are an ocean away. Nevertheless, these proposals do not stand in isolation but are accompanied by other initiatives that, together, suggest a genuine rearrangement of the division of Europe may be possible. For example, an article in *International Affairs*, noting the success of the INF agreement in resolving asymmetries of forces by the zero option, urges talks "in the nearest future . . . on deep cuts in the tank strengths of both Warsaw Treaty and NATO, or, better still, a complete elimination of all tanks in Europe.[36] Other proposals being made by Soviet officers involve transforming the Soviet armed forces into a small standing army supplemented by a territorial militia or moving from a conscript to a professional force.[37] The Soviet military establishment is resisting these proposals, arguing that they would reduce military effectiveness and increase costs. Another reason undoubtedly behind its hostility is the reduced role for the defense establishment that would accompany such developments.

In addition, in implementing their unilateral pledge to cut conventional forces in Europe, the Soviets are promising to concentrate on reducing the threat of surprise attack.[38] In this vein, an article in *Pravda* welcomed a proposal by two former American officials to create a demilitarized corridor in Europe.[39] Emphasizing the importance of this problem, Gorbachev has proposed the creation of "a European risk-of-war reduction center as a venue for cooperation between NATO and the Warsaw Treaty Organization."[40] Commenting on this initiative, a Soviet general notes that it is based on the U.S.-Soviet nuclear risk reduction centers and would establish "the first ever supranational body in European history."[41]

This apparent willingness to put their forces under the supervision of a supranational body is new for the Soviets and reflects their desire to create a "common European home." Although some Western observers have dismissed Moscow's initiatives for a common European home as merely a replay of earlier Soviet efforts to evict the United States from Europe, it is instead an effort to base peace in Europe on the integration of Western and Soviet values. Thus, in discussing the concept while visiting Paris in October 1988, Shevardnadze expressed interest in a French suggestion "to consider the concept of a European community under law," which "presupposes a comparison of the legal practices of European states and the highlighting of common norms in defending human rights."[42]

Astonishing as it may seem, respect for the Western concept of human rights has now been made the cornerstone of Soviet foreign and domestic policy. According to Shevardnadze:

> The image of a country in the eyes of the world is shaped definitively and above all from the overall orientation of its policies, from the values and ideals which the country upholds and implements, from the extent to which these values are in harmony with the predominating universal notions and norms and with its own conduct. . . .
>
> We should not pretend, Comrades, that norms and notions of what is proper, of what is called civilized conduct in the world community do not concern us. If you want to be accepted in it you must observe them. . . .
>
> Today we are shaping a foreign policy that will forever rule out the very possibility of our conduct being incongruous with our ideals. . . .
>
> . . . We cannot exhibit indifference to what others are saying and thinking about us. For our self-respect, our well-being, our position in the world hinge largely on the attitude of others toward us as well. . . .
>
> . . . *The image of a state is its attitude to its own citizens, respect for their rights and freedoms and recognition of the sovereignty of the individual.* . . .
>
> We are revamping our approach to human rights not because someone is pressuring us or speculating on this theme but because this approach is in tune with the ideals and principles of socialist society.[43]

In contrast to their earlier objections to American interference in what they considered to be solely their own affairs, Soviet diplomats now acknowledge that in a world in which human rights are violated, international security cannot be safeguarded.[44] Emphasizing the Soviet Union's need to learn from the West, an article in *Izvestia* in January 1989 drew explicit links between perestroika and the political philosophy of Ronald Reagan:

> In his farewell television address to the American people, recalling the first words of the U.S. Constitution, he said: "Ours was the first revolution in the history of mankind that truly reversed the course of government, and with three little words: 'We the people.' 'We the people' tell the government

what to do, it doesn't tell us. 'We the people' are the driver—the government is the car. And we decide where it should go, and by what route, and how fast."

Earlier we would have called this demagoguery. But now another word comes to mind: paradox. It's paradoxical, but *isn't there really a similarity between this credo of an American conservative and the strategic principles of the political reform that Soviet Communists are now conducting?!* We recognize that this common nature is grounded in the eternal idea of democracy. . . .

. . . To elevate society and social forces, to create channels for the effective expression and protection of the interests of social groups, and to put the state and the government "in their place," within the framework of the law, which in equal measure defines not only the duties but also the rights of citizens—it is completely possible to express these highly important, urgent tasks of ours in Reagan's image of the people who, taking the wheel, drive the car of government.

One of the most profound ideological and practical divergences between us and the Western-type democracies, divergences that Reagan "personally" emphasized, was our different view of the relations between the state and the individual. They assigned first place to the individual, while we assigned it to the state. . . . In recent years, while gradually breaking down the Stalinist and Brezhnevian stereotypes, *we have been gaining an understanding of the sovereignty of the human individual and have thereby found a common language with the West on a question that we used to regard as an infringement on our internal affairs—human rights.*[45]

The Gorbachev Revolution

What is occurring in the Soviet Union, therefore, is not simply a reform of the system that has existed for seventy years but rather a fundamental reorientation of its political philosophy and structure. Although efforts are made to justify this shift by references to Marx and Lenin, it actually is grounded in the study of Western political philosophers and institutions, with particular attention apparently devoted to the Enlightenment. In fact, if any single philosopher can be said to have influenced these changes, it is Immanuel Kant. In an article that appeared in *Kommunist* immediately following the Nineteenth Party Conference, which established the rule of law as the objective of perestroika, the head of the Institute of State and Law, Vladimir Kudryavtsev, wrote flatly that "the philosophical foundation of the rule-of-law state was formulated by I. Kant."[46] Drawing the link between domestic and foreign policy, Foreign Minister Shevardnadze himself has observed that "we cannot help being amazed at the prophetic power of many ideas about disarmament, in particular the one expressed by Immanuel Kant in his treatise *Towards Everlasting Peace.*"[47]

Carl Friedrich sums up Kant's philosophy in these words in the preface to his anthology, *The Philosophy of Kant:*

> [Kant] believed that of all freedoms that of speaking and writing with complete liberty on philosophical and scientific matters was the most important. . . . To make *that personal* freedom secure was the meaning and significance of laboring for constitutional government; i.e., for government under and according to law throughout the world.[48]

These themes—of turning the Soviet Union into a society governed by the rule of law, of making Soviet law consistent with international law, and of raising the importance of international law in the conduct of international relations—are now pervasive in the Soviet media. "In this context," proclaims Ambassador Lomeiko, "the task of bringing our own legislation further into line with international law becomes most important."[49] As Igor Blishchenko, head of the department of international law at Patrice Lumumba University in Moscow, has written in *International Affairs:*

> International law has been underestimated in our country. . . . This situation should be rectified immediately. . . .
> . . . We must first of all include in [the Soviet Constitution] a provision that a treaty signed by the USSR is to be applied on the entire territory of the Soviet Union as a national law, and in case of a contradiction it supersedes a national law.[50]

This Kantian obsession with the rule of law is also reflected in discussions of another Kantian theme, representative constitutional government, which was the basis of Kant's vision of perpetual peace. In contrast to their previous experience, Soviet officials and scholars are focusing on the importance of the separation of powers to guarantee individual rights and preserve international peace. "Marxists criticized the 'separation of powers' theory which drew a clear dividing line between legislative and executive power," acknowledges Kudryavtsev. "Yet, history has shown that it is not always useful to combine, or intermingle those functions."[51]

The need to shift power from a government dominated by an executive apparatus (which, in turn, is controlled by the Communist party) to a government embodying a separation of powers has been a dominant theme in the Soviet political literature since the June 1988 party conference. Unlike the American model, however, in which the executive and legislative branches are generally regarded as coequal, the Soviet system envisions the subordination of the executive to the legislature—for example, the Soviet president will not have a veto over legislation. Indeed, explicitly drawing the parallel, an article in *Kommunist* notes that the Soviet government now being formed does not duplicate "that part of the scheme of 'separation of powers' that reduces the role of parliament by means of providing the president broad powers allowing him to oppose himself to the legislative organ."[52]

To some degree, this caution with regard to executive power reflects the horrible experience the Soviet Union underwent during the Stalin era. "The danger," writes Kudryavtsev, "is not so much that a legislative body would assume executive, instruction-giving or control functions as the opposite, i.e., that executive machinery would begin to promulgate laws."[53] At their most benign, such laws would simply interfere with economic efficiency. At their worst, however, they could be used by the executive to rearrange the political system by suppressing opposition, thereby paving the way to a new reign of terror.

Just as important, though, this scheme also reflects the lesson of Afghanistan, in which a few top officials ordered the invasion. The Soviets, mindful of this experience and perhaps also observing the American debate on war powers, apparently have made a decision that the power to commit military forces abroad—not merely to declare war—should rest with the Supreme Soviet exclusively. "The present Soviet Constitution does not contain a provision allowing the Supreme Soviet to decide the question of using our armed forces abroad," states an article in *International Affairs*. "This is utterly absurd and cannot be tolerated under any circumstances."[54] Echoes an article in *Izvestia:*

> Most acts of aggression have been committed by expansionist countries under the pretext of acquiring "lebensraum." . . . It is now clear to everyone that neither unbounded lebensraum nor immense natural resources can at all guarantee a high living standard. . . .
> . . . It is difficult now to imagine a government in any highly developed country *with an effectively operating parliamentary system of control over executive power* being politically capable of such actions.[55]

This emphasis on legislative control over the war-making power, it should be noted, may also be indicative of Kant's influence. "If, as is necessarily the case under the constitution, the consent of the citizens is required in order to decide whether there should be war or not," he wrote in *Perpetual Peace,* "nothing is more natural than that those who would have to decide to undergo all the deprivations of war will very much hesitate to start such an evil game."[56]

NATO's Opportunity

These are extraordinary developments, which are full of hope that the state of military confrontation in Europe may be ending. If the Soviet Union withdraws all its forces to its own territory, if it eliminates all its tank forces in Europe, if it transforms its army into a much smaller volunteer force, and if it places the war-making power in the hands of a popularly elected legislature, then its conventional military threat to the European democracies would disappear. Indeed, even the partial implementation of these measures, and others that have been mentioned, would significantly reduce the potential for Soviet aggression.

To stop there, however, would miss the main point. As a Soviet commentator has observed, the objective of perestroika is "the development of a Soviet parliamentary system."[57] NATO, it must be remembered, was formed when the Western democracies confronted an expansionist Stalinist regime. NATO has endured because the Soviet Union, while shedding many of its Stalinist characteristics, remained fundamentally totalitarian. But if the Soviet Union becomes a parliamentary democracy, then the situation changes entirely. Simply put, NATO is not a military alliance of parliamentary democracies designed for the purpose of guarding against military aggression from other parliamentary democracies.

To be sure, we cannot know how events in the Soviet Union will develop, but we can no longer reasonably doubt the fundamental nature of the transformation now under way. The major question before us, therefore, is not one of force structure or burden sharing. Rather, the question is how we can encourage these developments in the Soviet Union and thereby help transform it into a parliamentary democracy sharing Western values. Specifically, the members of NATO should be engaging the Soviet Union and the other Warsaw Pact countries on two broad fronts.

The first, and most obvious, is arms control. In this regard, NATO should not hesitate to pursue the suggestions made by Gorbachev and Shevardnadze that they would be willing to remove Soviet forces from Eastern Europe if the United States would withdraw its forces from Western Europe. To be sure, in the light of the geographical asymmetry, such a negotiation would have to be conducted carefully. Nevertheless, one cannot help noting that if Soviet forces withdraw to their own territory, a surprise conventional attack against Western Europe becomes impossible. Indeed, a Soviet withdrawal would not only present a physical barrier to an invasion of Western Europe, but just as important, it would also amount to the liberation of Eastern Europe. The point must be made bluntly: having enjoyed the blessings of democracy, the members of NATO would be immoral if they did not pursue every reasonable opportunity to extend these benefits to the long-suffering people of Eastern Europe.

Another arms control proposal that should be pursued vigorously is a mutual East-West ban on conscription, which would have both military and political advantages for NATO. Militarily, a ban on conscription would reduce Warsaw Pact, and especially Soviet, forces much more than NATO forces and would also undercut the danger of surprise attack by reducing the

Soviet cadre of highly trained reservists. Politically, a ban on conscription would further weaken the military's grip on Soviet society, since it would no longer have the ability to indoctrinate all young men with its worldview.[58]

The second front is ideological and is designed to be responsive to the avowed desire of the Soviet leadership to incorporate universal human values into their political and economic system. Accordingly, we should vigorously pursue opportunities to encourage a freer flow of information and people between the two blocs. For example, in May 1989 the head of news for Soviet television, Eduard Sagalayev, told a Western delegation that "we do not see any political obstacles to accepting direct satellite broadcasting on our television sets."[59] This statement is a stunning repudiation of the previous Soviet position, and Western negotiators should waste no time in investigating its seriousness.

Opportunities should also be provided for Soviet students to study Western political, legal, and economic institutions. As a commentator wrote in *Pravda* in February 1989, "We are using the experience of the West, especially in matters concerning the protection of personal rights and freedoms."[60] Limited programs have already been established to allow Soviet lawyers to study the American legal system and work in the United States, and they should be expanded. Similarly, the response to President Reagan's speech at Moscow State University during the 1988 Moscow summit highlights the benefits that can be derived from having Western professionals in these areas lecture and study in the Soviet Union.

Western businessmen and financiers can also make a significant contribution to this process. Unfortunately, to date the debate in this regard has centered around questions of trade and loans. Although these issues are important, they ignore one of the fundamental transformations now under way in the Soviet bloc: the development of equity markets. Hungary has already established a stock market—albeit not very active—in which Westerners can buy shares.[61]

More important is the movement toward equity markets in the Soviet Union. In a little-noticed decree, "On the Issuing of Securities by Enterprises and Organizations," adopted in 1988, the Council of Ministers gave Soviet enterprises the right to issue two kinds of shares. The first kind is issued only to employees of a given enterprise and will allow them to share in the profits by collecting dividends but will not include any ownership rights. The second kind of shares will be sold to outsiders and apparently will convey some ownership rights. According to the chairman of the Soviet Gosplan, "Shareholders are to a greater degree in charge of production, and have a direct stake in the careful handling of state property placed at enterprises' disposal. A number of labor collectives are already utilizing this democratic form of involvement in management and are getting pretty good results."[62] An enterprise that buys another's shares, echoes Deputy Finance Minister Vyacheslav Senchagov, "joins in the active process of decision-making, not only at home but also in the associated enterprise."[63]

To be sure, these are only tentative initial steps, but they provide a wedge that should be widened. Already the Soviets are planning to create special economic zones in which Western companies will be able to own 100 percent of a plant.[64] It is only a short step from Western ownership of plants in special economic zones to Western ownership of enterprises elsewhere in the Soviet Union, especially if that ownership can be achieved by purchasing shares in a stock market. Such equity investment would provide a firmer basis for East-West economic relations than loans could. More important, the development of an equities market would necessarily involve a tremendous shift in Soviet attitudes toward capitalism, further integrating the Soviet Union and its allies into the Western community.

The attractiveness of these proposals is that they do not call for any unilateral Western concessions that would put NATO at risk. At the same time, they can hardly be dismissed as one-sided, since they are all responses to initiatives already made by the Soviet Union and its allies. What better "tests" could we want? If the Soviets reject these ideas, we shall have a much clearer understanding of the purposes behind Gorbachev's perestroika. On the other hand, if the Soviets are receptive, we should be able to make giant strides toward ending the East-West confrontation in both its military and ideological aspects.

We are living in a very exciting time, full of hope and challenges. In countries as different from the NATO members as China and Burma, common people are demonstrating for democracy. Increasingly the Soviet Union is also following this path; but whereas the Chinese and Burmese governments have suppressed their people's yearning for democracy, Gorbachev is leading the movement toward democracy in the Soviet Union. Although caution in responding to this new situation is understandable, given its extraordinary novelty and a history of bitter disappointments, it would be inexcusable to miss an opportunity to end the East-West rivalry. It is possible for NATO to safeguard its security while at the same time actively responding to the changes in the Soviet Union. Given the political tensions in the alliance, it may be impossible to safeguard its security any other way.

Notes

1. See *Argumenty i fakty,* no. 6 (1989), in Foreign Broadcast Information Service: Soviet Union: Daily Report (hereafter cited as FBIS:SOV), February 22, 1989, p. 3.

2. See Bernard E. Trainor, "Soviet Split Seen on Military Cuts," *New York Times,* December 8, 1988, p. A18.

3. Dale R. Herspring, "The Military Factor in East German Soviet Policy," *Slavic Review* (Spring 1988): 93.

4. Interview with Admiral of the Fleet V. Chernavin in *Izvestia,* February 23, 1989, in FBIS:SOV, February 27, 1989, p. 91.

5. M. Moiseyev, "Standing Guard over Peace and Socialism," *Krasnaya zvezda* [Red star], February 23, 1989, in FBIS:SOV, February 23, 1989, p. 101.

6. Mikhail Gorbachev, *Perestroika: New Thinking for Our Country and the World* (New York: Harper & Row, 1987), pp. 216–17.

7. Stanislav Kondrashov, "Impressions and Reflections after a Trip," *Izvestia,* April 2, 1988, in *Current Digest of the Soviet Press* (hereafter cited as *CDSP*), May 4, 1988, p. 11 (emphasis added).

8. T. Boykova, "Difficult Lessons of Democracy," *Selskaya zhizn,* February 23, 1989, in FBIS:SOV, February 28, 1989, pp. 44–45.

9. According to the *New York Times,* "In the current campaign to elect a new national congress, candidates are finding that two themes with strong voter appeal are cutting the defense budget . . . and abolishing the draft." Bill Keller, "A Dirty War Comes Home to the Soviet Union," *New York Times,* February 19, 1989, p. E1. Indeed, in the election a lieutenant-colonel who called for "radical reforms" in the armed forces, including the abolition of the draft, defeated a senior officer who opposed such measures. Other senior officers lost to civilian challengers. Bill Keller, "Soviet Voters Deal a Mortifying Blow to Party Officials," *New York Times,* March 28, 1989, p. A10.

10. M.S. Gorbachev, "Increase the Intellectual Potential of Restructuring," *Pravda,* January 8, 1989, in *CDSP,* February 1, 1989, pp. 4–5.

11. "The World We Are to Live In," *International Affairs,* no. 3 (1989): 85.

12. Igor Malashenko, "Non-Military Aspects of Security," *International Affairs,* no. 1 (1989): 49.

13. "In the USSR Ministry of Foreign Affairs," *Vestnik Ministerstva innostrannykh del SSSR* [Digest of the USSR Ministry of Foreign Affairs], no. 2 (1987): 31.

14. *New York Times,* December 9, 1987, p. A20.

15. V. Zhurkin, S. Karaganov, and A. Kortunov, "Challenges to Security—Old and New," *Kommunist,* no. 1 (1988): 44, 45.

16. Stanislav Kondrashov, Moscow Television Service, June 24, 1988, in FBIS:SOV, June 27, 1988, p. 9.

17. Interview in *Der Spiegel,* October 24, 1988, trans. in *Reprints from the Soviet Press,* November 30, 1988, p. 27.

18. Discussion by Pavel Kuznetsov, Radomir Bogdanov, and Sergei Plekhanov, Radio Moscow in English to North America, June 17, 1988, in FBIS:SOV, June 22, 1988, p. 43.

19. Vladimir Lomeiko, "Priority of Humanitarian Values," *International Affairs,* no. 2 (1989): 78–79.

20. Anatolii Adamishin, "Humanity's Common Destiny," *International Affairs,* no. 2 (1989): 11.

21. Interview in *Der Spiegel,* p. 27.

22. "Restructuring as a Social Revolution," *Izvestia,* December 24, 1988, in *CDSP,* January 18, 1989, p. 1.

23. "Restructuring the Party Apparatus. Its Work Must Be Distinguished by Glasnost, Businesslike Efficiency, and Contacts with the Masses," *Pravda,* August 11, 1988, in FBIS:SOV, August 11, 1988, p. 26.

24. V.P. Nikonov in *Pravda,* February 26, 1989, in FBIS:SOV, March 1, 1989, pp. 53, 54. Nikonov was a member of the Politburo and secretary of the Central Committee when he made this statement.

25. "Introduction: The Language of Perestroika," in Abel Aganbegyan, ed., *Perestroika 1989* (New York: Charles Scribner's Sons, 1988), p. 2. The author of this introduction is not identified, although clearly he is a Soviet. Whoever the author is, the appearance of other articles in the book by figures such as Alexander Yakovlev and Valentin Falin, the head of the Central Committee's International Deparment, lends weight to the introduction's description of perestroika.

26. It may be objected that this is an artificial distinction since the overwhelming majority of those elected are members of the Communist party. The response is that because they are elected, the deputies will shift their loyalties from the party to the voters. According to a staffer at the Institute of State and Law, deputies will be "subordinate to the law alone" and will be "guided by their civic conscience and the interest and mandates of the voters"—that is, not by the party. Interview with B. Kurashvili in *Argumenty i fakty,* no. 35 (1988), in FBIS:SOV, September 9, 1988, pp. 37–39. The election results would appear to confirm this reasoning, since many old-line party candidates, including some who had no opposition, were defeated. As the *Washington Post* reported, "Voters with a choice between party apparatchiks and advocates of reform almost invariably chose the reformers." David Remnick, "Party Candidates Beaten in Historic Soviet Vote," *Washington Post,* March 28, 1989, p. A1. Perhaps most significant, in the aftermath of these elections, Vadim Medvedev, the chief party ideologist, declared that henceforth "the party apparatus . . . is completely controlled by elected bodies." Vadim Medvedev, "Leninism and Restructuring: For Realism and Creativity," *Pravda,* April 22, 1989, in FBIS:SOV, April 24, 1989, p. 45.

27. Interview with V.I. Desyaterik, "Reading Lenin: More Democracy," *Pravda,* April 22, 1988, in *CDSP,* May 25, 1988, pp. 2–3. It is also worth noting that when the interviewer asked Professor Desyaterik about Lenin's statement that "the Revolution . . . requires the unquestioning obedience of the masses to a single will," he replied that "to read Lenin that way is a typical example of dogmatism" because "the quotation is taken out of context" (p. 1). Vadim Medvedev has also indicated that "the existence of several parties is not illegal for socialism or socialist countries." *Argumenty i fakty,* no. 17 (1989), in FBIS:SOV, May 4, 1989, p. 43.

28. See, for example, A. Karpychev, "The Commonwealth: Hungary, Familiar and Unfamiliar," *Pravda,* January 30, 1989, in *CDSP,* March 1, 1989, pp. 6–7.

29. "Hungarian-Soviet Talks," *Washington Post,* March 25, 1989, p. A12.

30. Interview with Oleg Bogomolov, Budapest Television Service, February 19, 1989, in FBIS:SOV, February 24, 1989, p. 31. (emphasis added). It is worth noting that in the light of recent history, Gorbachev's objections to a multiparty system should be taken with a grain of salt. For example, in February 1986 he said that "Stalinism" is a concept thought up by the enemies of communism and widely used to discredit the Soviet Union and socialism as a whole." Interview in *L'Humanité* reprinted in *Pravda,* February 8, 1986, in FBIS:SOV, February 10, 1986, p. CC7. Gorbachev has also

shown remarkable flexibility on other questions such as agriculture, first creating a superministry (Gosagroprom) and, after a few years, abandoning the idea. For an apparent explanation of why he is leery of a multiparty system in the Soviet Union "in today's conditions," see "The Vanguard Force of Renewal," *Kommunist,* no. 5 (1989): 22.

31. Vladimir Lukin in "August 1968," *Moscow News,* no. 35 (1988), in FBIS:SOV, September 9, 1988, p. 64.

32. L.S. Yagodovskiy, "Czechoslovakia: August 1968," *Argumenty i fakty,* no. 33 (1988), in FBIS:SOV, August 15, 1988, pp. 42–43.

33. Moscow Television Service, February 16, 1987, in FBIS:SOV, February 17, 1987, p. 24.

34. Interview in *Der Spiegel,* p. 33.

35. Eduard Shevardnadze, "The 19th All-Union CPSU Conference: Foreign Policy and Diplomacy," *International Affairs,* no. 10 (1988): 19.

36. Vitaly Shlykov, "Strong Is the Armor," *International Affairs,* no. 12 (1988): 48.

37. See Alexander Savinkin, "What Kind of Army Do We Need?" *Moskovskive novosti [Moscow news],* no. 45 (1988): 6, and the report by Michael Dobbs, "Soviet General Faces Challenge," *Washington Post,* March 24, 1989, p. A1.

38. See, for example, the interview with Phillip A. Karber in John J. Fialka, "Soviets Outline Troop-Cut Plan in East Germany," *Wall Street Journal,* March 14, 1989, p. A21. According to Karber, "If the Soviets had asked me to come in and design the cuts so that they would take away the disproportionate [Soviet] threat in Central Europe, I couldn't have done it any better—and I can't believe I'm saying that."

39. B. Tuzmukhamedov, "Security Corridor," *Pravda,* February 25, 1989, in FBIS:SOV, March 1, 1989, pp. 3–4.

40. Mikhail Gorbachev, *Bringing Out the Potential of Socialism More Fully* (Moscow: Novosti, 1988), p. 13.

41. Major-General G. Batenin, "New Ideas and Prospects for European Disarmament," *Pravda,* October 10, 1988, in *Reprints from the Soviet Press,* November 15, 1988, p. 28.

42. Moscow Television Service, October 12, 1988, in FBIS:SOV, October 13, 1988, p. 37.

43. Shevardnadze, "19th All-Union CPSU Conference," pp. 23–24 (emphasis added).

44. Lomeiko, "Priority of Humanitarian Values," p. 78.

45. Stanislav Kondrashov, "On Ronald Reagan and Other Matters," *Izvestia,* January 19, 1989, in *DCSP,* February 15, 1989, p. 5 (emphasis added). Perhaps even more astonishing, Kondrashov also admitted that "the developed capitalist countries . . . had done a better job than we had in resolving a number of questions that, historically, were put to the world by the October Revolution—the question of social protection for the working people, medical assistance and education, earnings and pensions."

46. V. Kudryavtsev and Ye. Lukasheva, "The Socialist Rule-of-Law State," *Kommunist,* no. 11 (1988): 45. Kudryavtsev repeats this statement in his article, "Towards a Socialist Rule-of-Law State," in Aganbegyan, *Perestroika 1989,* p. 110.

47. Eduard Shevardnadze, "Towards a Safe World," *International Affairs,* no. 9 (1988): 12.

48. Carl J. Friedrich, "Preface," in Carl J. Friedrich, ed., *The Philosophy of Kant* (New York: Modern Library, 1977), p. vii.

49. Lomeiko, "Priority of Humanitarian Values," p. 79.

50. Igor Blishchenko, "International Law in a Rule-of-Law State," *International Affairs*, no. 1 (1989): 85. Putting some force behind these words, the Soviet Union has accepted the jurisdiction of the International Court of Justice in disputes regarding five human rights agreements. Paul Lewis, "Soviets to Accept World Court Role in Human Rights," *New York Times*, March 9, 1989, p. A1.

51. Vladimir Kudryavtsev, "The Soviet State: Continuity and Renewal," *Social Sciences*, no. 3 (1988): 33.

52. B. Lazarev, " 'The Separation of Powers' and the Experience of the Soviet State," *Kommunist*, no. 16 (1988): 50. With regard to this issue, one cannot help noting that Thomas Jefferson wrote 200 years ago that "the tyranny of the legislature is the most formidable dread at present, and will be for long years. That of the executive will come in its turn, but it will be at a remote period." Thomas Jefferson to James Madison, March 15, 1789, in Michael Kammen, ed., *The Origins of the American Constitution* (New York: Penguin, 1986), p. 378. It is also worth recalling John Locke's words that "while the government subsists, the legislative is the supreme power; for what can give laws to another must needs be superior to him." John Locke, *The Second Treatise of Government* (Indianapolis: Bobbs-Merrill, 1952), p. 85.

53. Kudryavtsev, "The Soviet State: Continuity and Renewal," p. 33.

54. Blishchenko, "International Law," p. 86.

55. S. Blagovolin, "The Strength and Impotence of Military Might: Is an Armed Conflict between East and West a Real Possibility in Our Time?" *Izvestia*, November 18, 1988, in *CDSP*, December 14, 1988, p. 3 (emphasis added).

56. Friedrich, *Philosophy of Kant*, p. 438. For an argument that the U.S. Constitution also subordinates the executive to the legislature—notably the Senate—on such matters, see Leonard W. Levy, *Original Intent and the Framers' Constitution* (New York: Macmillan, 1988).

57. Fyodor M. Burlatsky, "Khrushchev, Andropov, Brezhnev: The Issue of Political Leadership," in Aganbegyan, *Perestroika 1989*, p. 214.

58. For a discussion of the conscription issue, see Stanley Kober, "To Reduce Military Tensions in Europe, Ban Conscription," Cato Institute Policy Analysis no. 116, March 10, 1989.

59. Quoted in Jerry Schwartz, "Soviet CNN Broadcasts Expected to Start Soon," *New York Times*, May 6, 1989, p. 35.

60. V. Bolshakov, "Reflections on the Shore of Lake Geneva," *Pravda*, February 23, 1989, in *CDSP*, March 22, 1989, p. 17.

61. Barry Newman, "The Hungarians Take Themselves Public," *Wall Street Journal*, April 20, 1989, p. A10.

62. Report by Yu. D. Maslyukov, "On the State Plan for the Economic and Social Development of the USSR in 1989 and the Progress of Plan Fulfillment in 1988," *Pravda*, October 28, 1988, in FBIS:SOV, October 28, 1988, p. 61.

63. Interviewed on *Vremya*, Moscow Television Service, October 21, 1988, in FBIS:SOV, October 24, 1988, p. 55.

64. Peter Gumbel, "Soviets Planning Economic Zones to Draw More Foreign Investment," *Wall Street Journal*, May 2, 1989, p. A3.

IV
Alternatives to
the Status Quo

13
The American Role in NATO

David P. Calleo

The NATO alliance has been celebrating its fortieth anniversary. Forty years is a long time for a modern alliance. The NATO partners have had some severe and intractable differences over the years, but the alliance has served the United States and its allies well. The long-standing predisposition to leave NATO's arrangements alone seems quite understandable. "If it ain't broke, don't fix it" has been the motto of the NATO bureaucracy and of a great many policymakers in the United States and Europe.[1] This complacency, however, has been fading rapidly. Today there is a widespread view that the status quo in NATO has become a bad deal for the United States.

Militarily, NATO is a hegemonic American protectorate. An American general is Europe's Supreme Allied Commander (SACEUR), and Europe's defense depends on the willingness of the United States to initiate a nuclear war rather than see Europe overrun, even by conventional forces. It is not that the Americans forced this arrangement on the Europeans. On the contrary, the Europeans embraced it warmly, and they still contemplate abandoning it with great reluctance.[2]

From an American perspective, the most obvious problem with this status quo is its high cost for the United States. Half the American defense budget, some $150 billion a year, is said by the Pentagon to be devoted to sustaining the NATO commitment.[3] It is significant that this $150 billion is double the entire defense budgets of France and Germany, which combined come to only a little more than $70 billion a year.[4] Not surprisingly, there is a widespread view that the Europeans are free riders who are not contributing enough to the alliance. There is strong pressure in Congress for more burden sharing, and there is increasing discussion of the possibility that the United States should disengage from NATO.

The reasons are not only economic but also military and diplomatic. Militarily, many think that the NATO commitment has become too dangerous now that the United States has lost its nuclear superiority.[5] Diplomatically, many hope that Gorbachev offers a chance to end the U.S.-Soviet military confrontation in Europe, a chance that should be seized to rid the United States of what has become an unsustainable strategic and economic burden.[6]

Devolution

My own position is that the status quo is no longer viable but that both burden sharing and disengagement are inadequate or inappropriate policies. Burden sharing I define as letting others pay more while the United States continues to run things. America has done quite well by this formula over the years but should not be surprised that the approach has limitations. Today burden sharing is no longer enough. But while an American protectorate no longer suits military, economic, and political realities, an American disengagement from NATO is an excessive and self-destructive solution. The American stake in Europe is enormous, and the geopolitical significance of the transatlantic connection remains vital. The problem, then, is to find some way to continue the alliance but to reform it so that the disproportionate and unsustainable diplomatic economic and strategic burden on the United States is relieved.

The only way to do this successfully, in my view, is through a policy of devolution.[7] By devolution I mean a shift of responsibility within the alliance. Europe's own major powers should take the primary responsibility for managing their own territorial defense. Such a policy does not preclude an American contribution to Europe's nuclear and conventional deterrence. The United States should continue to keep a substantial number of conventional forces in Western Europe. And it should continue to extend its nuclear guarantee, for whatever such a guarantee is worth under present circumstances.[8] But devolution does preclude a hegemonic alliance, that is, an alliance in which the United States takes the primary responsibility for organizing and managing Europe's defense. In the future, the United States should assume the role of an ally rather than that of a hegemonic protector managing Europe's defense.

Devolution in Europe ought to be the first move in a more general American strategy for adjusting to a more plural world. In general, devolution is the appropriate strategy for the United States to take advantage of the rising power of the European allies while at the same time conserving its own relatively shrunken resources.

Let me develop these arguments further.

Why is Western Europe so important to the United States? Militarily, three of the world's half-dozen major military powers, two of them nuclear, are in Western Europe. Commercially, Western Europe forms a market larger than that of the United States. Financially and industrially, its economy rivals that of the United States. And it is the other major center of world power where economic and political liberty is deeply implanted and reliably practiced. Culturally, the world would be very lonely for an American democracy alienated from Europe.

Geopolitically, the American alliance with Western Europe has allowed the United States to contain the Soviet Union on its own home ground. It has also given America the necessary margin of superior power to shape the postwar world. As a result of the European alliance, the United States has been able to build a "Pax Americana," an integrated, liberal world economy that comes reasonably close to its own postwar ideals.

This postwar Pax Americana is a great achievement, but it also has had certain predictable long-term consequences. Inevitably, as other countries in the world have developed, American power has declined in relation to them. This is not a result of American failure but rather of American success. The United States wanted Europe and Japan to recover. They have. The result, inevitably, is that they are now much more powerful economically and also militarily, in relation to the United States than they were in 1949, when NATO was established.[9] The United States also wanted Third World countries to develop. Success means that many of them are becoming formidable industrial competitors. They are also much harder to push around than they were in the immediate postwar years, a lesson that both Americans and Soviets have had to learn from painful experience.

Even the Soviet Union has benefited disproportionately from the Pax Americana. Again, this is not the result of a failure of American policy but of its success. The United States never wanted to destroy the Soviet Union but rather wanted to contain it. Containment has given the Soviet Union over forty years of peace, no small contribution considering the rest of twentieth century Russian history. Despite its subsequent follies, the Soviet Union is now a vastly more developed country than it was after the terrible destruction of World War II.

It cannot be stressed enough that this decline of American power is not absolute but relative. Relative decline, moreover, need not imply a loss of America's own vitality. There is no reason that the United States should not continue to be the world's leading nation for the indefinite future. But America's relative decline since the beginning of the postwar era does pose a major historical challenge for American policy. How is the United States to adjust its role to reflect its changing resources? And how can it do this while at the same time preserving the liberal global structure that it has created?

This is not only America's problem but also the rest of the world's. The international system has become highly dependent on American leadership and resources. Can other leading powers rise to the challenge of a more plural management now that there is a more plural distribution of resources?

These challenges have been growing more and more immediate. Clearly the United States is increasingly overstretched in its present role. The strain is reflected in the financial bad habits that have grown endemic to American policy over the past twenty years. The most obvious illustrations are the extraordinary fluctuation of the dollar since the beginning of the 1970s and the ballooning public debt of the 1980s.[10] Americans have grown so used to their fiscal and monetary disarray that its dangers have come to seem rather banal. We can only pray that the United States continues to be lucky enough to avoid a financial train wreck.

But even if Americans are spared the worst in the short run, they should not ignore the long-range costs for both the national economy and for the future of a global integrated economy. It is not possible for capitalist markets to work efficiently over the long term when the value of money is perpetually unstable. The dollar is the world's currency as well as America's own. From a global perspective, a United States unable to sustain a stable currency has become a sort of hegemon in decay, using its unique privileges as leader to exploit the international system it is supposed to be sustaining. At the same time, these same unstable and unsound economic policies undermine its own national economy. Relative decay thus threatens to become absolute decay.

Reorganizing NATO

In the beginning, NATO was the foundation of the postwar Pax Americana. Today, reforming NATO offers the best opportunity to deal with America's relative decline by putting in place a more plural structure of international management. Under its present arrangements, NATO has become both militarily unstable and economically unsustainable. The two deteriorating trends combine. NATO could be saved by being organized differently, if only the United States and its allies can rise to the occasion.

The reasons that NATO has become militarily unstable are well known. NATO has always depended on the willingness of the United States to initiate a nuclear war. The commitment was easy to undertake when the United States was essentially invulnerable to Soviet nuclear attack. It has become a very different sort of commitment as the American strategic position has declined from invulnerability to parity. The strategic shift has been a long time in developing and has also been long anticipated. The more it has become real, the more it has revealed a fundamental conflict of interest between the United States and Western Europe.

America's strategic interest is that any war that starts in Europe should stay there. As a result, American strategy has stressed flexible response. If at all possible, a European war should be limited to conventional forces. If not, there should be many firebreaks between limited nuclear war and all-out nuclear war. American nuclear strategy, the so-called counterforce doctrine, has sought to limit even intercontinental nuclear exchanges to very gradual increments. Again, the reasoning is clear and intimately related to America's European commitments. If there ever is a nuclear war, it should be kept as far away from the United States as possible. Should it reach the United States, it should do so in as limited a fashion as possible.

Europeans have had a contrary interest: there should be no nuclear war in Europe that does not spread automatically to the superpowers. European governments have favored this position not out of insensitivity to the horrors of a nuclear Armageddon but because they have believed the prospect of automatic escalation is the best way to deter a Soviet attack. What they feared was that a nuclear war between the superpowers would be confined to Europe. They found this belief a much greater risk than the certainty that any European war would immediately become intercontinental. In short, the United States and its NATO allies have been separated by a fundamental conflict of strategic interest.

Skilled diplomats on both sides have managed this conflict well enough over the years. NATO's official strategy of flexible response gives something to the Americans but not enough to alarm the Europeans. Essentially flexible response calls for sufficient forces to make certain that any Soviet conventional attack will result in a major battle. Flexible response does not expect to win that conventional battle but instead expects it to be large and long enough to make sure that the use of nuclear weapons before it is finished seems highly plausible.

Neither Americans nor Europeans have been satisfied, but both have been satisfied enough to continue their alliance. The Americans feel relieved that they are not required to use their nuclear weapons immediately. The Europeans feel reassured that nuclear escalation is sufficiently certain so that the Soviet Union will not be tempted to start a conventional attack. To prevent flexible response from turning into a real conventional strategy, Western Europe's big powers, other than the Federal Republic of Germany, have carefully limited their commitments of conventional forces. The compromise is therefore very expensive for the Americans. It absorbs half the U.S. defense budget and takes up ten of its eighteen standing divisions. Thus, although there is not a real conventional balance, the cost to the United States is enormous.

In recent years, Americans have become more and more conscious of the nuclear risk and the economic cost of extended deterrence for Europe. One significant sign of the strategic malaise was the no-first-use campaign of the early 1980s, sponsored by some of the leading American officials and planners of the postwar era. And then there is the intermediate nuclear forces (INF) episode. Europeans, prodded by Soviet SS-20s, grew anxious that American coupling be reaffirmed. The United States first decided to deploy new nuclear weapons in Europe but at the first opportunity took them out again. Allied governments that had supported the deployment were left angry and demoralized. Americans were greatly relieved. Both the left and the right in the United States seemed to share a strong disposition to downgrade nuclear forces in European defense.[11]

The problem with this inclination is that the United States cannot provide the conventional forces that such a shift in emphasis requires. One of the reasons that NATO costs the United States so much is its great comparative disadvantage in providing Europe with conventional forces. The cause is the Atlantic Ocean. When this basic geographical disadvantage is combined with America's fiscal crisis, it is clear that the more NATO's strategy comes to rely on conventional forces, the less the United States is suited to lead the alliance.

The solution is not American withdrawal but a shift in the American role. This is justified not only for political and economic reasons but also for military reasons. There is no military solution for the problems that arise from the diminishing credibility of American extended deterrence other than a European-directed alliance. Logically, there are two ways out of the military problems of extended deterrence: the Europeans could have a nuclear deterrent of their own, or there could be a genuine conventional balance. In practice, any successful solution would probably involve some combination of European nuclear forces and a more effective conventional defense.

The United States is incapable of providing either. On the one hand, the United States cannot, by definition, manage a European nuclear deterrent. Americans can provide Europeans with technological assistance; but if they control the deterrent, it becomes American and not European. On the other hand, if there is to be a genuine conventional balance in Europe, the forces will have to come from the Europeans. The United States is going broke providing its present conventional forces. Increasing its conventional forces for Europe is an utterly inconceivable notion under present fiscal circumstances. But if the Europeans are to strengthen and reorganize conventional forces for Europe, they will certainly not do so under American tutelage.

Do the Europeans actually have the military resources for such a shift? By and large, they do. Britain and France have nuclear deterrents in the process of a major upgrading. By 1995, they will have, between them, ten submarines and some 1,200 warheads, a force that seems more than adequate for a European strategic deterrent.[12] The major West European NATO countries already have large conventional forces and could certainly increase those forces if necessary.[13] France in 1914 was able to field an army of 8 million, and we hardly need remind ourselves what the Germans have been capable of. Today the principal obstacle to a serious European conventional defense is the nonparticipation of France in the alliance. For all intents and purposes, no conventional defense of West Germany is possible with the French army disengaged and French territory neutral.

For a long time, the French have made it clear that they will not integrate with an American-dominated alliance. There is an obvious solution: in a European-run NATO, the French could take on their proper responsibilities. Whether the Europeans could succeed depends, above all, on whether France and Germany could cooperate sufficiently in the military sphere. Since they never have but have preferred to rely on the Americans, they are often said to be incapable of military cooperation.

I prefer a different conclusion: Europeans have not developed a military coalition because they have not needed to do so. Their efforts have been pre-empted by the United States, and they have been more than happy with the arrangement. To see the real possibilities for European military cooperation, look at what is going on in other spheres. In economic matters, Europeans have achieved remarkable cooperation. The Common Market is unquestionably the most successful experiment in intergovernmental cooperation in modern times. France and Germany are the essential motors of the European Community.

Is military cooperation more difficult than economic cooperation? Quite the contrary. Economic interdependence involves interest groups throughout the whole spectrum of national politics and therefore enters intimately into the domestic politics of every country. Compared to these complexities, military cooperation is relatively simple. In fact, Europeans have greatly increased the military dimension of their cooperation in recent years. France and Germany, in particular, have been holding intensive talks for the past several years on how to increase their military cooperation. They have even begun experimenting with joint conventional forces.

Europeans have increased their military cooperation because they implicitly recognize that the American role must change and that they must prepare an alternative. They are not eager for the transformation, but they know it must take place. At this point, it is up to the United States to take the initiative to make clear that it would welcome a European-run NATO and indeed will eventually insist on it.

Devolution does not mean withdrawal. The United States should keep its nuclear commitment to Europe but should not be expected to bear the full weight of collective deterrence. The task should be shared with a parallel European deterrent. Similarly, the United States should continue to keep substantial conventional forces in Europe, to supplement West European armies, but it cannot continue to sustain the present ten divisions for NATO. Cutting out even half of those divisions would eventually have an appreciable impact on the U.S. fiscal situation. It would at least make it possible to begin to bring military spending under rational control and in some fashion commensurate with America's present geopolitical situation. Cutting military spending is certainly no panacea for America's fiscal disarray, but a reduced military budget that reflects a coherent geopolitical strategy is an essential part of any package to restore balance to American fiscal and monetary policy. In the long run, rebalancing the American economy will prove a far greater contribution to world order than a few more American divisions in Europe.

Arms Control: No Substitute for NATO Reform

These same arguments could have been made forcefully five or ten years ago. In the interim, the American position has grown more unstable and the European cooperation has intensified. These were trends already clear by the middle of the 1970s. What is new today is Gorbachev and his remarkable transformation of the Soviet scene. How does this affect the need and prospect for an American devolution within NATO?

One widespread reaction has been to regard Gorbachev's arms control negotiations as the heaven-sent opportunity to avoid changing the fundamental structure of the alliance and perhaps also to reduce America's defense burden. The tactic is tried and true. Fifteen years ago, the Mutual and Balanced Force Reduction (MBFR) negotiations were launched to delay or prevent changes in the structure of NATO. MBFR served its purpose extremely well. The negotiations achieved nothing in the way of arms reduction but did preempt any serious congressional discussion about American troop withdrawals from Europe.[14] Today such a tactic seems dangerous. Arms talks should not be used as a diversion from serious and long overdue reforms in the Western alliance. The military and economic difficulties of the American role have begun to reach a critical stage. For those who care about the alliance, it would be far more prudent to prepare an orderly transformation than to risk a sudden collapse of the American role. Moreover, it seems unlikely that Gorbachev will be able to accept changes in the Soviet military posture that would reduce NATO's requirements to the point that the United States could afford to continue its traditional protector's role.

To argue that the upcoming arms talks cannot be a panacea for NATO's problems is not to denigrate their importance. They may greatly improve Europe's political atmosphere. And they may greatly reduce the military danger of a surprise attack, a very significant accomplishment. But arms talks cannot negotiate away the need to maintain a military balance in Europe.

Inevitably the Soviet Union must remain a great military power—perhaps because of its inherent character, certainly because of its geopolitical situation. From Moscow, the Russians see themselves surrounded by Japan, China, India, the Muslims—including Iran—and Europe. Not surprisingly, they feel the need to remain a superpower. One can only imagine American behavior if suddenly placed in a similar geopolitical situation.

So long as the Soviets remain a military superpower, an independent Western Europe will need to have a military balance. So long as that European balance is necessary, the fundamental reform of NATO's internal arrangements cannot be avoided. Negotiations could be used as a cover for an American devolution and withdrawal. But the particular issues of arms control should not deflect us from our more fundamental purpose: to make the Western alliance viable over the long term. Moreover, the kinds of security arrangements likely to evolve out of Gorbachev's initiatives will hasten, rather than delay, the advisability of a diminished American role. If, for example, European security should come to depend more and more on reserve forces and defense in depth, the United States has less and less to offer. The United States is not well suited to organize that kind of defense. The sooner we can transfer the responsibility for it to the Germans and the French, the better it will be for Europe's security.

Devolution and Pan-Europa

When the broader political aspects of Europe's arms talks are considered, the case for American devolution becomes still more compelling. Negotiations about future security arrangements invevitably bear heavily upon the political and economic, as well as the military, character of some new pan-European system. The United States has a vital interest in the outcome of these talks but a lesser interest, nevertheless, than the European states themselves. The spring of 1989 witnessed an explosion of acrimonious misunderstanding between Bonn and Washington over plans for "modernizing" NATO's short-range missiles and negotiating their levels with the Soviets. This is only a foretaste of what may follow if the United States tries to hang on to its role of lead manager while formulating Western security proposals from an American perspective.

Traditionally Europeans have often preferred leaving Europe's military negotiations to the Americans while reserving the economic and political negotiations to themselves. Under present circumstances, this is a formula that puts the United States in a false position and threatens grave damage not only to the Atlantic alliance but also to Western Europe's own cohesion. As the prospects for political change grow, Europeans can no longer afford to allow American preoccupations to determine their security posture toward the Soviets. The United States should therefore encourage the Europeans, in particular the Germans and the French, to take the initiative in formulating the Western position. It is Europeans, after all, who will have to live most intimately with the results and provide the bulk of the forces upon which Europe's security will depend in the future. Meanwhile, the lingering American hegemony in NATO will not only lead to increasingly dangerous transatlantic friction but also encourage Europeans to procrastinate resolving a common position among themselves.

At this critical juncture in postwar Europe's evolution, it is hardly in America's interest to be subsidizing European disunity while delaying America's own geopolitical adjustment. The United States, of course, continues to have a vital interest in European stability. But that interest is no longer served by playing the traditional hegemonic role in NATO. Devolution is the answer.

Conclusion

Reflecting on the Soviet geopolitical situation helps put America's problem of overextension in better perspective. It is sometimes observed that both superpowers face a common problem of overextension and may look to resolve it through some form of European disengagement. The parallel is obvious, but so is the difference. The difficulty for the United States arises not from having failed but from not knowing how to take advantage of success. It has sustained Europe through its period of weakness and promoted the remarkable transformation of Japan. In recent years, it has also helped sustain the Chinese. Today these countries provide the essential elements of an indigenous Eurasian balance. It is absurd that the United States should be bankrupting itself, and destabilizing the world economy, by trying to sustain a balance against the Soviets that could almost exist without it. In short, the West has won the cold war. The United States needs to take advantage of that victory. America has to learn how to harness the forces of its allies for purposes that are very much in the common interest. To do this, Americans must finally abandon that bipolar perspective that cannot see how much this victory has changed the world since 1950.

Notes

1. A notable study extolling the virtues of the transatlantic system is Anton W. DePorte, *Europe between the Superpowers: The Enduring Balance* (New Haven: Yale University Press, 1979). More recently, see Gregory Treverton, *Making the Alliance Work: The U.S. and Western Europe* (Ithaca, N.Y.: Cornell University Press, 1985).

2. French foreign minister Robert Schuman observed as his country decided to sign the Atlantic Treaty: "Today, we attain what we hoped for in vain between the two wars: the United States recognizes that there can be neither peace nor security for the United States if Europe is in danger." On West European support for the Atlantic Treaty at the time of its origin, see Alfred Grosser, *The Western Alliance* (New York: Vintage Books, 1980), pp. 82–95. For a discussion of current European enthusiasm for the U.S. commitment, see Josef Joffe, *The Limited Partnership* (Cambridge, Mass.: Ballinger, 1987).

3. See Richard Halloran, "Europe Called Main U.S. Arms Cost," *New York Times,* July 20, 1984. This estimate is reported to be derived from FY 1985. Also see

Alice C. Maroni and John J. Ulrich, *The U.S. Commitment to Europe's Defense: A Review of Cost Issues and Estimates* (Washington, D.C.: Congressional Research Service, November 7, 1985). In a recent U.S. Congress report, this figure was criticized as too low because it did not take into account the cost of U.S. strategic forces. See *Interim Report of the Defense Burdensharing Panel of the Committee on Armed Services House of Representatives* (August 1988), p. 38.

4. The West Germans deploy twelve divisions, twenty-four combat aircraft squadrons, and a small naval force in the Baltic, costing $30.3 billion in 1988. The French deploy six smaller armored divisions and eleven light infantry divisions, forty-six squadrons, and a larger navy—and they possess a strategic deterrent—all costing $31.8 billion in 1988. International Institute for Strategic Studies, *The Military Balance, 1988–1989* (London: IISS, 1988), pp. 60, 65.

5. The vulnerability of American territory to a Soviet nuclear attack has long been seen as undermining extended deterrence. As Henry Kissinger observed in Brussels in 1979: "it is absurd to base the strategy of the West on the credibility of the threat of mutual suicide. . . . European allies should not keep asking us to multiply strategic assurances that we cannot possibly mean, or if we do mean, we should not want to execute because if we execute, we risk the destruction of civilization." Reprinted in Henry Kissinger, "NATO: The Next Thirty Years," *Survival* (November–December 1979): 266. Those arguing for a U.S. policy of no first use are also particularly cognizant of the risks to the American homeland posed by an alliance policy that relies on initiating nuclear strikes to stem a Soviet conventional assault. See McGeorge Bundy et al., "Nuclear Weapons and the Atlantic Alliance," *Foreign Affairs* (Spring 1982): 753–68.

6. The former NATO SACEUR, General Andrew Goodpaster (Ret.), advocates taking advantage of the current thaw in East-West relations to negotiate a 50 percent reduction in U.S. forces in Europe in return for major Soviet withdrawals from Eastern Europe. General Andrew Goodpaster, *Gorbachev and the Future of East-West Security: A Response for the Mid-Term* (Washington, D.C.: Atlantic Council, April 1989).

7. See David P. Calleo, *Beyond American Hegemony* (New York: Basic Books, 1987); also see David P. Calleo, "NATO's Middle Course," *Foreign Policy* 69 (Winter 1987–1988): 135–47.

8. The likelihood of a U.S. nuclear response to a Soviet attack has been in doubt since early in the nuclear age. Robert McNamara, secretary of defense in the Kennedy and Johnson administrations, has written that "in long conversations with successive Presidents—Kennedy and Johnson—I recommended, without qualification, that they never initiate, under any circumstances, the use of nuclear weapons. I believe they accepted my recommendation." Robert McNamara, "The Military Role of Nuclear Weapons," *Foreign Affairs* (Fall 1983): 79. In the mid-1970s, as East-West tensions were on the increase, Paul H. Nitze, a key figure in U.S. security policy, feared that the United States was increasingly becoming "self-deterred" and thus unlikely to carry through on its nuclear guarantee to Europe. See Paul H. Nitze, "Deterring Our Deterrent," *Foreign Policy* 25 (Winter 1976–1977): 195–210.

9. One method of demonstrating the relative decline of American economic power is to look at the U.S. share of world exports of manufacturers. In 1960 that figure stood at 25.3 percent; it dropped to 16.8 percent in 1980, and 13.9 percent in 1987. See *Statistical Abstract of the United States* (Washington, D.C.: U.S. Govern-

ment Printing Office, 1980), 813; and *Statistical Abstract of the United States* (1989), 731.

10. The following table illustrates the fluctuation of the dollar against the Deutschemark and the yen between 1970 and 1986.

Year	Yen	Deutschemark
1970	369	3.66
1972	303	3.19
1974	292	2.59
1976	296	2.52
1978	210	2.01
1980	226	1.82
1982	249	2.43
1984	237	2.85
1986	168	2.17

Figures cited in Organization of Economic Cooperation and Development Economic Outlook, *Historical Statistics: 1960–1986* (Paris: OECD, 1988), p. 19.

11. The American case against NATO's reliance on nuclear weapons can be found in the classic statement by McGeorge Bundy, George F. Kennan, Robert S. McNamara, and Gerard Smith, "Nuclear weapons and the Atlantic Alliance," *Foreign Affairs* 60, 4 (Spring 1982): 753–68. Reagan strategists also came to promote a greater U.S. emphasis on non-nuclear or limited nuclear force. Report of the Commission on Integrated Long-Term Strategy, Fred C. Iklé and Albert Wohlstetter, cochairmen, *Discriminate Deterrence* (Washington, D.C.: U.S. Government Printing Office, January 1988).

12. On British and French modernization plans, see George M. Seignious II and Jonathan Paul Yates, "Europe's Nuclear Superpowers," *Foreign Policy* 55 (Summer 1984): 40–53; and Robbin F. Laird and Susan Clark, *The Impact of the Changing European Nuclear Forces on Theater Deterrence,* IDA Paper P-2065 (Alexandria, Va.: Institute for Defense Analyses, 1988).

13. Data on the armed forces of the major European NATO powers are as follows:

Country	Personnel	Tanks	Aircraft	Naval Combat Vessels
United Kingdom	318,700	1200	596	59
Federal Republic of Germany	488,400	4887	604	21
France	546,900	1540	520	45

International Institute of Strategic Studies, *The Military Balance 1987–88* (London: IISS, 1987).

14. On the MBFR talks and Senate majority leader Mike Mansfield's proposed drawdown of U.S. troops in Europe, see Jonathan Dean, *Watershed in Europe* (Lexington, Mass.: Lexington Books, 1987), p. 100; on the Mansfield amendments and the Nixon administration's attempts to head them off, see Henry Kissinger, *The White House Years* (Boston: Little, Brown, 1979), pp. 938–49.

14
Disengagement from Europe: The Framing of an Argument

Earl C. Ravenal

The Name of the Game

The purpose of this chapter is not so much to make the substantive case for American strategic disengagement from Europe but to indicate how I think the case should be made (and to distinguish my argument from those of others who may come out in the same place but for reasons that I either would not share or do not think really arrive there). In the method is where much of the trouble lies between those (still few) critics who "advocate" American disengagement from the defense of Western Europe and those (still many) loyalists who argue for its indefinite continuance.

The problem is how the question is framed. The typical debate on the future of NATO is entitled, "Should the United States disengage from Europe?" That conveys and invites an air of pure prescription; it even suggests or allows arguments based on animus, on one side, countered by sentiment, on the other. It almost demands a normative tone. My version of the debate is entitled: "Should the United States accommodate, or adjust to, the actual, progressive dissolution or disintegration of NATO?" That form properly indicates the complex predictive-prescriptive nature of the problem. This is not the ordinary normative or prescriptive argument. It is not: "NATO: for or against?" If that were the question, I might even join the NATO loyalists.

Almost all Americans are "for" NATO in some such sense, which they are led to construe as almost a moral sense. Europe is where the political sympathies of many Americans lie; it is where many would prefer to draw the American defensive frontier, if such frontiers were matters of pure—and free—preference. There is, however, a small but growing band of neoconservatives and new rightists, who have a real animus against Europeans—so-called Eurowimps. This band of articulate and well-published conservatives includes such commentators as Irving Kristol and Melvyn Krauss,[1] and it also includes the editorial board of the *Wall Street Journal*. They favor an active—indeed, an aggressive—role for the United States in the world, but they think that the Europeans trammel the United States and inhibit its political-military initiatives even, in the "peripheral" areas of the world, including some that are not much of the Europeans' business, such as Central America. These conservative critics favor an American military withdrawal, partial or total, "from" Europe—but stop short of denial of a U.S. commitment—and a shift of American defensive "emphasis" to other parts of the world, usually Southwest Asia, the Western Hemisphere, and the sealanes. Sometimes these moves are suggested more as gambits to induce or coerce greater European sharing of the burdens of the still-common defense, in which case the moves are proposed as not absolute or irrevocable but reversible on the condition of certain European behavior. Perhaps the most extreme version of the neoconservative anti-NATO case is that of Melvyn Krauss, who posits that the alliance is a net negative—in terms of defensive output or defensive efficiency—for all parties, not just the United States but the European allies themselves and the present collectivity of NATO as a whole.

My approach is different. The argument I put forth is not normative or even purely prescriptive. It is prescription mingled with prediction—and even with some empirical description. It pivots on a description of NATO. What is the essence of this alliance? The answer is that NATO is not the ordinary pooling of defensive (or, in other times, offensive) resources by the participant nations. Its necessary—and I dare say sufficient—condition is the unilateral American nuclear guarantee—what is known as extended deterrence. With this, you have an alliance, a compact. Without it, you have nothing, except a semblance, a label.

Indeed, you could say that the mere label "NATO" is the future of the alliance—or, worse, its present. We are celebrating NATO's fortieth birthday. The loyalists congratulate themselves on NATO's remarkable (and initially unexpected) longevity and toast "a thousand years." But the situation can be summed up in this metaphor: after forty years, NATO is an old, unused medicine on the shelf. The bottle is still there, and the label remains the same, but the contents have long since evaporated or spoiled. That is why it may be misplaced to urge the dissolution of NATO, certainly not its instant and formal abrogation. NATO is an alliance that is less dependable, year by year, as objective changes in circumstances erode the validity of the essential condition of the alliance—the American guarantee. Conversely, the loyalists should not take as compelling proof of the perpetual durability of the alliance the fact that something called NATO has not been formally repudiated. NATO can dissolve without a scrap of paper being torn up, without a journalist reporting it. The failure of almost any part of the practical condition for the integrity of NATO—and that is, preeminently, the predictive reliability of the American commitment to defend against a wide range of Soviet pressures—will mean the effective demise of the alliance. NATO need not even perish in acrimony (though that may attend its demise); it can expire in skepticism. The strategic content of the alliance can drain away, measured by the confidence allies repose in the ritual American commitment and by the hedges they erect against the guarantees the alliance still pretends to offer. NATO need not lose its form, at least until long after it has lost its substance.

And so I would change the question to this: Does it make sense to continue to meet the increasing requisites of maintaining the alliance—and this in the face of recurring recriminations among the allies; increasing technical, physical, and fiscal demands; and risks that increase in scale (though they may, for periods of time, be diminished, through benign diplomacy, in incidence)? Such a reformulation captures the combined predictive-prescriptive nature of this inquiry, and in a way that might even elicit a certain cooperation by open-minded NATO loyalists.

More specifically, instead of looking at NATO in quasi-moral terms and as a policy object in itself, I view it as, at once, more parochial in terms of the problems that NATO poses for America's domestic economic-social-political system) and more cosmic (in terms of the significance of NATO as a large piece of America's quasi-"empire"). In turn, the continued appropriateness of America's guarantee of Western Europe is a matter of the way the U.S. system works (its political economy) and the way the international system works (geopolitics). In other words, I view NATO in terms of America's expenditures on it and America's net advantage in doing so and in terms of America's larger scheme of containment of Soviet power, Soviet proxies, and indigenous but Soviet-oriented revolutionaries around the world.

The question of NATO is often posed in falsely moral terms: Are America's allies worthy of its help? That is not an operational formulation. The important question is this: Is America getting its own money's worth out of the alliance? Foreign policy—like a Renaissance landscape—must be looked at from some point of perspective, not from none, or from all; and it is appropriate for American disputants to view NATO from an American point of reference. It may seem crass to inquire about the problems of NATO from an American viewpoint and to weigh those problems primarily on the grounds of cost to Americans. Yet it is perfectly fair, as well as inevitable, to observe that NATO's future will be disposed within America's political, economic, and social process and largely on grounds of cost (and cost traded off against the risk involved in holding its nuclear umbrella over its European allies).

The Logic and Logistics of the Problem

There are questions of logic and logistics involved in America's commitment to NATO and, indeed, to the larger enterprise of containment. Although America's guarantee to protect Europe may be vitiated or void, something is yet entailed. Nothing is free, particularly alliance guarantees. To the United

States, NATO is a tangible disposition, a set of preparations to intervene in conflict. Thus, the alliance has its requisites. And it is these tangible requisites of alliance that suggest the argument for letting NATO wind down over, say, the next decade or so.

In a nutshell, the requisites of NATO are risk and cost. The essence of NATO is the American nuclear commitment, that is, the coupling of America's strategic nuclear retaliatory force ultimately to the outbreak of a conflict in Europe. But because deterrence is not perfect and because we want to avoid excessive risk, we set conventional defense at as self-sufficient and "confident" a level as possible.

Thus, the commitment to Europe presents the United States with a choice between high, and perhaps unsupportable, costs, associated with the confident conventional defense of Europe, and unassumable risks attributable to reliance on the earlier use of nuclear weapons. The direction in which this tension is resolved by any particular American administration is not rigidly determined. To some extent, cost can be transmuted into additional risk, and risk can be transformed into mere cost. That is what is meant by lowering or raising the nuclear threshold. But as long as the United States is committed to Europe, the choice itself is inescapable.

The Europeans have a somewhat parallel choice: costly generation of sufficient conventional forces or acquisition or expansion of their own national nuclear arsenals, with more resolute and risky doctrines of employment. But there is an obvious difference. The European allies are situated along the forward line of defense; the United States can decide whether it wants to pitch its own security perimeter along that common line. That statement begins to suggest the disabilities of shared risk, which is what alliances are about in the age of nuclear damage.

The consequences of shared risk—the coupling of America's strategic nuclear arsenal to the outbreak of conflict, at any lesser level, in Europe—are twofold. They exhibit themselves in the character of America's nuclear strategy and in the history of NATO, which is a tapestry of crises of strategic confidence.[2]

The Verdict of History

There is a structural reason for NATO's present, and persistent, debility: the danger, and yet the incredibility, of the American military guarantee of Europe, including the nuclear umbrella. The cracks in America's guarantee in turn form a tension inherent in the American assumption of this strategic commitment to Europe forty years ago.

The alliance of Atlantic nations has been beset by many problems: the periodic recrudescence of commercial and agricultural disputes; the irreconcilable antagonisms of pairs of nations, such as Greece and Turkey; the threat of Eurocommunism; the acrimony over burden sharing; the complaints about the one-way street of American military production for the alliance; the assaults of neutralists and anti-American political groups; the failures of consultation; and the recriminations about American hegemony. But whatever else is wrong with the Atlantic alliance, its essential problems are strategic.

From its beginning in 1949 to the present, NATO's history could be written in terms of a series of strategic crises: the isolationist challenge in the great debate of 1950–1951 about dispatching American troops to Europe; the rejection of the European Defense Community (EDC) in 1954; the thwarting of the Suez adventure of Britain and France by the United States in 1956; the failure of the United States to aid the Hungarian uprising in 1956; the Cuban missile crisis of 1962; the unilateral American cancellation of the Skybolt air-to-ground missile in 1962; the defeat of the multilateral nuclear force (MLF) in the mid-1960s; de Gaulle's withdrawal of France from the NATO structure in 1966; the Soviet invasion of Czechoslovakia in 1968; Kissinger's "Year of Europe" in 1973; the European denial to the United States of bases and overflight in the Mideast war of October 1973 and disputes over oil sharing during the ensuing embargo; divergent reactions to the Soviet invasion of Afghanistan in 1979; European criticism of America's conduct in Central America; and the emplacement of intermediate nuclear forces (INF) in Europe between the 1979 decision and the mid-1980s.

The last deserves special comment. Although the deployment of American missiles (now withdrawn according to the 1987 INF treaty) was a response to German chancellor Helmut Schmidt's 1977 plea for some regional balance to the Soviet SS-20s, the compromise two-track decision opened an abyss between the European and American allies: the United States bent on a considerable deployment of the INF, the Europeans intent on negotiations with the Soviet Union. True, the cohesion of NATO weathered five years of Soviet bluster and the excitement of West European peace groups; but the crisis illustrated a point of deeper significance. One might ask why European governments would have wanted these longer-range nuclear weapons in the first place. The additional protection they afforded was illusory; they were not even subject to European control. The missiles were not an increment to NATO's strength; rather, they represented another European attempt to secure America's commitment to the defense of Europe. They were a symbol of Europe's abiding distrust of America's extended deterrence.

What does all this history prove? First, NATO's crises are not random. There is a common thread; they are all tests of confidence among the allies. Second, the crises are not accidental or superficial. They would not be crises if they did not have deep causal roots; in fact, they derive from the divergent conceptions of alliance, the divergent security needs, and the divergent geopolitical situations of the United States and Europe. Third, the crises are not novel. They stem from problems that have been implicit in the alliance from its inception.

In short, the crises lie along the dimension of risk—shared risk. Forty years after the founding of NATO, the defense of Western Europe still rests on the proposition that an American president will invite the destruction of U.S. cities and the incineration of 100 million Americans to repel a Soviet incursion or resist a Soviet ultimatum in Western Europe. On its face, America's war plan—never denied by any president from Truman to Bush or by any secretary of state from Marshall to Baker—is the first use of nuclear weapons, if necessary, to defend Europe. But under the surface, America's nuclear commitment to Europe is not so sure. The word that encapsulates this problem is *coupling*—a term of art used by strategic analysts to connote the integrity of the chain of escalation, from conventional war in Europe to theater nuclear weapons to the use of America's ultimate strategic weapon.

In a larger sense, coupling connotes the identity of the fates of the peoples, societies, and political systems on both sides of the Atlantic. The root of the problem is that America, the alliance guarantor, hoping to escape the destruction of nuclear war, will seek to put time between the outbreak of war in Europe and the decision to escalate to nuclear weapons and will take whatever advantage it can of its distance from Europe. (Not that an adversary is likely to test American will with an attack on Europe. Odds of, say, 65 percent of an American nuclear response will almost certainly restrain a potential aggressor. Even a whiff of American nuclear retaliation is probably enough to keep the Soviet Union from invading Western Europe. But those odds will not convince allies. There is a nagging asymmetry about nuclear protection: it takes more credibility to keep an ally than to deter an adversary.)

Virtually every American strategic move—the multilateral nuclear force (MLF), flexible response, the Schlesinger doctrine, the neutron bomb, INF— has evoked the specter of decoupling in one or another of its forms: either the avoidance of a nuclear response altogether or the attempt to confine even a nuclear conflict to the European theater. The Strategic Defense Initiative (SDI), a design to protect American society from Soviet missiles, stirred European concern that the United States could afford a "Fortress America" mentality and ignore forward defense in Europe. And America's attempt to endow NATO forces with emerging technology has had the significance, for some Europeans, of further detaching the United States from its commitment to escalate to nuclear weapons, specifically by promising conventional coverage of some targets that otherwise require nuclear systems.

At issue here is not whether these American strategic moves are well planned or well meant—they might even have the declared or ostensible purpose of affirming coupling—but whether they have the possible effect of attenuating the American connection with Europe; whether they provide reasons, or pretexts, for the United States to make its escalation to strategic nuclear weapons less than prompt and automatic; whether they give the United States additional firebreaks. Coupling is the essence of alliance protection in a nuclear age, and firebreaks are an imperative of American security. But coupling and firebreaks are inversely related.

A Crisis of Solvency

When the issue of NATO's cost[3] is presented, to Americans and from an American perspective, it translates into two questions: (1) Is America getting its money's worth out of the alliance? And (2) can America continue to pay the price of NATO? Increasingly, the answer to both of those questions is no.

Obviously these two ultimate questions transcend the issue of burden sharing. Burden sharing itself breaks down into two subsidiary points. First, in terms of shares of gross national product devoted to defense (and also in terms of per capita defense expenditures), it is apparent that America's European allies pay far less of their "share" of the common defense than does the United States. Comparative contributions of certain NATO allies are as follows; United States, 6.4 percent; West Germany, 3.1 percent; Britain, 5.4 percent; France, 3.9 percent; Netherlands, 3.0 percent.[4]

But second, in other terms, usually cited by those who support the present dispositions, America's European allies appear to be making the lion's share of the contributions of forces in Europe itself. A typical estimate has it that "of the ready forces currently available in Europe, about 91 percent of the ground forces and 86 percent of the air forces come from European countries, as do 75 percent of NATO's tanks and more than 90 percent of its armored divisions."[5] Another reads: "If the Soviet Union were to launch an attack against Western Europe tomorrow, our NATO allies would provide 90 percent of the ground forces, 80 percent of the tanks, and 75 percent of the naval and air units available to repulse the invasion."[6]

But comparing burdens is not the point, or the problem. The question has always been whether the United States is getting its money's worth out of its forward strategy and would be getting its money's worth even after some putative redistribution of burdens. In any case, it is increasingly doubtful that the United States, taken as an entire political-social-economic system, will be able to continue to provide the resources for a confident conventional defense of Europe. What the United States faces at this juncture is a crisis of solvency—the solvency of its national strategy and, beyond that, of its foreign policy. Thirteen years ago, I said that the implementation of our foreign policy was outrunning our material and social resources.[7] That proposition still holds.

There are two senses of solvency, representing two phases of the problem, which operate in tandem. The first is the one that has been most persistently remarked. It is, in the words of Samuel Huntington, the "Lippmann Gap."[8] Almost half a century ago, Walter Lippmann, in a classic critique, said: "In foreign relations, as in all other relations, a policy has been formed only when commitments and power have been brought into balance." This judgment was echoed by James Forrestal, the first secretary of defense, in his initial report to Congress in 1948: "It is our duty to see that our military potential conforms to the requirements of our national policy; in other words, that our policy does not outstrip our power."

Lippmannesque critiques have been experiencing something of a revival.[9] But most of the arguments from solvency function better in the critical than the creative mode. They tend to pose the choices, not make the choice. Often they end merely in a reiteration of the alternatives. (For instance, do we reduce our commitment to Europe after all, or do we resign ourselves to bearing the domestic costs of providing the requisite forces?) Which term would the critics insist on as fixed, and which would they allow to float?

The intractable problem of choice lies not in the rather obvious way that Lippmann framed the question. Lippmann failed to distinguish between policies based simply on inadequate means and policies based on means that are impossible or improbable for a society to generate. The question of solvency has now entered a post-Lippmann phase. It is not enough just to invoke the potential power that would balance U.S. commitments. To test the validity of those commitments, it is now necessary to assess the underpinnings of that power, which are mostly domestic.

Thus we have a second gap, which is the one on which I have insisted, for its empirical primacy in shaping, ultimately, a nation's strategies and foreign policies. It is the gap that is at the root of the "imperial problem." This is the gap between the strategic means themselves, which are held to be necessary to execute or validate a chosen foreign policy, and the resources— or, more properly, the resource base that is called upon to generate the resources—needed to validate the requisite strategy.[10]

Faced with that stern requirement, even the solvency critics sometimes suggest that we can find some way to avoid the ultimate choice. This second gap, the post-Lippmann gap, is a hard, objective, and intractable datum. It will not do, as many writers would, to assume that the United States can physically generate, and has historically generated, the resources (usually stated in terms of a percentage of gross national product) necessary to fund whatever level of "national security" (or, more properly, whatever extent of strategic exertion) is deemed appropriate to its status in the international system or the moral universe. A typical example of such an argument is this: "Under John Kennedy in 1961, this country spent 9 percent of its gross national product—half the federal budget—on defense. Today we allocate only a bit more than 6 percent of GNP, a quarter of the federal budget, to defense.

. . . What has changed in this country over two decades is the addition of so many other costly activities and income-redistribution programs."[11] This may be historically true, but we are situated in a web of economic and political factors, and our choices are where we find them now, not where they might have been more than a quarter of a century ago. And the fact that domestic social welfare expenditures have overtaken—and putatively preempted—defense expenditures (a point made by defense conservatives as well as defense liberals) does not mitigate the situation; it certainly does not make defense more affordable. Quite the contrary, it makes it even less affordable. If anything, it argues for reducing both social welfare spending and defense spending.

Sooner or later, the constraints of the domestic system will prevail. It is of such domestic stuff, in the last analysis, that foreign policy is made, or unmade. It has been said that foreign policy begins at home; it may also be true that foreign policy ends at home.

Partial Remedies

Could the United States continue to defend Europe yet save significant amounts of money without compromising the effectiveness of the common defense? Various remedies have been proposed, of widely differing kinds and levels, by NATO loyalists and by NATO's critics. These remedies purport to provide sufficient conventional defense, or to adjust the American relationship to the alliance, or otherwise to meet the challenge within acceptable parameters of European and American sacrifice and exposure to risk.

A summary conclusion is that these proposed solutions, though generally right-minded and full of individual points of merit, in the end prove insufficient or contradictory or improbable of execution. After reviewing them, we will find the problem of NATO, as it presents itself to American policy, more or less where it is now and has always implicitly been.

Quick Fixes

Over the years, NATO has invented, and to some extent proceeded with, a long list of schemes to patch up its tactical deficiencies and repair its basic defensive stance. Energetic and often imaginative efforts have been made by the Office of the Secretary of Defense beginning in the Carter administration. These moves fall mainly into the category of quick fixes in NATO's existing posture: increasing armaments and firepower, including precision-guided antitank weapons and heavier American army divisions; improving electronic warfare; bringing about greater military integration of NATO in the areas of logistics, air defense, weapons procurement, communications, and intelligence; refining doctrine and stressing maneuver; improving mobility and readiness; fostering greater use of reserves; and correcting the maldeployment of forces along the front.

Many of these moves have been accomplished. Most are sensible as long as the alliance exists in roughly its present form, with more or less its present mission. But some of the quick fixes are not as quick or cheap as they might seem. And some moves—such as logistics integration and weapons standardization—would reduce U.S. autonomy of decision making and flexibility of action in the event of hostilities. There is also a question of sufficiency, even if all these measures were taken. For one thing, there remains the lack of maneuver depth and the vulnerability of supply lines resulting from the French withdrawal from NATO in 1966. For another, there is the probable inability of the navy to resupply the army in Europe in a sustained conventional war; the attrition of American convoys or individual ships would be fearsome, even if we exacted an equivalent toll of attacking Soviet undersea and surface naval forces. Also, even the proposed (or imagined) "emerging technology," and associated tactical concepts—revolutionary developments in long-range surveillance and target acquisition, and in lethal specialized submunitions and accurate terminal guidance; bold attempts to target second-echelon Soviet armored units, logistical installations, choke points, and airfields, usually far behind the forward edge of battle—raise serious questions. Some doubts center on the technical feasibility and high cost of the new systems. Still other critics challenge their relevance to the specific threat—the Soviet operational maneuver groups (OMGs). Another objection is that the new munitions, although conventional, use the same delivery vehicles that are assigned to nuclear weapons; this might create a fatal ambiguity in a war.

Devolution

A more far-reaching approach to mitigating America's burdens in NATO has been labeled devolution.[12] Devolution comprises a deliberate, orderly, and militarily adequate effort by the United States to confer defensive capability and responsibility on Western Europe. More than the other remedies, devolution is premised on European unity; there would have to be a fit political and strategic receptacle for the increased security capabilities and responsibilities. But the integration of the European states has not been impressive on the political plane (although considerable economic integration will be realized in the unified market of 1992). And there is the more challenging question of combined military competence, particularly in nuclear arms. True nuclear allies must share strategies, decision making, and targeting, not merely financing and technology. Even if it could be achieved, an independent European nuclear force would be at best useless to the United States and at worst a considerable embarrassment.

The question here is not whether the West European nations could defend themselves in some measure; it is whether the United States would benefit from continuing to be a party to such an alliance. The trouble with devolution for the United States is that it combines aspects of commitment and decommitment, arraying them in a series of contradictions: it would have participation without authority, risk without control, involvement without the clear ability to defend, and exposure without adequate deterrence.

Arms Control

Any contemporary critique of NATO must be against the backdrop of the Gorbachev factor—that is, the impressive offers of unilateral and disproportionately large mutual force cuts by the Soviet Union[13], and the far-reaching new agenda of conventional arms control that comes with them, amounting to the promise—or the attractive illusion—of mutual reductions that would preserve the balance of conventional forces in Europe with lesser, and more sustainable and tolerable, effort by the United States.

The current forum for thrashing out conventional arms control proposals is the twenty-three-nation (sixteen NATO and seven Warsaw Pact) talks called Conventional Armed Forces in Europe (CFE), meeting in Vienna (replacing the immediately prior designation, Conventional Stability Talks, or CST, and the original forum, Mutual and Balanced Force Reductions, or MBFR). But even with mutual conventional force reduction, America's commitment to Europe, its forces for Europe, and its annual budgetary costs on account of Europe would remain in their present range.

No doubt some such cuts will be made, but several matters are being confused. The Gorbachev cuts alter mostly the probability of a war in Europe. To the extent that they are reciprocated by the NATO allies, they somewhat reduce American forces for the European theater and thus the continuing cost to Americans of supporting NATO. (We now have on the table Bush's proposal of a cut in U.S. and Soviet ground and air troops to a common theater ceiling of 275,000, amounting to a cut of 30,000 U.S. troops and 325,000 Soviet troops; Bush's 30,000 troop cut would save a maximum of $3 billion a year.) Therefore, even with the arms cuts proposed by Gorbachev and by NATO, America's continuing participation in the common defense of Western Europe would require more or less the same nuclear and conventional dispositions as now. And the distribution of comparative burdens between the United States and its European allies would remain more or less what it is now, and so the same command arrangements would probably persist. The disabilities of the alliance on two levels—strategy and resources—would remain; the oscillations of American national strategy, between emphasis on conventional forces and reliance on nuclear weapons, would continue; and the mutual recriminations would go on.

All of the above are virtually built into the structure and dynamic of NATO—indeed, of any unequal multilateral alliance based on one country's provision of the ultimate defense of the alliance.

Troop Withdrawal

One of the most frequently proposed remedies for the high cost of the disproportionate American contribution to NATO is "troop withdrawal." This is a unilateral withdrawal of part of the American forces that are deployed in Europe. The salient version was the Mansfield amendment, or resolution, offered annually in Congress for eight years until 1975. In its various forms, it would have reduced American troops in Europe by as much as two-thirds, redeploying them to the United States but not (in all but one year's version) deleting them from the active force structure. But withdrawal of units saves nothing unless they are also deactivated. Nor would the Mansfield proposal have touched the forces kept in the United States for European contingencies. (Forces the United States keeps in Europe are only about one-third of the forces it maintains for the support of NATO.) Most significant, the U.S. commitment to European defense would have remained in full force. This is not a virtue but a flaw; the Mansfield type of initiative represents withdrawal without decommitment, a precarious stance.

Most versions of troop withdrawal are more trivial, some merely symbolic. An example was the amendment sponsored in 1982 by Senator Ted Stevens (R–Alaska), chairman of the Senate Appropriations Subcommittee on Defense, which would have lowered the ceiling on U.S. deployments in Europe in such a way as to return some 23,000 troops to the United States. As Morton H. Halperin said, in rebuttal, it is cheaper for the United States to keep its troops in Europe—cheaper, that is, then keeping its defensive commitment and just relocating its forces to the United States, providing even more prepositioned equipment in Europe and more airlift and sealift to return the forces there at the first sign of trouble.[14] But it is not cheaper than absolving itself of the commitment, disbanding most of the forces it devotes to it, and also saving the tactical air and surface naval units that go along with it. What makes the difference is not the troops but the commitment.

The Case for Strategic Disengagement

The foregoing ideas for remedying or mitigating America's situation in Europe might have some value and are often ingenious, but they do not constitute a policy that would close the gap between conventional requirements and available resources or obviate nuclear strategies that are precarious yet still lack credibility.

What would meet the test of sufficiency is a progressive disengagement of American forces from NATO, accompanied by a substantive withdrawal from the commitment to come to the defense of Europe in the event of attack or military pressure. This would be an actual, tangible disengagement. It would not be merely verbal, and it need not even be formal. Disengagement would be a matter of annulling, operationally—that is, in terms of real predictable propensity to intervene in conflict—the U.S. commitment to defend.

A thorough and consistent disengagement from Europe would shed the responsibilities, as well as the burdens, of alliance. The United States would devolve defensive tasks upon the European states but not insist on the orderly and sufficient substitution of capabilities or harbor illusions of maintaining American political weight in subsequent European decision making. Withdrawal from Europe would take a decade of preparation, diplomacy, and logistical rearrangement. The United States would progressively reduce Europe's strategic dependency on it and insulate itself from the consequences of conflict in Europe.

Disengagement from the defense of Europe would make sense only as part of a broad alternative conception of foreign policy and national strategy for the United States. The resolution of its defense predicament and its fiscal dilemma suggests a wholesale remedy. Globally it would draw back to a line that has two mutually reinforcing characteristics, credibility and feasibility—a line that it must hold, as part of the definition of its sovereignty, and a line that it can hold, as a defensive perimeter and a strategic force concept that can be maintained with advantage and within constraints over the long haul.

If the United States were to disengage—in general from all regions of the world—it could save on the order of $150 billion a year from the current defense budgets. (Another $80 billion to $100 billion or more, to close the federal budgetary gap that looms each year for the next several years, at least, should come from stringent cuts in entitlements and other domestic programs.) America could defend its essential security and central values with a much smaller force structure than it now has. It would provide the following general purpose forces: eight land divisions (six army and two Marine Corps), twenty tactical air wing equivalents (eleven air force, four Marine Corps, and five navy), and six carrier battle groups. With the addition of a dyad of nuclear forces, submarines and cruise-missile-armed bombers, this would mean manpower of 1,125,000 (330,000 army, 300,000 air force, 360,000 navy, and 135,000 Marine Corps). The total defense budget at the end of a decade of adjustment would be about $150 billion in 1990 dollars. In contrast, the parting request of the Reagan administration for 1990, modified to reflect the stance of the incoming Bush administration, consists of twenty-one land divisions and forty-four tactical air wing equivalents, with fourteen carrier battle groups; this force requires about 2,121,000 military personnel and a budget authorization of $296 billion.

Unless the United States changes its course, these numbers will multiply considerably. By 1999, the defense budget will be about $435 billion, and cumulative defense spending during the decade from now until then will be $3.6 trillion. Under a noninterventionist policy, the 1999 defense budget would be $213 billion, and the cumulative cost over a decade would have been about $2.5 trillion.[15]

The savings to the United States from its present European spending would amount to a greater fraction than the savings from the overall defense budget, since Atlantic-oriented forces would constitute only 26 percent of the noninterventionist program, compared to the current European-oriented forces that constitute 43 percent of the present defense program. At the end of a decade of adjustment, there would be no American forces in Europe; but in and around the United States, oriented toward the Atlantic, there would be three (army) divisions, seven tactical air wing equivalents (five air force and two navy), and three carrier battle groups. By 1999, after a decade of retrenchment, the United States could be spending (in then-year inflated dollars) only $55 billion a year on the residual forces deliberately retained in the force structure, out of those it now keeps for European contingencies. This compares with $187 billion that it would be spending in 1999 for the forces that it is now keeping for NATO. (The costs now attributable to NATO, $127 billion for fiscal year 1990, are not entirely avoidable, but as much as 70 percent of them could be eliminated over a ten-year period.) Cumulatively, over ten years, instead of spending $1.6 trillion on NATO, the United States would have spent only $874 billion.

If the United States is to cut defense spending significantly, it must change its national strategy and foreign policy. The only way to save significant sums from the defense budget is to remove large, noticeable units from the force structure. And this would make it necessary, somewhere along the line, to reduce its defensive commitments in the world; specifically, both of the cardinal elements of the present American national strategy would have to change. Instead of deterrence and alliance, it would pursue war avoidance and self-reliance. Self-reliance is a response to (as well as a precipitant of) the dissolution of alliances, nuclear proliferation, and the practical demise of extended deterrence. Precisely because America's stance in the world is essentially defensive rather than aggressive and expansive, it would benefit from a compartmentalization of deadly quarrels between other nations. Compartmentalization must mean the delegation of defensive tasks to regional countries and the acceptance of the results of this, win or lose. It would, over time, accommodate the dissolution of defensive commitments that obligate it to overseas intervention—not just in Europe but in the western Pacific and the Middle East.

The other phase of this alternative national strategy, war avoidance, is a response to the diffusion of power, the attainment of nuclear parity by the Soviet Union, and the risk of nuclear destruction to itself. It is based on the fact that the United States can no longer intricately and reliably manipulate or manage conflict. It will always need a strategy that discourages direct nuclear attacks on the homeland or intolerable coercion of national political choices through nuclear threats. But today safety for the United States depends on maintaining crisis stability, where both sides have a strong incentive to avoid striking first with their nuclear weapons. A design for stability must include an unconditional doctrine of no first use of nuclear weapons. And a consistent policy of no first use implies the dissolution of the American defensive commitment to NATO.

The Strategic Self-Sufficiency of Europe

One answer to the doubts that follow upon American disengagement would be the demonstration that Europe by itself has a strong basis for self-defense and therefore could achieve a good probability of deterrence.

What disengagement implies for America's relationship to Western Europe is not necessarily the instant dismantling of the formal alliance. In this century, old alliances seldom die; they waste away. They become drained of their real strategic content, and nations hedge against the guarantees that the alliances still pretend to offer. Something like that seems already to be happening to NATO under the surface of the formalities and under the cover of some energetic programs for modernizing and strengthening forces.

Yet my proposal is substantive disengagement, in prescription and in lively prospect.[16] Conceptually, it goes beyond the proposals of troop withdrawal and burden sharing that have by now become commonplace in American journals. Therefore, in contemplating a scenario of American disengagement, it is important to consider the probable status of Europe without American protection.

The least likely, though most obvious, scenario is a calculated large-scale Soviet invasion of Western Europe. A more plausible challenge is that the withdrawal of the American presence might lay Western Europe open to Soviet manipulation (which could take the form not of unremitting pressure but even of alternating sharp threats and peace offensives). This is what is meant by Finlandization. But this possibility cannot exist by itself. It must be a derivative of the ability of the Soviet Union to apply direct military pressure; therefore, its analysis follows the same lines as the rejoinder to that other asserted threat.

The real question is: Does the model of Finlandization apply with much force to a large, populous, rich, industrially capable, socially whole, politically resolute country, with a military force that would have far more than nuisance value—a country, in short, such as West Germany? Hardly. Unlike direct attack, Finlandization takes a willing victim as well as a determined aggressor. The recipient of pressure or pointed suggestion by the Soviet Union could simply turn its back on the démarche—and what then? What could the

Soviets do? Much, of course, but how effectively? how productively? To argue such a point as Finlandization, there has to be more than the concept, however plausible in the abstract; there has to be a scenario (a demonstration of how you get from here to there).[17]

What would America's European allies do in the event of disengagement? Their options range from acquiring national nuclear forces, to improving their conventional defenses, forging a new European military community, adopting unconventional defensive strategies (often suggested are forms of territorial defense or mobilization on the Swedish, Yugoslavian, Swiss, or Israeli models or even less orthodox strategies of denial or attrition), or doing all or several of the above—or none.

Each nation, according to its external and internal situation, would adopt some combination of these moves. It is far from certain that West Germany would independently go nuclear.[18] That would worsen its position not only with the Soviet Union but also with its Western European partners. And since the aim of disengagement is not to shock or punish, the United States would not withdraw its forces, or even its commitment, precipitately. There would be time for European countries to deliberate, plan, and act.

I envisage a Western Europe that is independent politically and diplomatically and autonomous strategically and that acts in greater military concert, though not political unity or strategic unanimity. Actually Europe could go quite far toward defending itself without American help. If the United States were to withdraw, the principal European countries would probably increase their defense spending gradually, perhaps to 5 percent or so of their gross national product. This would produce as much absolute military output as the Soviet Union. Although the national defense budgets might be uncoordinated, this aggregate measure is not meaningless. No one can predict whether Europe would opt to do this, but that would be Europe's choice.

In theory at least, if Western Europe were to coalesce, not only in a military compact but in a sort of federal union, it could become the second most powerful entity in the world—more powerful than the Soviet Union (and in a few respects even more than the United States). Even now, Western Europe has greater population (401 million), more ample economic potential ($4.8 trillion in gross national product), in the same area of military manpower (over 3.1 million), a respectably competitive military technology, and the reckonable nuclear forces of Britain and France. Europe's aggregate defense spending, however, is markedly inferior ($167 billion).[19]

Of course, European political unity is conjectural (despite the impending economic union of 1992). In this calculation, I do not imply its probability or its contingent probability in the event of a deliberate American withdrawal. In any case, we do not need the premise of European unity and collective military superiority or equivalence to argue for American disengagement (as opposed to devolution, which may depend for its full validity on a unified political receptacle for the military power, particularly nuclear, to substitute for the withdrawn American support). The proposals of military analysts (including quick fixes such as restructuring forces, adding equipment, and revising tactical doctrines, mobilization plans, and reserve arrangements), though they are designed in the first instance to improve NATO so it would be bearable for the United States to perpetuate its commitment, ironically hold possibilities for Western conventional defense without the United States, and even without European unification.

Actually, the most convincing proposals for strengthening NATO overshoot the mark. If NATO forces have had weaknesses that are now beginning to be addressed (they have been maldeployed, stretched thin, immobile, wrongly configured, badly integrated); and, further, if the Warsaw Pact countries could have achieved their military advantages from inferior production and manpower bases and from weaker economic and social systems, then it is not fanciful to imagine that the Western European countries—together or even powerful ones such as West Germany individually—if they were to make the most of their assets, could generate self-reliant military forces that could be formidable in defense and also in deterrence.[20]

How Containment Will End

Deciphering the future of NATO is too often attempted within the confines of the immediate regional problem, an exercise that will lead to frustration and perhaps a myopic fixation on the status quo. Rather, NATO must be seen as the linchpin of America's entire structure of alliances, as the keystone of the global arch of containment. Containment, in turn, must be viewed as the American version of empire, a sort of quasi-empire—not the traditional brand but something clearly protective, oriented to commercial objectives, and tinged with political sentimentality. America has paid dearly for this expression. From its inception, containment has cost it $5 trillion to $6 trillion; NATO alone has cost $2½ trillion over the years. And as part of the demanding and distracting enterprise of containment, NATO not only has contributed to debilitating the American economy but has helped to warp American society and skew its domestic governance.

NATO, along with containment itself, is widely considered to be successful. But if it is true that the United States can now live—and could have always lived—with a wide range of international outcomes, then everything that has been sacrificed, everything that it has taken to bring about the differential outcome we now have, has been for external influence and control, not for essential security.

With some hindsight, we see that we have come to the end of a strategic

era. The world that is likely to follow will be marked by a more diffuse possession of power and a more diffuse definition of power. There will be a new
array of regional competitors. More areas are becoming politically and
militarily inaccessible to both superpowers, ironically just when both have
acquired the technical means to penetrate any area. Rather than perpetuating
their preemptive confrontation—the cold war—or sharing the global condominium fleetingly spied by Nixon and Brezhnev (and perhaps offered, in a
renewed gambit, by Gorbachev), the present superpowers themselves will
probably shrink, toward the end of the century, to the status of regional
powers.

Also traditional alliances will be less meaningful. Interdependence will
mean more pressure points for terrorists, more opportunities for resource
blackmail, more shortages and price instabilities because of other nations' patterns of harvests and food demand and administrative failures, more monetary chaos because of some countries' economic abuse and incompetence. The
homeopathic theory says that the cure for interdependence is more interdependence, but the likelier remedy would be less of it. What we will probably
get is a world of buffers and bulkheads, both geographical and functional.

In that kind of world, Europe would be less central and indispensable to
the United States. With longer-range and more varied means of essential
deterrence, as well as the global mobility of its military forces, the United
States would not need Europe for the same defensive purposes, though it
would continue to be some sort of a frontier of Soviet and American interests.
Other relationships would persist. America would continue to cooperate with
Western Europe in many categories—trade, monetary and investment
arrangements, energy, access to resources, environmental measures, food and
population, restricting arms transfers both nuclear and conventional, and
even some peacekeeping exercises. But the principal strategic function of
Europe for the United States would be as a massive early-warning system.

The Geopolitical Perspective

My analysis of the international system and its evolution offers a vision of
how containment will end. There are, in this, grounds for a kind of cosmic
optimism. The world seems to be settling and transcending the agenda of the
wars and the revolutions that are to be seen as the legacy of the problems of
the nineteenth century. These are the great global military conflicts, World
Wars I and II, and the communist revolutions, of Russia in 1917 and China
in 1949. Both of these sets of events formed the matrix of the cold war and
the American imperative of containment.

It may well be that the twenty-first century will see not only a new agenda
but the prevalence of a new perspective on world politics and foreign policy-

making, and also a new relation of the national state to the the international system and, in the other direction, to its own society (that is, the larger body in which it exists and out of which it arises). In other words, the international system may evolve into, and containment may devolve into, a different set of relationships.

In the more concrete terms of America's historical experience, containment will end when America completes the long arc of "its" century and become again, as it was on the threshold of that century, part of a multiple order of substantively unaligned powers—then, some eight great powers, now, perhaps a dozen and a half—in other words, when America sheds the ultimately unsupportable burden of empire, or quasi-empire—a burden without sufficiently compensating advantages—and becomes a nation among nations.

Notes

1. See Melvyn Krauss, *How NATO Weakens the West* (New York: Simon & Schuster, 1986).

2. For the purposes of this chapter, I must slight the matter of America's nuclear strategy—an orientation toward counterforce targeting, which implies a doctrine of first use–first strike, and a force posture capable of implementing those doctrines of targeting and precedence of use. This nuclear strategy, I argue, is a consequence of America's alliance commitments, principally to NATO, which is the cardinal American alliance. I elaborate this argument in "Counterforce and Alliance: The Ultimate Connection," *International Security* (Spring 1982). But the following section, on NATO's recurrent crises, should adequately illustrate both the entailments and the disabilities of extended deterrence.

3. I judge that the Bush administration intends the following regional attribution of a total of 21 active land divisions: NATO/Europe, 11-2/3; East Asia, 3-2/3; Other Regions and the Strategic Reserve, 5-2/3 divisions. Applying these fractions to the total cost of our general purpose forces, $228 billion, we can calculate the rough cost of our three regional commitments. Europe will account for $127 billion; Asia will absorb $40 billion; and the requirement for the Strategic Reserve and other areas of the world will be $61 billion, of which about $46 billion is for CENTCOM, that is, primarily the Persian Gulf.

4. Figures are derived from *The Military Balance, 1988–1989* (London: International Institute for Strategic Studies, 1988). The figures are from 1987 and represent outlays on a "NATO definition" basis.

5. Stanley R. Sloan, *Defense Burden Sharing: U.S. Relations with NATO Allies and Japan* (Washington, D.C.: Congressional Research Service, July 8, 1983).

6. Congressmen Stephen J. Solarz, "To Buoy Europe's Defenses," *New York Times,* January 10, 1983.

7. Earl C. Ravenal, "After Schlesinger: Something Has to Give," *Foreign Policy* (Spring 1976).

8. Samuel P. Huntington, "Coping with the Lippmann Gap," *Foreign Affairs,* "America and the World" (1987–1988). The emblematic quotation is from Walter Lippmann, *U.S. Foreign Policy: Shield of the Republic* (Boston: Atlantic–Little, Brown, 1943).

9. Some prominent examples are: James Chace, *Solvency: the Price of Survival* (New York: Random House, 1981); and David Calleo, "Inflation and American Power," *Foreign Affairs* (Spring 1981), *The Imperious Economy* (Cambridge: Harvard University Press, 1982), and *Beyond American Hegemony: The Future of the Western Alliance* (New York: Basic Books, 1987).

10. A somewhat different set of two gaps is cited in my critique of the Nixon doctrine in "The Nixon Doctrine and Our Asian Commitments," *Foreign Affairs* (January 1971): "The Nixon Doctrine reveals an apparent contradiction between objectives and strategy. . . . The Administration's defense planning procedure allows a second contradiction: between strategy and forces." A third gap (the one I refer to here as the post-Lippmann gap) is adumbrated by the phrase "in the face of budgetary pressures that arise not out of absolute scarcity of resources, but out of the nation's unwillingness to make large sacrifices for objectives that cannot be credibly invoked by its leadership." It should be clear that a resource base is made available to a government's purposes only through the medium of a society's support. Thus, the frequently invoked "political will" is not a solution; it is part of the problem.

11. John G. Kester, "War and Money," *Washingtonian* (January 1983). In this argument, administration and congressional conservatives are joined by liberal critics, whose devotion to taxes as a sort of infinite resource (as in the parable of the loaves and the fishes) is impressive.

12. This is essentially the proposal of David P. Calleo in *Beyond American Hegemony* and other works, as well as that of Robert E. Osgood, in various writings in the mid- and late 1970s.

13. The Gorbachev proposals, announced in his December 7, 1988, speech to the United Nations General Assembly, were that the Soviet Union, during the next two years, would unilaterally and unconditionally reduce its total armed forces by 500,000 (about 10 percent); remove 10,000 tanks from the area between the Atlantic and the Urals, including 5,000 from East Germany, Czechoslovakia, and Hungary (of these, disbanding six tank divisions with 2,000 tanks); withdraw 50,000 troops, including assault landing and bridging units, from East Germany, Czechoslovakia, and Hungary: cut 8,500 artillery systems and 800 tactical aircraft from Europe; and remove a substantial part of the Soviet forces stationed along the Chinese border in Mongolia. In addition, the remaining Soviet divisions in Eastern Europe are to be reorganized into a defensive posture. Subsequently, Soviet foreign minister Shevardnadze announced that the Soviets would also remove the short-range nuclear systems associated with the six tank divisions to be withdrawn from Central Europe.

14. "Keeping Our Troops in Europe," *New York Times Magazine,* October 17, 1982.

15. These figures, based on official Pentagon estimates, modified to reflect the initial Bush stance, assume the same rates of year-to-year increases that the secretary of defense uses for the first five years (inflation of under 4 percent plus somewhat less than 1 percent real increase), extrapolating them for a further five years. My alterna-

tive assumes a pared-down 1990 defense budget of $290 billion, and, thereafter, my prescribed cuts taken over a ten-year period and adjusted only for 4 percent inflation.

16. It should be noted that in such existential terms, the "formula" put forward by President Reagan at the Reykjavik summit meeting with Chairman Gorbachev in October 1986 was also a blueprint for eventual American disengagement from defensive responsibility for Western Europe (and was widely read that way by America's European allies). Reagan, in both assenting to the extensive denuclearization of the European military balance and insisting on the integrity of America's Strategic Defense Initiative, was adumbrating a strategically decoupled United States and a militarily self-sufficient Western Europe. This would equate to the substantive disintegration of NATO.

17. Now, with the Gorbachev-inspired prospect of loosening the Soviet grip on Eastern Europe, "Finlandization" has become a plus-word, taken to mean a sort of halfway station (or three-quarters-way station) in freeing the Eastern European states from Soviet control.

18. For an advocacy of this, see Doug Bandow, "The Germans Need a Nuclear Arsenal," *New York Times,* May 2, 1989.

19. In this calculation I include the European NATO countries (including France and Spain) but exclude Austria, Ireland, Sweden, and Switzerland. Figures are derived from *The Military Balance, 1988–89.* The figures are generally from 1988, with a few from 1987. By comparison, the figures for the superpowers are: population, U.S. 245 million, Soviet Union 285 million; gross national product, U.S. $4.5 trillion, Soviet Union $2.3 trillion; military manpower, U.S. 2.2 million, Soviet Union 3.6 million (excluding 1.5 million command and general support troops); and defense spending, U.S. $289 billion, Soviet Union $345 billion (a figure that seems to be at the high end of the range).

20. Admittedly, in resorting selectively to the arguments of Steven Canby and others, I am taking them in a direction that they would not follow. Certainly they do not argue for American disengagement. But their arguments could be enlisted to support such a strategy. See Steven L. Canby, "NATO Muscle: More Shadow than Substance," *Foreign Policy* (Fall 1972); "NATO: Reassessing the Conventional Wisdoms," *Survival* (July–August 1977); "European Mobilization: U.S. and NATO Reserves," *Armed Forces and Society* (February 1978); "Mutual Force Reductions: A Military Perspective," *International Security* (Winter 1978). Canby's later studies, on the same theme, include "Military Reform and the Art of War," *Survival* (May–June 1983), and (with Ingemar Dörfer) "More Troops, Fewer Missiles," *Foreign Policy* (Winter 1983–1984). One particularly interesting observation (from "Mutual Force Reductions: A Military Perspective") stresses the organization and use of reserves: "Europe has the wherewithal to deploy the forces necessary for its own defense, if its trained conscripts exiting from military service were organized into structural units . . . using these trained conscripts in a rapid mobilization system. . . . NATO could triple its divisions at a cost of roughly 25 percent of current army expenditures. . . . NATO could solve its military deficiencies unilaterally and at *zero* additional cost. The true deficiency is not the inadequacy of resources, the lack of standardization, or the like. The problem is rather NATO's tactical doctrine, its organization for combat, and its deployment" (pp. 130–34).

15

Ambivalent Past, Uncertain Future: America's Role in Post–Cold War Europe

Christopher Layne

A lthough NATO has been the anchor of U.S. foreign policy for 40 years, from the alliance's very beginning Americans have been ambivalent about this nation's engagement in European affairs. That ambivalence is not surprising. The North Atlantic Treaty was a reversal of America's historic policy of shunning entangling European alliances and attempting to steer clear of Old World conflicts. In the years between 1945 and 1949, U.S. isolationism ended out of necessity; but the vestigial attitudes of America's insular past remain, and throughout the postwar era Americans have been reluctant internationalists. Moreover, imbedded in America's political culture is a striking duality about this country's relations with Europe: the United States has always been simultaneously attracted to and alienated from Europe. As William Pfaff explains, the different historical experiences of America and Europe are

> at the heart of a largely unconsidered but absolutely basic American perception of Continental Europe as entirely different from us—and as insecure, unstable, and somehow dangerous. It is not just the fact that we were drawn into two world wars that lies behind this perception. The whole political evolution of Europe over the past 200 hundred years contrasts with our own national experience.[1]

In the postwar era, America's concern with protecting Western Europe from a Soviet threat has alternated with resentment of the burdens imposed by this commitment and what has been (and still is) viewed as West European ingratitude for America's exertions. Nevertheless, the basic U.S. political commitment to Western Europe has been steadfast and supported by a relatively stable domestic consensus, albeit one that has rarely been tested seriously. However, there has never been equally firm agreement about the extent of America's military undertakings on behalf of the alliance, and on at least four previous occasions—1948 to 1951, 1954, 1957 to 1959 and 1966 to 1974—latent doubts about America's proper role in European security affairs erupted in searching debates as to whether U.S. forces should be deployed in, or brought home from, Western Europe.

What accounts for these recurring episodes of introspection? Why, despite sometimes severe transatlantic tensions and an outpouring of plans to "reform" NATO, has the alliance remained intact and essentially unchanged structurally? Those questions have a new urgency today because the future of America's role in Europe is again at issue. Spurred by momentous developments in the Soviet Union, Poland, Hungary and the German Democratic Republic (GDR) in 1989—and by the realization that the European Community's 1992 process portends a politically as well as economically unified Western Europe—the American foreign policy community has belatedly begun to come to grips with the implications of post-cold war Europe. That discussion has been grafted onto two other debates. During the early and mid-1980s discussion about the U.S. commitment to NATO intensified but was, for the most part, parochial and disjointed, focusing on burden sharing, nuclear strategy, and trade protectionism. In the late 1980s, however, that dialogue became linked to a broader examination of NATO in the context of secular trends in international politics, especially the hypotheses that the world was becoming more multipolar, America's relative economic power was declining, and the United States was overextended strategically.

As those three debates blend into one, pressure to redefine America's commitment to Western Europe is already mounting. Born in the cold war's darkest and most dangerous hour, NATO has enjoyed 40 years of remarkable success. But it is an open question whether the alliance will be the victim or the beneficiary of its achievements. NATO was erected as a bulwark against the Soviet military and ideological menace; but as that threat recedes, it has become an institution in search of a rationale. Whether the new NATO debate will be a replay of earlier ones—which ended by reaffirming the alliance's centrality—remains to be seen. The critical issue posed by the new debate is whether the factors that gave birth to and sustained NATO remain relevant and compelling in a time of rapid geopolitical change.

For most of the past forty years, the conventional wisdom held that Europe's postwar security order was immutable. However, the events of 1989 shook the old conventional wisdom to its core. As the underpinnings of the old order collapsed one by one, statesmen were forced to remember what they should not have forgotten: postwar Europe was shaped by historical circumstances and was not the product of any overreaching design or vision. Inevitably, the durability of the postwar system is put in doubt by the transformation of the conditions that brought the system into being. In the suddenly fluid and uncertain European political environment, it is no longer possible to defer thinking about what new arrangements will replace the post-1945 order. Thus, questions once thought firmly settled have been reopened and will dominate the diplomatic agenda during the 1990s: the nature of America's relationship with Western Europe, the fate of the Soviet empire in Eastern Europe, and the German question.

Those issues are not new. Although frequently submerged by the cold war, they have been considered on several occasions during the past four decades. Washington's deliberations about joining NATO, the disengagement proposals of the late 1950s, and the Mansfield amendments of the late 1960s and early 1970s are particularly relevant to today's reexamination of America's NATO policy. In 1948 some U.S. policymakers and analysts used the occasion to think about the basic geopolitical implications of the triangular relationship among the United States, Europe, and the Soviet Union. This was a theme in the late 1950s also, and the various disengagement plans prefigured today's issues of how to end the cold war in Europe and transcend the Continent's division. Although framed in terms of burden sharing, the Mansfield amendments occurred at a time when America and Europe began drifting apart on a broad range of issues and when Vietnam foreshadowed the end of America's postwar hegemony.

In the coming years, the United States will need to make important decisions about its European policy. How should Washington respond to Mikhail Gorbachev's foreign policy initiatives and domestic reforms? What should the United States do with respect to an increasingly volatile Eastern Europe? Should America regard the prospect of a unified Western Europe as a challenge to its political (and economic) primacy, or as an opportunity to establish a more mature—and stable—relationship with Western Europe? Can NATO remain a vital institution without major changes, or should it be reformed or replaced by a new framework for United States/Western European political and security relations? How will developments within Western Europe and between the United States and the Western Europeans affect the Soviet Union and Eastern Europe? What stance should the United States take on the German question? History cannot dictate the choices Washington should make, but it can impose a conceptual framework on the analysis of present options. Also, at a time when statesmen have been set adrift from the cold war's familiar analytic moorings, history can provide a useful compass by which to navigate. Only those who believe history has ended can fail to profit from studying it.

Proposals for a More Limited Commitment

In 1947 critics like diplomat George F. Kennan and commentator Walter Lippmann questioned both the necessity and desirability of a formal alliance between the United States and Western Europe. Both downplayed the threat of Soviet military aggression and believed that internal subversion and malaise were the main dangers to Western Europe's security. A military buildup, they feared, would divert European efforts away from the critical tasks of political and economic recovery.[2] Moreover, they believed the proposed North Atlantic Treaty would militarize containment and result (in Kennan's words) in an "irrevocable congealment of the division of Europe" into Soviet and American spheres of influence.[3] If the Soviets were in Eastern Europe because of concerns about national security, the way to get them out, Kennan and Lippmann believed, was to alleviate those fears by negotiating a simultaneous withdrawal of U.S. and Soviet forces from Central Europe.[4]

Kennan (like many others in official Washington at the time) also believed that America's interests lay in Western Europe's reemergence as an independent power center in the global balance—a third force in world politics—and he was apprehensive that NATO would retard rather than facilitate the then promising movement toward West European integration. The alliance, he predicted, "will come to overshadow, and probably replace, any development in the direction of European Union" as Western Europe became habituated to U.S. leadership in political and military affairs.[5] Both he and State Department counselor Charles Bohlen, among others, worried that the kind of U.S. commitment represented by the North Atlantic Treaty would sap the West Europeans' will to defend themselves and result in the Old World's becoming a strategic appendage of the United States.[6] The realist critique of NATO advanced by the Kennan-Lippmann school retains its intellectual freshness forty years later.

The mid- and late-1950s were a time of hope and tension. On the one hand, the post-Stalin thaw within the Soviet Union, and the spirit of Geneva and Austrian State Treaty (both in 1955) raised hopes for an easing of cold war tensions. But the upheaval in Eastern Europe in 1956 and the 1958–1959 Berlin crisis were stark reminders that Europe was still volatile. It was during this time too that West European governments were first afflicted with creeping doubts about the credibility of America's nuclear umbrella over NATO and West European publics (especially West German) grew troubled about the implications of the U.S. doctrine of using nuclear weapons to defend Western Europe.

Against this backdrop, the mid-1950s produced an outpouring of various schemes for mutually disengaging America and the Soviet Union from Europe and more modest plans for demilitarizing Eastern Europe. It was, as Kennan observed, not by accident that Poland proposed the Rapacki plan for a Central European nuclear-free zone, presumably as a first step to easing the Soviets out of Eastern Europe.[7] In the West, at the 1955 Geneva Summit, British prime minister Anthony Eden floated the notion of a Central European demilitarized zone. In the wake of Hungary's November 1956 rebellion, interest in disengagement deepened. By 1957 important British Labour party leaders like Hugh Gaitskell and Denis Healy embraced the concept, and West Germany's Social Democrats (who saw NATO membership as a barrier to reunification) sounded similar themes in West Germany's 1957 election.[8]

The disengagement debate was crystalized by Kennan's BBC Reith Lectures in late 1957.[9] His starting point was that the events of 1953 (East Germany) and 1956 (Poland and Hungary) had shown that Eastern Europe was dangerously unstable and that the U.S. policy of rolling back Soviet influence and "liberating" Eastern Europe was bankrupt. Post-Stalin liberalization in the Soviet Union and Eastern Europe had not reconciled that region's people to Soviet domination; on the contrary, it illustrated the depth of their disaffection. Unless Eastern Europe's situation was ameliorated, Kennan (like Hugh Gaitskell) foresaw a stark choice for the West: either acquiescing in Moscow's long-term domination of Eastern Europe or risking renewed unrest, with all that implied for the maintenance of peace.[10] The only escape from this dilemma, he believed, was the departure of Soviet troops from Eastern Europe. "Only when the troops are gone," Kennan said, "will there be possibilities for the evolution of these nations toward institutions and social systems most suited to their needs."[11] But the Soviets would not leave Central Europe as long as that region remained a focal point of East-West competition. Thus, to get the Soviets out of East Central Europe, Kennan said, it would be necessary for the United States to withdraw its troops from West Germany.

Kennan understood that the prospect of mutual disengagement would require both superpowers and the Europeans to come to terms with the German question; however, he thought it impossible to overcome Europe's division without ending Germany's division.[12] While recognizing that negotiations about Germany's future would be laborious, Kennan was highly critical—for both geopolitical and moral reasons—of those who would accept permanent Soviet domination of Eastern Europe in order to keep Germany split. Consistent with the position he had taken while still at the State Department, he believed that German reunification should occur within a broader framework of all-European political and economic integration.

The disengagement proposals sparked a lively debate among foreign policy intellectuals but had little impact on official circles. Disengagement was predicated on several assumptions: (1) the Soviets could not for long maintain their position in Eastern Europe and an explosion in that region was imminent; (2) the Germans would not tolerate their nation's indefinite partition; and (3) the Soviets were interested in new European security arrangements. As long-term propositions, these assumptions contained a good deal of truth, but they had little immediate relevance to the world of the late 1950s.

From 1966 to 1974 Senator Mansfield raised anew the question of the U.S. commitment to Europe as he pressed repeatedly for cutbacks in America's NATO forces. Starting from the premise that Western Europe should take its own security as seriously as the United States did, he rekindled long-standing American burden-sharing grievances that went back to NATO's inception. In the late 1940s, the Marshall Plan, the North Atlantic Treaty, and the Mutual Assistance Program had been presented to Congress as short-term measures that would spur West European self-reliance and obviate the need for a long-term American military presence in Europe. During the great debate of 1950–1951, Secretary of Defense George C. Marshall and General Dwight Eisenhower, NATO's first Supreme Allied Commander Europe, reiterated that U.S. troop deployments to Europe were designed to be temporary and to give Western Europe a breathing spell to build up its own self-defense capabilities.[13]

Burden sharing resurfaced as a major issue in the mid-1960s and early 1970s because of important changes in America's external and domestic situations. Western Europe's economic recovery and America's persistent balance of payments deficit inclined many Americans to think the United States was doing more than its fair share for NATO and the West Europeans not enough. Vietnam had a critical impact. The view took hold that the United States was overextended strategically, and the lack of West European support for Washington's Southeast Asia policy fanned American resentment of the West Europeans. If America needed to retrench, many felt, NATO was the place to begin. By mid-1966, the first serious cracks in NATO's facade appeared as a result of French president Charles de Gaulle's challenge to America's nuclear, diplomatic, and economic preeminence in Atlantic relations. In fact, Mansfield's first sense of the Senate resolution on troop reductions was introduced just after France withdrew from NATO's integrated military command. France's defiance was especially galling because it rested explicitly on the calculation that America's interest in European security was so paramount that Western Europe could, with impunity, follow political and economic policies that put it at odds with Washington, and pursue a separate détente with Moscow, without risking U.S. protection.

Mansfield amendments, which would have been binding on the executive branch, were defeated in 1971, 1973, and 1974. On the first two occasions, the Nixon administration was forced to engage in intensive lobbying to defeat the amendments.[14] Ironically, however, even as the Mansfield amendments were being turned down in the early 1970s, the seeds of the present crisis in U.S.–West European relations were being sown. In 1972, SALT (Strategic Arms Limitation Talks) I codified strategic nuclear parity between the superpowers and thus, in West European eyes, undermined the credibility of extended deterrence. It was to restore confidence in the U.S. nuclear guarantee and keep America coupled to West European security that West German chancellor Helmut Schmidt delivered his famous 1978 Alistair Buchan Lecture at London's International Institute of Strategic Studies.[15] His initiative led to NATO's fateful decision to deploy U.S. intermediate-range nuclear forces (INFs) and to the decade-long crisis of the 1980s that has eroded the alliance's nuclear strategy.

Even as strategic issues began clouding the U.S.–West German relationship, West German chancellor Willy Brandt's Ostpolitik foreshadowed a growing rift between Bonn and Washington over how to manage relations with the Soviet Union and Eastern Europe. Vietnam and the 1973 Yom Kippur War raised questions about whether NATO was relevant to out-of-area theaters of East-West conflict. And in the economic sphere, the United States found itself confronting a prosperous and assertive rival, the European Community (EC). By the mid-1970s it was also apparent that the EC was becoming more than just an economic organization; increasingly it was the focal point for a new West European identity that found expression by challenging America's leadership on a broad range of political and economic issues.

Prospects for a New Debate

Will there be an American reassessment of NATO in the 1990s and, if so, will it—unlike similar exercises in the past—produce significant changes in U.S.– West European relations? There is good reason to answer "yes" to both questions. Forty years of change in world politics have finally caught up with NATO. Because it is increasingly less relevant to the European security environment, the alliance is suffering from old age, not from midlife crisis.[16]

Political perceptions on both sides of the Atlantic are finally catching up with the reality and implications of nuclear parity. Meanwhile, a relatively declining America is facing worrisome budget and trade deficits. Thus, the staples of transatlantic controversy—nuclear strategy and burden sharing— have new urgency and will underlie the coming reconsideration. More significant, however, these old issues will appear in new guise as they blend with the three critical trends that are reshaping the geopolitical context of U.S.– West European relations: the emergence of a politically unified Western Europe (an overlooked aspect of the 1992 process); the emergence of a politically, as well as economically, powerful West Germany that is increasingly pursuing its national interests; and the Gorbachev factor, which has rekindled hopes on both sides of the Elbe that Europe's division can be replaced by an all-European security order.

Western Europe will be infused in 1992 with economic vitality. The unified economic market, however, will heighten the rivalry between the United States and the EC, placing new strains on the U.S. commitment to NATO. Although economic issues have always been a source of divisiveness in transatlantic relations, so far they have proved manageable because of a broad Atlantic consensus on political and military concerns and because of a U.S. economic predominance that has made it possible for America to sacrifice its short-term economic interests in order to maintain alliance cohesion. As these buffering factors dissipate, the firewall that has usually insulated trade and financial issues from security issues may be breached. Economic competition and a growing political estrangement from a unified Western Europe may cause an economically straitjacketed America to ask the question recently posed by the House Defense Burdensharing Panel: why should the United States subsidize the security of a wealthy and powerful competitor?[17]

Transcending in importance 1992's economic aspects is its geopolitical impact. Likened (by Paul Kennedy) at its present stage of political development to mid–nineteenth century Germany, Western Europe is a superpower-in-embryo that could, Samuel P. Huntington notes, become "the preeminent power of the 21st Century" if it fulfills its potential.[18] Since the end of World War II, the United States has lent its support—always rhetorically and occasionally concretely—to the concept of West European unity. Yet the closer that goal has come to reality, the deeper American misgivings have become about the prospect of a politically unified, economically buoyant, and independent Western Europe.

What America has always wanted, it seems, is the best of both worlds: a Western Europe strong enough to relieve the United States of its burdens but not so strong as to challenge Washington's primacy in Atlantic relations. Thus U.S. initiatives like President John F. Kennedy's "Grand Design" and Secretary of State Henry A. Kissinger's ill-fated "Year of Europe" have placed the concept of West European unity within the framework of an Atlantic partnership—with the United States as senior member of the firm. The paradox of transatlantic relations, however, is that the stronger Western Europe becomes, the more self-confidently it will articulate and pursue its own interests.

As Europe achieves greater political cohesiveness in the 1990s, transatlantic conflicts will sharpen. The EC vindicates de Gaulle's vision of a Europe with its own external identity and vocation.[19] The declining reliability of U.S. security guarantees and the melting of cold war tensions will contribute further to Western Europe's separateness by giving the West Europeans new incentives to formulate their own strategic policies and initiatives toward the Soviet Union and Eastern Europe. "It's now clear that 1992 will mark an important step in Europe's construction," says French defense minister Jean Pierre Chevènement. "And international events are encouraging us to take our own security into our own hands, at the same time offering us new possibilities to do so."[20] For the first time in the postwar era, the West Europeans are mounting a concerted, across-the-board attack on the transatlantic status quo, and this certainly will have an effect on the U.S. domestic debate about NATO.

In his recent book, *The Grand Illusion*, French writer Alain Minc argues that there is no European question, only a German question.[21] And the German question is, as Renata Fritsch-Bournazel puts it, "the question of where in Europe the Germans belong: looking Westwards or wandering between East and West; recognizing their geographically central position or breaking out of it?"[22] Today the German question is being played out through the media of nuclear strategy and relations with Moscow. West Germany is the linchpin of America's security policy. But as Bonn and Washington drift apart on these issues, the geopolitical underpinnings of the U.S. NATO commitment are coming unstuck, raising questions—German questions—to which U.S. policymakers have no answers.[23]

The postwar compact that bound America and West Germany together was a two-part bargain. On the security side, Bonn was linked to the West strategically by the protective mantle of the U.S. nuclear deterrent. However, for Bonn, over the years the reliability of the nuclear guarantee has declined and its potential costs have risen. There is a deep, ultimately unbridgeable conflict between U.S. and West German strategic interests that is summed up in two competing aphorisms: "The shorter the range, the deader the Germans" (a NATO strategy that emphasizes conventional defense or assigns a prominent role to SNFs is dangerous for West Germany) versus "The longer the range, the deader the Americans" (a tight coupling of American strategic nuclear forces to Western Europe's security is dangerous for the United States).[24]

Parity has vitiated the worth of U.S. nuclear assurances. Worse, from the German viewpoint, America seems to be reducing its own nuclear exposure by increasing West Germany's. As has often been true since 1949, Washington fails to understand how its own actions contribute to transatlantic tensions. However, the Reagan shocks (SDI and the Reykjavik summit), the INF treaty (which removed the only European-based U.S. missiles capable of reaching the Soviet Union), and the semiofficial Iklé-Wohlstetter report (which strongly suggests that the United States should attempt to confine the use of nuclear weapons to Europe) raised German fears about U.S. strategic intentions. U.S. demands for SNF modernization—backed up by "no nukes, no troops" threats—confirmed these suspicions.[25]

As a result of the prolonged INF crisis, a new strategic culture has taken root among West Germany's elites and public. Most of the ideas underlying the post-INF strategic culture were co-opted from the peace movement by the Social Democratic Party and have gained widespread public acceptance. Consequently, the contours of the West German security debate are now effectively delineated by the left and even the Christian Democratic Union/ Christian Social Union must trim its sails accordingly.[26]

Moreover, security issues have been linked to revival of the national question.[27] Both East and West Germany—and the relations between them—are seen as potential victims of the superpower rivalry, and both are thought to share a community of responsibility for ensuring that war never begins again on German soil. As NATO's front-line state, West Germany has a far more immediate interest than its allies in ending the cold war in Europe. Bonn's policies are driven by the lure of positive payoffs too. As a divided nation,

West Germany has a paramount interest in Deutschlandpolitik—its outreach to the German Democratic Republic. Moreover, as the traditionally pre-eminent nation in Central Europe, West Germany has compelling reasons to use its diplomatic influence and economic power to improve ties with Moscow and Eastern Europe. From Bonn's perspective, instability in Eastern Europe is the major threat to West Germany's (and Europe's) security. Moreover, West Germany's long-term goal is to overturn peacefully the postwar political status quo. As designed by Brandt and Egon Bahr, Ostpolitik seeks to wean Eastern Europe gradually away from the Soviet Union and to substitute an all-European security order for the "stalemate system" represented by two blocs.[28] Ultimately, it is believed, the process of East-West convergence and diminishing superpower influence will make possible at least the informal reconstitution of the German nation.

West Germany's reassertion of its sovereignty and its national interests—expressed in President Richard von Weizsacker's declaration that West Germany is not the plaything of other powers—is irreversible. Support for a more national policy is reflected in West German public attitudes. More West Germans support the alternatives of neutrality, equal relations with both superpowers, or closer cooperation with the EC than support a policy of standing by the United States. And while West Germans strongly support NATO membership in the abstract, most oppose the alliance's specific security policies (especially with respect to nuclear strategy). The two most striking changes in West German attitudes are the surge of support for more cooperative relations with Moscow and the declining support for the U.S. troop presence.[29]

The Washington-Bonn connection is certain to be severely tested by West Germany's assertiveness and self-awareness and by clashing U.S. and West German views about nuclear strategy and East-West relations. In the 1990s, NATO's political rationale will be doubly challenged by West German uncertainty about U.S. nuclear protection and by the changing nature of the Soviet threat, which paradoxically reduces Bonn's need for that protection while increasing its scope for diplomatic maneuver. West German policy cuts across Washington's belief that it should have a monopoly on setting NATO's diplomatic agenda in relation to the Soviet Union and also contradicts the prevailing American understanding of the second part of the original trans-atlantic compact: that in exchange for U.S. protection, West European resources would not be put at the Soviet Union's disposal.[30] But West Germans see things differently: for them, the Atlantic compact was premised on an explicit recognition of West Germany's right to pursue a special relation-ship with the other German state and, by extension, with the Soviet Union.

Transatlantic differences over nuclear risk sharing and burden sharing, the emergence of a unified Western Europe, and the resurfacing of the German question are sufficient conditions for restructuring NATO and the overall U.S.–West European relationship. However, the necessary condition for change is the Soviet Union's transformation into a normal great power—one pursuing a nonideological foreign policy and focusing primarily on its own domestic problems. Yet Washington is far more skeptical than Western Europe about the authenticity and staying power of the changes underway in the Soviet Union. National Security Council and Pentagon hard-liners predict (perhaps hope) that Gorbachev's reforms will fail, warn that the cold war continues unabated, and enjoin that the West's "view of the Soviet Union cannot be based on the personality of one or another leader, but must be based on the nature of the Soviet system itself."[31]

This view is excessively narrow and fails to grasp the dynamics driving Soviet policy. Moscow's policies have changed because much of the Soviet elite has lost faith in the utility of ideology as an adjunct of foreign policy while realizing that the opportunity costs of the Brezhnev era's policies were unacceptably high.

The overseas empire Moscow acquired in the 1970s proved a costly drain on the Soviet Union's material (and in Afghanistan, human) resources. Moscow's strategic nuclear and conventional arms buildup provoked a Western counterresponse. The ideological component of Moscow's foreign policy had a paradoxical effect: nowhere was the Soviet Union perceived as a political or cultural model worthy of emulation, yet by clinging to Marxist-Leninist orthodoxy, the Soviet Union solidified Western suspicions that it was a revolutionary, destabilizing power with insatiable ambitions. By heightening Western fears, the Kremlin contributed to its own geopolitical encirclement by fostering an anti-Soviet coalition comprised of the United States, Western Europe, Japan, and China. Finally, it became clear that the Soviet Union's domestic economy—burdened by its stifling institutional inefficiencies—could not sustain the military competition against the West.[32]

Retrenchment abroad and reform at home came to be seen as the only way of ensuring (as Serewyn Bialer puts it) that the Soviet Union's systemic crisis of efficiency did not degenerate into a crisis of survival. The Soviet Union's deteriorating situation (externally and domestically), not the personality or identity of its leaders, explains Moscow's rejection of the Brezhnevite policies of stagnation. Gorbachev could disappear, but the objective constraints on Soviet policy would remain.

Soviet foreign policy is driven by the need to relax external tensions in order to allow Moscow to confront its daunting internal problems. West Europe has a special role in Soviet foreign policy "new thinking." Moscow looks to West European markets, technology, and credits to infuse life into perestroika. And as evidenced during Gorbachev's visit to Bonn, the Soviets regard West Germany as a privileged interlocutor in this respect. The Soviets apparently regard the EC as a source of economic deliverance for Poland and Hungary as well. However, to achieve the objectives of its Westpolitik, the

Soviet Union needs to be seen by Western Europe as a reliable partner. By draining the ideological content from its policy, Moscow is attempting to demonstrate to Western Europe that it can be a steady partner on a broad range of political, military, and economic issues.

For some time, Western Europe has had a more relaxed view than the United States of the Soviet threat. The INF treaty, Soviet proposals to eliminate SNFs, Gorbachev's December 1988 announcement of a unilateral 500,000-man force reduction (including removal of six divisions from Eastern Europe), and Foreign Minister Eduard Shevardnadze's acceptance of troop and equipment parity from the Atlantic to the Urals have all further lowered West European perceptions of the Soviet military threat.[33] At the same time, the political liberalization within the Soviet Union and Moscow's tolerance of pluralistic reforms in Poland and Hungary have removed the lingering traces of the ideological dimension of the East-West rivalry in Europe. Soviet foreign policy thus strikes directly at NATO's most sensitive point: in times of danger, alliances hold together, but when the danger recedes or is thought to recede, alliances tend to break apart. As political scientist Kenneth Waltz has observed, "Alliances are made by states that have some but not all of their interests in common. The common interest is ordinarily a negative one: fear of other states."[34]

Rethinking the Transatlantic Relationship

For nearly four decades, Europe's postwar security system seemed to be a permanent feature of the international system, a structure to which there were no viable alternatives. Yet as George F. Kennan wrote in 1948, "A divided Europe is not permanently viable and the political will of the U.S. people is not sufficient to enable us to support Western Europe indefinitely as a military appendage."[35] Put another way, the postwar settlement could last only as long as the United States—and the Soviet Union—were prepared to uphold it and as long as the Europeans were willing to accept it. Neither of these conditions is likely to hold true much longer.

In the 1990s, America's willingness to maintain its European commitment will be tested by Western Europe's drive toward political unification and by changes in the Soviet Union and Eastern Europe that make it realistic to think that Europe's post-1945 division can be overcome. Ironically, the U.S. link to NATO encourages Western Europe and West Germany to go their own way in relations with Moscow; alliance incentives have become skewed, and the payoff from acting independently exceeds that of remaining in lockstep with Washington. Judging from resurgent congressional burden-sharing irritations and the "no nukes, no troops" response to Bonn's stance on Lance modernization and short-range nuclear forces negotiations, the U.S. political system is increasingly unable to tolerate Western Europe's self-interested behavior. The danger of such a situation is apparent, and an abrupt, acrimonious transatlantic rupture is not an unthinkable prospect.

What is needed instead is a thoughtful consideration of what the triangular relationship among the United States, Europe, and the Soviet Union should look like at the end of the 1990s. The transatlantic relationship needs to be restructured to forge a new post–cold war partnership between the United States and a unified Western Europe. Acting in concert, the United States and Western Europe must frame a new political strategy toward Moscow and Eastern Europe. The critical issues in European security are now primarily political, not military, in nature, and U.S. force structures must be related to America's long-term diplomatic objectives in Europe.

By 1992, the United States must confront the tension—unresolved for forty years—between its commitment to an American-led NATO and its support for greater West European political, military, and economic unity. As Henry Kissinger wrote a quarter-century ago and subsequently restated, Western Europe's unity comes at a price for America, which, while worth paying, must be recognized.[36] It has always been doubtful that

> Europe would unite in order to share *our* burdens or that it would be content with a subordinate role once it had the means to implement its own views. Europe's main incentive to undertake a larger cooperative role in the West's affairs would be to fulfill its own distinctive purposes.[37]

For Western Europe to assume the responsibilities of independence, however, the United States must yield its hegemonic prerogative of insisting that Western Europe's external and security policies must be preapproved in Washington. A post–cold war U.S. policy toward Western Europe would encourage the emergence of a united Western Europe by actively supporting a West European supreme commander for NATO; the development of an independent West European nuclear deterrent; and West European initiatives for a closer defense collaboration, such as the West European Union and the Franco-German military axis.

The United States is a world power with a long-term interest in Europe's security and stability. Washington should reaffirm that it will remain involved in Europe as long as the West Europeans believe a U.S. presence is required. At the same time, however, the risks and costs of the American commitment to Europe must be reduced to acceptable levels. A more limited U.S. involvement in Europe is dictated by America's strategic and economic requirements.

Because rational governments do not base their strategy on a pledge to commit suicide to protect other nations' security, the United States should move to limit its nuclear exposure. While not ruling out the possibility that it might use nuclear weapons in response to a Soviet attack on Western Europe, U.S. strategy should be restructured to ensure that Washington has the option and flexibility to decide whether American nuclear forces would be used. Because NATO's present strategy all but locks the United States into a posture of automatically using nuclear weapons in the early stages of a European conflict, it is an unacceptably risky strategy.

The United States should also cut the costs of its NATO obligation by significantly reducing its conventional force commitments to NATO. The American commitment to Western Europe is the most expensive item in the U.S. defense budget. By demobilizing the bulk of its NATO-earmarked conventional forces, the United States could realize substantial savings and ease its budget crisis. Such a move would make strategic, as well as financial, sense. It is now widely accepted that cost, geography, and the extent of its other worldwide military obligations put the United States at a severe comparative disadvantage in providing NATO with conventional forces. The West Europeans, by contrast, are well placed to provide these forces (assuming they decide NATO needs more robust conventional defenses).[38]

Unilateral cuts in the U.S. military presence can be made without affecting the prevailing military balance. Any shortfalls could easily be made good by the Western Europeans. A scaling back of the American commitment should be undertaken because it is in the best interest of the United States.

Moreover, *all* U.S. forces should eventually be withdrawn from Europe. But that final step must be contingent on tangible confirmation that the present favorable trends in European security are unlikely to be reversed. The ultimate withdrawal of those forces should not be taken as a signal of U.S. disinterest in the affairs of the continent. Although the United States is not a European country, it is a world power with an interest in Europe's stability and security. When full disengagement becomes possible, the United States should nevertheless maintain a close political and strategic association with the NATO community, even if it is no longer manifested in a formal alliance. In the final analysis, it has always been America's European interests—not the form in which those interests are expressed—that have been the real bond between the United States and Western Europe. As German Social Democratic spokesman Karsten Voigt put it in an address to the Cato Institute on NATO's fortieth anniversary, America's security-political presence in Europe need not remain linked to the presence of U.S. troops and weapons in Europe.

A more circumscribed U.S. role in NATO would further America's interests by lowering the excessive risks and costs currently imposed by the alliance. In effect, America's role in Western Europe's security would revert to what was originally envisioned by the North Atlantic Treaty's framers. NATO would thus be transformed from a protectorate into the true alliance it was intended to be, where the greatest costs and risks are borne by the countries in the gravest danger. In contrast to the late 1940s, there is no question today that Western Europe has the wherewithal to become an equal pillar of a transatlantic security arrangement. And the West Europeans themselves increasingly realize that their aspirations to play a more prominent and independent role in world affairs require them to become more self-sufficient strategically.

The initial U.S. goal should be to reduce its NATO-committed ground forces to two European-deployed divisions and one U.S.-based division (with prepositioned equipment stored in Europe). By the end of the 1990s America's remaining European-committed forces would be gradually demobilized. Preferably this outcome should be achieved as part of the European conventional force reduction talks in Vienna (CFE), and Washington and Western Europe should stipulate that NATO cuts under CFE will come from U.S. forces until the American presence is reduced to the two-division level. However, if CFE fails to produce an agreement by 1995, America and Western Europe should establish a reasonable timetable to effectuate these troop reductions. To keep the CFE door open, under this alternative the NATO-committed troops in the United States would be disbanded before U.S. troops in Europe were reduced.

Although some might claim that this action would dangerously weaken NATO on the critical Central Front, such arguments are faulty. In fact, U.S. troop levels in Europe have never been related to any conventional defense or war-fighting objective. As Zbigniew Brzezinski has written, "There is no special magic to any particular number of U.S. troops in Europe. The total is not the consequence of a purely military calculus."[39] U.S. forces are in Europe for symbolic and crisis management purposes. By explicitly abandoning the pretense that they have a war-fighting function, the number of U.S. troops committed to Western Europe can be cut to a number compatible with their true function—as a symbol of America's continuing interest in Europe's security.

The United States should also agree to open negotiations with Moscow to eliminate all SNFs. The argument that this step would lead to Western Europe's denuclearization is a canard. The United States has always firmly insisted that France's and Britain's independent nuclear forces be excluded from U.S.-Soviet arms talks and should continue to do so. A redesigned American commitment to Europe would not adversely affect Western Europe's security. U.S. SNFs have no warfighting utility and contribute almost nothing to deterrence; removing them will not increase the remote possibility of a Soviet bolt-from-the-blue strike at Western Europe. Moscow is constrained by a number of factors, including a global balance of power that includes such potential Soviet adversaries as China and Japan and by the unreliability of the East European nations. Furthermore, the critical military balance (NATO forces in West Germany versus Soviet forces in East Germany and Czechoslovakia) is quite stable and makes highly doubtful the possibility of a successful Soviet surprise offensive. Moreover, the Soviets have little to gain by attacking because the very prize they might attempt to seize—Western Europe's industrial and technological resources—almost certainly would be destroyed.

Finally, the risk-benefit calculus is strongly tilted against Moscow; the Soviets must assume that the United States has a greater interest in protecting Western Europe than they have in overrunning it. Even without U.S. tactical nuclear weapons on the ground, the Soviets would know that an attack would lead to a direct superpower showdown, with incalculable consequences. That is the real basis of deterrence. It is worth recalling that in 1969 the United States was able to deter the Soviet Union from attacking China, notwithstanding that the United States had no security relationship or diplomatic links with Beijing—much less troops or tactical nuclear weapons on the ground.[40]

An altered U.S. strategic posture in Europe would have many advantages. Most important, the removal of U.S. SNFs from Europe would enable America to regain the power to decide if and when its long-range nuclear forces would come into play. The SNFs are intended to act as a hair-trigger mechanism to ensure that a Soviet conventional attack on Western Europe would automatically escalate to a full-scale nuclear exchange between the superpowers. This kind of reflexive commitment is far too dangerous; American strategy should seek to retain decision-making autonomy and discretion with respect to using nuclear weapons. Moreover, a negotiated third zero solution would remove a source of poison from U.S.–West German relations and relieve German anxieties that America is lowering its nuclear risks by increasing West Germany's. Finally, by removing its European-based SNFs and circumscribing its nuclear guarantee, the United States would lower the entry barriers to Western Europe's strategic self-sufficiency and provide the Europeans with an incentive to build an independent nuclear deterrent. Although a reconfigured U.S. strategic posture would significantly de-Americanize European deterrence, it should not lead to Europe's denuclearization.

Reduction of U.S. ground forces in Europe would have a similar incentive effect. If the West Europeans were dissatisfied with the resulting conventional balance, they could opt to make good the shortfall caused by withdrawal of three front-line U.S. divisions. (Moreover, if the United States relinquished its decision-making control within the alliance and encouraged NATO's Europeanization, France might fill the gap by rejoining NATO's integrated command.) Alternatively, the West Europeans could decide to live with the new security environment. The United States should respect whatever decision the West Europeans make and refrain from badgering them about burden sharing.

The traditional weakness of America's European security policy, reflected in President Bush's CFE initiatives, is a tendency to focus narrowly on military issues while glossing over more fundamental political concerns. For example, any reduction in the U.S. military presence in Western Europe helps to lower the barriers to Soviet withdrawal from Eastern Europe. This is implicit in the CFE process. But any change in the present military balance has crucial political implications for Eastern Europe and, hence, for European stability.

The partial withdrawal of Soviet forces in Eastern Europe would be a mixed blessing for the West. In an immediate sense, Western Europe's military security would be increased, but from a broader perspective, Europe could be a far more dangerous place. Wars are not caused by armies; they are caused by political crises that spin out of control. Unless CFE-type talks are put in a political context, force reduction agreements could actually create conditions that increase the possibility of war. The departure of some Soviet forces could embolden East Europeans to seek even greater sweeping political and economic changes than those that took place in Poland and Hungary in 1989. Yet the presence of remaining Soviet forces could encourage beleaguered communist regimes (or elements within them) to crack down rather than risk being swept out of power altogether. And if European events threaten to get out of hand, Moscow might be tempted to intervene again in Eastern Europe's domestic affairs. It will be hard for experiments in multiparty politics and "socialist market" economic reforms to take root securely as long as Soviet troops remain in Eastern Europe. But the Soviets will not leave Eastern Europe as long as American troops remain in Western Europe in more than token strength.

Eastern Europe is Europe's unfinished agenda, a volatile region where nothing is settled. In the 1990s, NATO's agenda will be dominated less by strictly military issues and concerned more with managing the process of stable, evolutionary change in Eastern Europe. Overcoming the cold war will become NATO's primary task, and the alliance must transform itself into an instrument for East-West negotiations on this issue.

Framing a comprehensive political strategy to construct a post–cold war European security system is a formidable challenge. But sometimes the best new ideas actually are old ones. George F. Kennan's mutual disengagement proposal merits a fresh look. Suitably modified to allow for a residual American presence in Europe, it could provide the framework for a comprehensive Western approach to managing East-West relations in Europe in the 1990s. In contrast to the late 1950s, the factors that Kennan then believed made disengagement necessary are now present.

The German question is again a live issue, and new attention must be paid to resolving it in an all-European context. More important, the Soviet position in Eastern Europe is being severely challenged. Eastern Europe was intended to be a defensive glacis that strengthened the Soviet Union's security, but the Kremlin now seems to recognize that a restive, alienated Eastern Europe is actually a major source of insecurity and an unaffordable drain on Soviet resources. Although the prospect of mutual superpower disengagement in Central Europe was once visionary, it is now conceivable, and many Soviet officials have hinted that Moscow would be interested in exploring such an arrangement.

Mutual superpower disengagement in the 1990s would erect a new post–

cold-war European settlement based on (1) removal to national territory and asymmetrical demobilization of both superpowers' military forces and nuclear weapons from Central Europe (East and West Germany, Poland, Hungary, and Czechoslovakia), and (2) a pledge that neither superpower will be the first to introduce its forces into that region. Mutual disengagement would dramatically reduce the chances of war in Europe by lowering the political tensions that could cause a conflict. A Soviet pullback from Eastern Europe, coupled with an American pledge to refrain from interfering in the region, would enable the Eastern Europeans to work out their own internal political arrangements and thus help ensure that that region does not become the Sarajevo of the 1990s. Stable change—not upheaval—is what is needed in Eastern Europe, and both superpowers—and all Europeans—have a common interest in achieving Eastern Europe's Austrianization by reconciling legitimate Soviet security concerns with Eastern Europe's desire for autonomy and political and economic reform.

Moreover, in a strictly military sense, mutual disengagement would bolster Western Europe's security by neutralizing Moscow's presumed conventional superiority. The Soviet army's size would be reduced, and it would be put back where it belongs—in the Soviet Union. Western Europe's strategic depth and warning time of an impending attack (currently serious weaknesses) would be greatly improved by moving Soviet forces hundreds of miles to the east of their present positions.

The assertion that the West could be disadvantaged by mutual disengagement—because the Soviet Union could easily move back into Central Europe while the United States, for geographic reasons, could not—does not hold up. Mutual disengagement would transform Eastern Europe into a protective buffer between Western Europe and the Soviet Union. The East Europeans probably would forcibly resist an attempted Soviet reentry. Indeed it is widely believed that the Soviets refrained from directly intervening in Poland in 1980–1981 because they were apprehensive about the prospect of a military confrontation with the Polish army (or a potential civilian uprising). Moreover, any forced reentry into Eastern Europe would produce a rupture in Moscow's crucial ties with Western Europe. Eastern Europe's credibility as a neutral barrier could be further bolstered by stipulating that the region's armies be placed outside the Soviet command structure and configured for independent territorial defense (along the lines of the Yugoslavian and Rumanian armies). Moreover, the United States could reorient its declaratory policy and strategy to the specific task of deterring Soviet reentry. Finally, disengagement can be reconciled with America's role as a European power. The Soviets have already acknowledged that they must make additional concessions in CFE because of the geographical asymmetry in the superpowers' proximity to Europe. This principle would easily be extended to permit the United States to leave in place in West Germany the headquarters and support skeletons, and prepositioned equipment, for three divisions and their tactical air support. In a crisis, the reinsertion of these U.S. forces into Western Europe would be a powerful demonstration of America's commitment to Western Europe's security. Such a modified form of mutual disengagement would be a prudent hedge against a Soviet violation of an agreement.

Finally, mutual disengagement is a substantive policy that would shift the political momentum in Europe in Washington's favor. Gorbachev's ideas resonate in Western Europe not because of his Madison Avenue–style wizardry but because they appeal to its desires for independence, an end to the arms race, and a reunited Europe. Unlike CFE—which is likely to become bogged down in the technical minutiae of arms control and messy details of verification—mutual disengagement is a pristinely simple concept that could easily be grasped by all Europeans and would clearly align the United States with European aspirations.

In the 1990s American leaders will be called upon to display statesmanship and vision. A post–cold war European settlement requires that the United States continue to play an active role in European affairs but also that Western Europe trades (and Washington accepts) an attenuation of its security links with America in order to obtain greater freedom for Eastern Europe. At the same time, the United States must balance its support for emergence of an independent Western Europe with the need to reassure Moscow that such a Western Europe will not be an instrument of an anti-Soviet policy orchestrated in Washington. This, too, requires a distancing between America and Western Europe. And with respect to Eastern Europe, the United States will need to exercise considerable restraint and abjure a closet rollback policy.

These imperatives can be reconciled by insisting that the European security dialogue be a three-cornered negotiation that includes the EC as well as the superpowers and by allowing the West Europeans to take the lead for the West. This would give a substantial boost to the process of West European political unification and simultaneously encourage the West Europeans to bargain hard and responsibly while carefully weighing Ostpolitik's implications. Moreover, because of their historical and cultural ties, the West Europeans are best placed to take the lead in the post–cold war European security process—a process concerned fundamentally with restoring to Eastern and Western Europe their common heritage.

Instead of pursuing the unattainable goal of using external pressure to change the Soviet Union's internal system, American diplomacy should concentrate on channeling Moscow's diplomacy into more acceptable directions and securing agreements that promote both superpowers' interests and security. As they enter the 1990s, America, Europe, and the Soviet Union stand on the threshold of the post–cold war era. The coming decade will be a time of dramatic change and unparalleled opportunity. For both superpowers and for all of Europe, a disengagement agreement would bring down the curtain on the cold war's final act on the Continent. The time has come for both superpowers to stand aside and let Europe be Europe. "Someday," Kennan wrote in 1948, "our forces must leave Central Europe. Someday Soviet forces must leave. The question is when?" That is the question the United States and the EC should jointly put to Mikhail Gorbachev.

Notes

1. William Pfaff, *Barbarian Sentiments: How the American Century Ends* (New York: Hill and Wang 1989): p. 26.

2. George F. Kennan, *Memoirs, 1925–1950* (Boston: Atlantic–Little, Brown, 1967), 1:410; Ronald Steel, *Walter Lippmann and the American Century* (Boston: Atlantic–Little, Brown, 1980), p. 459.

3. Quoted in John Lewis Gaddis, *The Long Peace* (New York: Oxford University Press, 1987), p. 63.

4. PPS 43, "Considerations Affecting the Conclusion of a North Atlantic Security Pact," November 23, 1948, in Thomas H. Etzold and John Lewis Gaddis, eds., *Containment: Documents on American Policy and Strategy, 1945–1950* (New York: Columbia University Press, 1979), p. 157; Steel, *Walter Lippmann*, p. 445.

5. Quoted in Gaddis, *Long Peace*, p. 63.

6. Kennan, *Memoirs*, 1:407. Geir Lundestad, "Empire by Invitation? The United States and Western Europe, 1945–1952," *SHAFR Newsletter* (September 1984): 7.

7. George F. Kennan, "Disengagement Revisited," *Foreign Affairs* (January 1959): 190.

8. For a contemporary overview of the disengagement debate, see Michael Howard, *Disengagement in Europe* (London: Penguin, 1958), pp. 26–38. Gaitskell's views were set out in "Disengagement: Why? How?" *Foreign Affairs* (July 1958). For a discussion of the SPD position on the relationship between West Germany's NATO membership and German unity, see Fritz Erler, "The Struggle for German Reunification," *Foreign Affairs* (April 1956).

9. Published in the United States in "A Chance to Withdraw Our Troops in Europe," *Harper's* (February 1958).

10. See, Gaitskell, "Disengagement," p. 54.

11. Ibid., p. 35.

12. Kennan expanded on this point and expanded his argument for disengagement in "Disengagement Revisited."

13. For a concise account of Marshall's and Eisenhower's testimony and an overview of the 1950–1951 great debate, see Ted Galen Carpenter, "United States' NATO Policy at the Crossroads: The 'Great Debate' of 1950–51," *International History Review* (August 1986).

14. For a description of the Nixon administration's 1971 effort to turn back the Mansfield amendment see Henry A. Kissinger, *White House Years* (Boston: Little, Brown, 1979), pp. 938–49.

15. Schmidt's lecture is reprinted in *Survival* (January–February 1982).

16. As François Heisbourg has put it, "As a result of a number of recent developments the alliance is now exposed to a new, more diffuse peril: senility, possibly leading to death from natural causes. Put another way, it faces the possibility of gradual spontaneous disintegration after a period of growing incoherence." François Heisbourg, "Can the Atlantic Alliance Last Out the Century?" *International Affairs* (1987).

17. *Report of the Defense Burdensharing Panel, House of Representatives Armed Services Committee* (Washington, D.C.: U.S. Government Printing Office, 1988).

18. Samuel P. Huntington, "The U.S.—Decline or Renewal?" *Foreign Affairs* (Winter 1988–1989): 93.

19. See Stanley Hoffman's penetrating and prescient analysis, "The European Process at Altantic Crosspurposes," *Journal of Common Market Studies* 3, no. 2 (1964).

20. Quoted in Philip Revzin, "Europeans Begin Planning for the Day When the U.S. Pulls Troops Back Home," *Wall Street Journal*, February 17, 1989, p. A6.

21. Quoted in James M. Markham, "When Europe's Walls Tumble, Who'll Rush In?" *New York Times*, March 21, 1989, p. A4.

22. Renata Fritsch-Bournazel, *Confronting the German Question: Germans on the East-West Divide* (Oxford: Berg Publishers, 1988), p. 80.

23. The U.S. foreign policy community has been caught off guard by the reemergence of the German question. Yet as early as 1984 it was obvious that the German question would be the central issue in European security during the late 1980s and early 1990s. See Christopher Layne, "Toward German Reunification?" *Journal of Contemporary Studies* 3 (Fall 1984): 7–37.

24. For a more detailed discussion of these issues, see Christopher Layne, "Continental Divide—Time to Disengage in Europe," *National Interest* (Fall 1988); Alan Tonelson and Christopher Layne, "Divorce, Alliance-Style," *New Republic*, June 12, 1989.

25. As Helmut Schmidt told the North Atlantic Assembly in November 1988: "One hears a lot about burden sharing nowadays. But, Ladies and Gentlemen from the other side of the Atlantic, what about risk sharing? Given the geopolitical situation there is nobody arguing for undertaking greater risks . . . in the State of Washington or the State of Virginia or elsewhere. But last winter I read a report . . . under the title of 'Discriminate Deterrence.' It seemed to try to minimize the risk of nuclear escalation for America—and, by the way, also for the Soviet Union—and enlarge the nuclear risks for others, in the main in Europe. Or let me mention the SDI Utopia. If it ever could be put into reality . . . it points in the same direction: it would shelter Americans but obviously not those living in Europe."

26. The CDU-CSU is badly split over SNFs. Its Gaullist wing (the so-called Stahlhelm Fraktion) has argued that with the INFs gone, West Germany is dangerously singularized by the presence of U.S. SNFs, which can only reach targets on German soil. The Stahlhelm Fraktion favors removing the SNFs and moving toward a closer Franco-German military relationship, which will be the foundation of a European pillar to supplement the now unreliable American commitment. See James M. Markham, "Angst in Bonn: Debate over the Missiles," *New York Times*, February 10, 1988, p. 8; Stephen F. Szabo, "Post-INF Germany: The Changing Politics of Defense in the Federal Republic of Germany" unpublished manuscript presented to the Woodrow Wilson International Center for Scholars, December 1, 1988). The CDU main-

stream, concerned about balancing the U.S. commitment against German public opinion, favors limited SNF modernization coupled with reduction of NATO SNFs to the absolute minimum level. On Ostpolitik and Deutschlandpolitik, the Kohl government has carefully held to the course established by the SPD-FDP coalitions led by Brandt and Schmidt.

27. On the rise of this new West German strategic culture, see Jeffrey Boutwell, "Politics and the Peace Movement in West Germany," *International Security* (Spring 1983); Jeffrey Herf, "War, Peace and the Intellectuals: The West German Peace Movement," *International Security* (Spring 1986); Harald Mueller and Thomas Risse-Kappen, "Origins of Estrangement: The Peace Movement and the Changed Image of America in West Germany," *International Security* (Summer 1987).

28. Walter F. Hahn, "West Germany's Ostpolitik: The Grand Design of Egon Bahr," *Orbis* (Winter 1973).

29. The data upon which this paragraph's analysis of West German public opinion is based were presented at the Konrad Adenauer Stiftung conference, "40 Years of the Federal Republic of Germany—Experiences and Perspectives for the 1990s and Beyond," Los Angeles, June 24–27, 1989.

30. This description of the compact is Robert W. Tucker's. See Robert W. Tucker, "The Atlantic Alliance and Critics" in Robert W. Tucker and Linda Wrigley, eds., *The Atlantic Alliance and Its Critics* (New York: Praeger/Lehrman Institute, 1983), pp. 176–77.

31. Robert M. Gates, "Gorbachev and Change in the Soviet Union: Implications for the West" (speech delivered to Center for Strategic and International Studies Conference, "The 1990s: Critical Change," April 1, 1989).

32. Anders Aslund suggests that Soviet military spending may have risen to 22–30 percent of GNP, far above the accepted Central Intelligence Agency estimate of 15–17 percent. See Anders Aslund, *Gorbachev's Struggle for Economic Reform* (Ithaca, N.Y.: Cornell University Press, 1989).

33. Even hawkish U.S. defense analysts agree that if implemented, the switch to a defense-only posture and the unilateral withdrawal of four tank divisions from East Germany would substantially reduce the Soviet Union's ability to attack Western Europe. See John J. Fialka, "Soviets Outline Plan in East Germany," *Wall Street Journal*, March 14, 1989, p. A7; Michael Parks, "East Bloc Defensive Rule by '91 Seen," *Los Angeles Times*, March 4, 1989, p. 3.

34. Kenneth N. Waltz, *Theory of International Politics* (Reading, Mass.: Addison-Wesley, 1979), p. 209.

35. Quoted in Gaddis, *Long Peace*, p. 64.

36. Henry A. Kissinger, *The Troubled Partnership* (New York: McGraw-Hill, 1965), p. 40.

37. Henry A. Kissinger, *Years of Upheaval* (Boston: Little, Brown, 1982), p. 131.

38. This argument is ably made in David P. Calleo, Harold van B. Cleveland, and Leonard Silk, "The Dollar and the Defense of the West," *Foreign Affairs* (Spring 1988). Also see David P. Calleo, *Beyond American Hegemony* (New York: Basic Books, 1987). Similar arguments have been made by Henry Kissinger, Zbigniew Brzezinski, Jeffrey Record, and Eliot Cohen.

39. Zbigniew Brzezinski, *Game Plan* (Boston: Atlantic Monthly Press, 1986), pp. 178–79.

40. William G. Hyland, *Mortal Rivals: Superpower Relations from Nixon to Kissinger* (New York: Random House, 1987), pp. 15–27; Kissinger, *White House Years*, pp. 183–86.

Index

About the Contributors

Paul Bracken is a professor of public policy and political science at Yale University. Previously he was on the senior research staff at the Hudson Institute for nine years. He is the author of *The Command and Control of Nuclear Forces,* along with several articles and book chapters on European strategy, arms control, and crisis management. He serves as director of the Yale International Security Program and is a member of the Council on Foreign Relations. He holds a Ph.D. in operations research from Yale University.

David P. Calleo is Dean Acheson Professor and director of European studies at the Paul H. Nitze School of Advanced International Studies, The Johns Hopkins University. He has also taught at Brown University and at Yale and has served as a consultant to the U.S. undersecretary of state for political affairs. He has authored a number of books, including *The Atlantic Fantasy, The Imperious Economy,* and, most recently, *Beyond American Hegemony: The Future of the Western Alliance.* He has written for many journals including *Political Science Quarterly* and *Foreign Policy* and has contributed chapters to several recent books. He holds a Ph.D. from Yale University.

David Garnham is a professor of political science at the University of Wisconsin–Milwaukee. The author of *The Politics of European Defense Cooperation: Germany, France, Britain, and America,* he has written articles in various journals, including *International Security* and the *Journal of Peace Research,* on defense policy and international conflict. He holds a Ph.D. from the University of Minnesota.

Robert E. Hunter is vice-president for regional programs and the director of European studies at the Center for Strategic and International Studies. He served on the National Security Council from 1977 to 1981, and from 1977 to 1979 he was its director of West European affairs. He has also served as foreign policy adviser to Senator Edward Kennedy, lead consultant to the Kissinger Commission on Central America, and special adviser on Lebanon to

272 • NATO at 40

the Speaker of the House of Representatives. Hunter contributes regularly to the *Los Angeles Times* and other publications. He holds a Ph.D. from the London School of Economics.

Josef Joffe is foreign editor and a columnist for *Süddeutsche Zeitung* and a contributing editor to *U.S. News and World Report.* From 1982 to 1984 he taught international relations at the Johns Hopkins School of Advanced International Studies, was a fellow at the Woodrow Wilson Center for Scholars, and was a senior associate of the Carnegie Endowment for International Peace. He has written on international politics and strategy for *Foreign Affairs* and other journals, written extensively in the international press, and has appeared on discussion shows. His most recent book is *The Limited Partnership: Europe, the United States and the Burdens of Alliance.* He holds a Ph.D. in government from Harvard University.

Stanley H. Kober has worked for a variety of research institutions—SRI International, Center for Naval Analyses, and Hudson Institute—on a diverse range of defense issues but focusing on East-West relations. Educated at the Georgetown University School of Foreign Service and the Fletcher School of Law and Diplomacy, Dr. Kober has published in the *New York Times, Washington Post, Wall Street Journal, Foreign Policy, International Affairs,* and a number of other publications. He is writing a book examining why the democracies have flourished.

Melvyn Krauss is a professor of economics at New York University and a senior fellow at the Hoover Institution. He has written widely for scholarly journals and is a regular contributor to such publications as the *New York Times* and the *Wall Street Journal.* Krauss is also the author of a number of books, including *How NATO Weakens the West, Development without Aid,* and *The New Protectionism.* He has taught at colleges and universities in the United States and Canada and throughout Western Europe.

Christopher Layne is an attorney at the Los Angeles law firm Kaye, Scholer, Fierman, Hays and Handler and an adjunct scholar at the Cato Institute. A widely published expert on foreign policy issues, he has written for such publications as *Foreign Policy, Journal of Strategic Studies, SAIS Review, Orbis,* and the *National Interest.* He is also a frequent contributor to the *Los Angeles Times,* the *Wall Street Journal,* the *Chicago Tribune,* and the *New Republic.* He holds a Ph.D. in political science from the University of California at Berkeley, a diploma in historical studies from the University of Cambridge, an LL.M. in international law from the University of Virginia Law School, and a J.D. from the University of Southern California Law Center.

William S. Lind is the director of the Center for Cultural Conservatism of the Free Congress Foundation. He also serves as president of the Military Reform Institute and is an adviser to U.S. Representative Denny Smith. From 1977 through 1986 he worked as a legislative aide for armed services for Senator Gary Hart and coauthored with him *America Can Win: The Case for Military Reform.* He also coauthored with William H. Marshner *Cultural Conservatism: Toward a New National Agenda.* He has written extensively for military journals, including *Naval Institute Proceedings* and the *Marine Corps Gazette.* He holds an M.A. in history from Princeton University.

Earl C. Ravenal, a former official in the Office of the Secretary of Defense, is Distinguished Research Professor of International Affairs at the Georgetown University School of Foreign Service and a senior fellow at the Cato Institute. He is one of the nation's most prominent foreign policy experts and the author of a number of books, including *NATO: The Tides of Discontent, Never Again: Learning from America's Foreign Policy Failures,* and *Defining Defense: The 1985 Military Budget.* He is also the author of over 150 articles and has been a fellow of the Woodrow Wilson International Center for Scholars and the Washington Center for Foreign Policy Research. He has lectured or taught at more than fifty American and foreign universities and academies. He holds a Ph.D. from the Johns Hopkins University School of Advanced International Studies, as well as degrees from Cambridge and Harvard universities.

Jeffrey Record is a senior research fellow at the Hudson Institute. He also works as military commentator for the *Baltimore Sun* and is an adjunct professor of modern military history at Georgetown University. Formerly legislative assistant for national security affairs to Senator Sam Nunn, he has written numerous books and articles on defense topics, including *Revising U.S. Military Strategy: Tailoring Means to Ends* and *Beyond Military Reform: American Defense Dilemmas.* He received a Ph.D. from the Johns Hopkins School of Advanced International Studies in 1973.

Patricia S. Schroeder is a U.S. Representative from Denver, Colorado. She is the chairman of the burden-sharing panel of the House Armed Services Committee and the coauthor of the Schroeder-Ireland amendment calling for the withdrawal of American troops assigned to INF. Known as a fiscally conservative liberal, she is active on a wide range of issues, including arms control and wasteful defense spending. In 1983 Schroeder was cited as one of the 100 most influential women in America by the *Ladies Home Journal* and has received many other honorary degrees and achievement awards. Prior to her election to Congress, Schroeder lectured at Denver colleges and practiced law. She is a graduate of Harvard Law School.

Jed C. Snyder is a senior research fellow at the National Strategy Information Center and chairman and founder of the Washington Strategy Seminar. Currently a consultant to the office of the secretary of defense, he served in 1981–1982 as an official in the State Department's Bureau of Politico-Military Affairs. Snyder has also worked for several research organizations, including the Hudson Institute, the Woodrow Wilson International Center for Scholars, and the RAND Corporation. He is the author of *Defending the Fringe: NATO, the Mediterranean and the Persian Gulf* and the coeditor of *Limiting Nuclear Proliferation* and the forthcoming *Soviet Power in Transition*. Snyder holds an M.A. in political science from the University of Chicago.

Ronald Steel is a professor of international relations at the University of Southern California. He was previously a senior associate at the Carnegie Endowment for International Peace and a fellow of the Woodrow Wilson International Center for Scholars and the Wissenschafts-kolleg zu Berlin. A former recipient of a Guggenheim fellowship, he has taught at a number of American universities, including Yale, Rutgers, Dartmouth, and Texas. He writes frequently on foreign affairs for the leading American journals, including the *New Republic* and the *New York Review of Books*. He is the author of several books on foreign policy, including *Pax Americana* and *The End of Alliance: America and the Future of Europe*, as well as the prize-winning biography, *Walter Lippmann and the American Century*.

Alan Tonelson is a project director at the Twentieth Century Fund, for which he is writing a book on redefining U.S. foreign policy interests. Previously he was an associate editor of *Foreign Policy*, the *Wilson Quarterly*, and the *Interdependent*. He has lectured on U.S. foreign policy at the Johns Hopkins University School of Advanced International Studies and at the White Burkett Miller Center for Public Affairs at the University of Virginia. He is a frequent contributor to many publications, including *Foreign Policy*, the *Atlantic*, the *New York Times*, the *Washington Post*, and the *New Republic*. He is a summa cum laude graduate of Princeton University.

About the Editor

Ted Galen Carpenter is the director of foreign policy studies at the Cato Institute. An expert on defense and foreign policy issues, he is the editor of *Collective Defense or Strategic Independence? Alternative Strategies for the Future* and the author of more than forty articles and book chapters. His work has appeared in various professional journals, as well as the *New York Times, Wall Street Journal, Harper's, Chicago Tribune, Reason,* and other publications. His article "Pursuing a Strategic Divorce: The United States and the ANZUS Alliance" received the Olive Branch Award from the New York University Center for War, Peace and the News Media in 1987. Carpenter received his B.A. and M.A. in U.S. history from the University of Wisconsin–Milwaukee and holds a Ph.D. in U.S. diplomatic history from the University of Texas.